William Banks and his accomplices attacking the Reverend William Warrington and his wife
(*page 169*)

The New Newgate Calendar

Edited with an introduction by
Lord Birkett

London
The Folio Society
1960

PRINTED IN GREAT BRITAIN

Printed and bound by W. & J. Mackay & Co Ltd, Chatham

Set in Bell 11 point leaded 1 point

Illustrations printed by gravure by The Grout Engraving Co Ltd, Bromley

CONTENTS

Illustrations

INTRODUCTION

THE publication of a further volume of criminal trials taken from the *Newgate Calendar* needs no apology or justification. The reception given to the Folio Society's volume of 1951 proved quite conclusively that selected criminal trials that are interesting in themselves for special reasons, and at the same time illustrate some aspect of the criminal law, will always be attractive to the discerning reader. It is well that this is so, for the sanctions of the criminal law ultimately depend upon an instructed public opinion for their enforcement, and the wider the public interest in all that appertains to the problems of the criminal law the better the law will be, and the more enlightened and effective will be its administration.

The trials of the nineteenth century here presented do not differ very greatly from the trials of the previous century, and compared with the trials of our own day they seem to belong to quite a different world. It is true that the nineteenth century saw the beginnings of law reform but it may serve to show how terribly slow reform can be, if it is remembered that it was not until 1898, at the very end of the century, that a prisoner was allowed to give evidence on his own behalf and the wife or the husband became a competent witness for the defence. Subsequent experience has shown that this reform was not the boon to the prisoner that the reformers had prophesied, but it has certainly promoted the ends of justice, for it is undoubtedly a great boon to those who have a good defence, though it is a terrible handicap to those who have not. It was not until 1827 that the law was amended which had formerly decreed that all felonies were to be punishable by death, even down to the stealing of anything above the value of twelve pence; and it was not until 1836 that counsel were allowed to address the jury on behalf of the prisoner who was charged with felony. The substantial reforms of the twentieth century began with the report of the Gladstone Departmental Committee in 1895 and from that date progress has been slow but continuous, and all the modern procedure dealing with the treatment of the offender has been slowly built up until it culminated in the Criminal Justice

Act of 1948 with all its wise and beneficent provisions. The trials presented in this volume, therefore, belong to another age where other ideas were dominant, but they reveal in a dramatic way the imperfections of the criminal law and its procedure, and demonstrate the urgent need for reform both in the substance of the law and in its administration. Here will be found the fascinating case of Abraham Thornton who was tried for murder and acquitted at the Warwick Assizes. It reads to us like a work of pure fiction yet it actually took place in 1818. Today if a jury returns a verdict of *Not Guilty* the prisoner is for ever freed from prosecution on that same charge; but the case of Thornton records the process of an Appeal of Murder, long obsolete, which permitted an acquitted man to be tried again. When this procedure was invoked Thornton claimed to be tried by *Wager of Battle* and the judges after long argument were compelled to allow it and to declare that that method of trial was still the law of England. This trial recalls *Trial by Ordeal* and all these strange methods by which men in other ages strove to arrive at truth, and to fulfil their conception of justice.

If the case of *Thornton* reads like fiction, the case of the *Dorchester Labourers* reads like an unrelieved tragedy. In these days of ours, when all industry is liable to be disrupted at a moment's notice by a sudden strike of workmen in some vital process of manufacture, it is of the deepest interest to read the trial of the six farm labourers at the Dorchester Assizes in 1834 who are now known as the Tolpuddle martyrs. All the crime they were ever alleged to have committed was to try and form a primitive trade union to raise agricultural wages from 7*s* to 10*s* a week. In the course of so doing they administered an oath to prospective members binding them to be loyal to the union and its objects. These six respectable, God-fearing men, Methodists all, did not deny administering the oath and the jury found them guilty under an old Act which dealt with mutiny. It so happened that the presiding judge, Baron Williams had for years been a Whig politician and appears to have been made a judge for that reason. He thereupon passed the appalling and almost unbelievable sentence of seven years transportation beyond the seas. The men were taken in chains to Portsmouth, kept in the hulks for six weeks, and then shipped like cattle to

Australia. The most intense suffering was caused by the methods of transportation and the herding together of convicted men and women, whose crimes varied so much in gravity, but again it may serve to show the difference in outlook of one age from another, that the Lord Chief Justice of England, Lord Ellenborough could describe the punishment of Transportation as a 'summer's excursion, in an easy migration, to a happier and better climate'. Because of a great public agitation these six men received a free pardon, but not until 1836, and the punishment of Transportation continued until 1857 and was then discontinued only because Australia would no longer tolerate it. It is useless now to fulminate against the barbaric sentence, or the barbarous judge who pronounced it, and treated these six men as though they were wicked mutineers who had attacked the safety of the State and had taken a secret oath to continue to do so. It should be recognized that the trial took place in another age and in almost another world, and the law and its officers are not to be judged by the experience or garnered wisdom of subsequent ages and events.

The purpose of this volume, it must be emphasized, is to entertain the reader by exhibiting in these trials the extraordinary behaviour of men and women when their obscure lives are suddenly brought into a glare of publicity, when the thing done in secret is proclaimed from the house-tops, and the frailties and perversities, the cruelty and courage of human nature are subjected to the inexorable analysis of a court of law. But it is hoped that the book will also be of interest to the reader for the light it sheds on the administration of the law. We ourselves happen to live in a most remarkable age. Newgate, with its seven centuries of suffering and sorrow, seems very far away, and the revelations of Elizabeth Fry and John Howard have no modern counterpart. But we have no cause to be complacent in any way. Crime continues to increase in the most startling way and is a matter of the gravest concern to all who are concerned with just and orderly government.

This steep increase is true of all classes of crime and of every age group and is most marked in the years between seventeen and twenty-five. It is indeed a lamentable thing that whilst the records of indictable crime show such great increases, all the remedial and redemptive agencies engaged in trying to prevent crime were never more active or more efficient and the questions of punishment, and probation, and after-care, were never more carefully considered and so constantly reviewed. The present Home Secretary, Mr Butler, one of the most enlightened and humane of a long line of distinguished Secretaries of State, has summed up the present situation in words of the utmost value. He said:

'From whatever cause this delinquency comes, the fact is that our spiritual force is not strong enough, our educational influences are not enduring enough, our knowledge of what is happening is not profound enough, and the diagnosis of the effect of alleged prosperity upon the individual is not sufficiently understood.'

It is not without significance therefore that an Institute of Criminology has been established at the University of Cambridge to study the causes of crime with a scientific thoroughness never perhaps seen before. There can be no doubt that the power of the criminal law to prevent or overcome crime has been greatly exaggerated at all stages of our history. The terrible severity of the eighteenth century, and terrible indeed it was, proved a failure in the long run. Every method of deterrence was invoked. The punishment of death for most offences was not thought to be enough, and horror such as hanging in chains or dissection after hanging must be added to it. But it was all of no avail, and today because of the increase in crime, voices are heard calling loudly for the re-imposition of flogging and for the repeal of the provisions of the Homicide Act of 1957 which reduced the number of capital murders. In days past, a thousand writers have informed the world of the causes of crime and almost every evil in the world has been held to blame in some measure at least. A thousand writers have expounded their views on the prevention and cure of crime. Many of the suggestions so passionately advocated have been tried, and at the end of it all the Home Secretary in our day has been most reluctantly compelled to say of the prevalence of crime and its great increase in our time:

'. . . it is particularly disturbing when it occurs after the most massive educational and social reforms for a century.'

The dream of a society without crime has always been dear

to the idealists and the reformers, but the sad truth appears to be that crime is a constant factor in the history of all nations, ancient and modern. So great an authority as Dr Radzinowicz, the Head of the Institute of Criminology at Cambridge, said some wise and memorable words in a paper which he read before the Royal Institution in February 1958, which we do well to remember when considering the administration of the criminal law and the steps to be taken to enforce it. He said:

'We should not relax in our efforts to elucidate the causation of crime, the conditions conducive to it and the measures likely to prevent it; without however weakening the barrier against crime which the criminal law has erected and without condoning the atrophy of individual responsibility. But the inevitability of crime should be accepted with that sanity which one ought to preserve and foster, as one humbly confesses the mysterious enigma of the human mind and the unpredictable vicissitudes of human society.'

All this leads me to repeat that we should refrain from passing severe judgements on other ages for their attitude to crime, because the passage of centuries has brought us a wider experience. It is well to reflect upon the many agencies that are continually affecting the nature of the criminal law in any particular age. In the nineteenth century Chief Justice Cockburn, one of the greatest legal figures of his day, presented a memorandum to a Royal Commission as late as 1862, in which he had opposed very strongly the idea of reformation in the treatment of offenders. He referred the impression produced by suffering as being much more efficacious and lasting. Today, of course, reformation is an integral part of all theories of punishment but the methods of achieving it are the subject of much controversy. The evolution of society from a primitive community into a highly organized and infinitely complex industrial community, the steady growth of knowledge, the examination by the psychologists and the psychiatrists into all the various forms of human behaviour and into the springs of motive, the immense advances in science investigating mental processes, the profound changes in social outlook from one generation to another—all these things affect the criminal law and explain in some measure why the law and procedure of one age may differ so fundamentally from another. The criminal law will continue to interest the public mind because very deeply embedded in the public consciousness are the ideas of expiation, retribution and deterrence. The state of the criminal law at any time is the reflection of the prevailing ideas of the age and perhaps the recent discussion of the law relating to homosexual offences indicates how powerful public opinion can be. For a crime is some conduct that the State forbids, and the purpose of the penal law is to express for the public what it believes to be the kind of conduct that ought to be forbidden. What kind of conduct the community considers worthy of condemnation to be punished by interference with life and liberty or property is therefore dependent in the last resort on the moral and social ideas prevailing.

Fifty years ago a youthful Home Secretary, Mr Winston Churchill, with that distinction of language which has always characterized his public speeches, and which was to prove of inestimable service in the nation's most grievous hour, made this speech in the House of Commons and his fine words might well be taken to heart by everybody concerned with the treatment of the offender wherever he or she is to be found:

'The mood and temper of the public with regard to the treatment of crime and criminals is one of the most unfailing tests of any country. A calm, dispassionate recognition of the rights of the accused; a constant heart-searching by all charged with the duty of punishment; a desire and eagerness to rehabilitate in the world of industry those who have paid their due in the hard coinage of punishment; tireless efforts towards the discovery of curative and regenerative processes; unfailing faith that there is a treasure, if you can only find it, in the heart of every man; these are the symbols which, in the treatment of crime and criminal, mark and measure the stored up strength of a nation and are sign and proof of the living virtue in it.'

BIRKETT

The New Newgate Calendar

THOMAS PICTON, ESQ. Indicted for applying the Torture to LOUISA CALDERON, to extort a Confession

THE cruelty of the application of the torture to extort confession, cannot but be universally admitted in the present enlightened age. Who does not shudder at the idea? St Augustin opposed such cruelty. The Romans tortured their slaves only; and Quintilian, recollecting that they were men, reproved the Romans for such want of humanity.

The defendant, Thomas Picton, Esq., was indicted for putting to the torture a female, Louisa Calderon, one of His Majesty's subjects in the island of Trinidad in the West Indies, in order to extort confession.

Mr Garrow stated the case for the prosecution, and, whilst he expressed the strongest desire to bring to condign punishment the perpetrator of an offence so flagrant as that charged upon the defendant, yet much more happy would he be to find that there was no ground upon which the charge could be supported, and that the British character was not stained by the adoption of so cruel a measure. The island of Trinidad, he said, surrendered to Sir Ralph Abercrombie in the year 1797; and he entered into a stipulation, by which he conceded to the inhabitants the continuance of their laws, and appointed a new governor, until His Majesty should extend to this new acquisition to his empire all the sacred privileges of the laws of England. He had the authority of the defendant himself for stating that the system of jurisprudence adopted under the Spanish monarch, for his colonial establishments, was benignant, and adapted to the protection of the subject.

In December 1801, when this crime was perpetrated, Louisa Calderon was of the tender age of ten or eleven years. At that early period she had been induced to live with a person named Pedro Ruiz, as his mistress; and although it appeared to them very singular that she should sustain such a situation at that time of life, yet it was a fact that, in that climate, women often became mothers at twelve years old, and were in a state of concubinage, if, from their condition, they could not form a more honourable connexion. While she lived with Ruiz, she was engaged in an intrigue with Carlos Gonzalez, the pretended friend of the former, who robbed him of a quantity of dollars. Gonzalez was apprehended, and she also was taken into custody, as some suspicion fell upon her, in consequence of the affair. She was taken before the justice, and, in his presence, she denied having any concern in the business. The magistrate felt that his powers were at an end, and whether the object of her denial were to protect herself, or her friend, was not material. The extent of his authority being thus limited, the officer of justice resorted to General Picton and he had now to produce, in the handwriting of the defendant, this bloody sentence: 'Inflict the torture upon Louisa Calderon.' There was no delay in proceeding to its execution. The girl was informed in the jail, that, if she did not confess, she would be subjected to the torture; that under this process she might probably lose her limbs or her life; but the calamity would be on her own head, for, if she would confess, she would not be required to endure it. While her mind was in the state of agitation this notice produced, her fears were aggravated by the introduction of two or three negresses into her prison, who were to suffer under the same experiment for witchcraft. In this situation of alarm and horror, the young woman persisted in her innocence: and a punishment was inflicted, improperly called picketing. That was a military punishment, perfectly distinct in its nature. This was not picketing but the torture. It was true, the soldier exposed to this did stand with his foot on a picket, or sharp piece of wood; but, in mercy to him, a means of reposing was afforded, on the rotundus major or interior of the arm. Her position might be easily described. The great toe was lodged upon a sharp piece of wood, while the opposite wrist was suspended in a pulley and the other hand and foot were lashed together. Another time the horrid ceremony was repeated, with this difference, that her feet were changed.

[The learned counsel here produced a drawing in water-colours, in which the situation of the sufferer, and the magistrate, executioner and secretary, was described. He then proceeded]:

'It appeared to him, that the case, on the part of the prosecution, would be complete when these facts were established in evidence;

Louisa Calderon under the torture

but he was to be told that, though the highest authority in this country could not practise this on the humblest individual, yet that, by the laws of Spain, it could be perpetrated in the island of Trinidad. He would venture to assert, that if it were written in characters impossible to be misunderstood, that if it were the acknowledged law of Trinidad, it could be no justification of a British governor. Nothing could vindicate such a person, but the law of imperious necessity to which all must submit. It was his duty to impress upon the minds of the people of that colony, the great advantages they would derive from the benign influence of British jurisprudence, and that in consequence of being received within the pale of this government, torture would be for ever banished from the island. It was not sufficient for him, therefore, to establish this sort of apology: it was required of him to show that he complied with the institutions, under circumstances of irresistible necessity. This governor ought to have been aware that the torture was not known in England, and that it never would be, never could be tolerated in this country.

'The trial by rack was utterly unknown to the law of England, though once, when the Dukes of Exeter and Suffolk and other ministers of Henry VI had laid a design to introduce the civil law into this kingdom, for a beginning thereof they erected a rack for torture. This was called in derision the Duke of Exeter's daughter, and still remained in the Tower of London, where it was occasionally used as an engine of state, not of law. But when, upon the assassination of Villiers, Duke of Buckingham, by Felton, it was proposed in the Privy Council to put the assassin to the rack in order to discover his accomplices, the judges, being consulted, declared unanimously, to their own honour and the honour of the English law, that no such proceeding was allowable by the laws of England.

'Such was the effect of the observations of the elegant and learned author of the Commentaries of the Law of England on this subject; and as the strongest method of showing the horror of the practice, he gave this question in the form of an arithmetical problem: "The strength of the muscles and the sensibility of the nerves being given, it was required to know what degree of pain would be necessary to make any particular individual confess his guilt."

'But what were they to say to this man who, so far from having found torture in practice under the former governors, had attached to himself all the infamy of having invented this instrument of cruelty? Like the Duke of Exeter's Daughter, it never had existence until the defendant cursed the island with its production. He had incontestible evidence to show this ingenuity of tyranny in a British governor, and the moment he produced the sanguinary order, the man was left absolutely without defence. The date of this transaction was removed at some distance. It was directed that a commission should conduct the affairs of the government, and among the persons appointed to this important situation was Colonel Fullarton. In the exercise of his duties in that situation, he attained the knowledge of these facts, and with this information he thought it incumbent on him to bring this defendant before the jury; and with the defendant the victim of this enormity would also be produced.'

Louisa Calderon was then called. She appeared about eighteen years of age, of a very interesting countenance, being a Mulatto or Creole, and of a very genteel appearance. She was dressed in white, with a turban of white muslin, tied on in the custom of the country. Her person was slender and graceful. She spoke English but very indifferently, and was examined by Mr Adam, through the medium of a Spanish interpreter.

She deposed that she resided in the island of Trinidad in the year 1798, and lived in the house of Don Pedro Ruiz, and remembered the robbery. She and her mother were taken up on suspicion and brought before Governor Picton, who committed them to prison, under the escort of three soldiers. She was put into close confinement, and before she was taken there the governor said, 'If she did not confess who had stolen the money, the hangman would have to deal with her.'

She was afterwards carried to the room where the torture was prepared. Her left hand was tied up to the ceiling by a rope, with a pulley: her right hand was tied behind, so that her right foot and hand came in contact, while the extremity of her left foot rested on the wooden spike. A drawing representing the exact situation, with the negro holding the rope by which she was suspended, was then shown to her, when she gave a shudder, expressive of horror, which nothing but the most painful recollection of her situation could have excited; on which Mr Garrow expressed his concern that his Lordship was not in a position to witness this accidental, but conclusive, evidence of the fact.

The remainder of the witness's evidence corroborated the statement of Mr Garrow. She remained upon the spike three-quarters of an hour, and the next day twenty-two minutes. She swooned away each time before she was taken down, and was then put into irons, called the 'grillos', which were long pieces of iron, with two rings for the feet, fastened to the wall, and in this situation she remained during eight months. The effect produced by the torture was excruciating pain: her wrists and ankles were much swollen, and the former bore the marks of the barbarity employed towards her to the present day.

Don Rafael Shandoz, an alguazil in the island, bore testimony to his having seen the girl immediately after the application of the torture. The apartment, in which she was afterwards confined, was like a garret, with sloping sides, and the grillos were so placed that, by the lowness of the room, she could by no means raise herself up, during the eight months of her confinement. There was no advocate appointed to attend on her behalf, and no surgeon to assist her. No one but a negro, belonging to Ballot the gaoler, to pull the rope. The witness had been four or five years in the post of alguazil. He never knew the torture inflicted in the island, until the arrival of the defendant. There had been before no instrument for the purpose. The first he saw was in the barracks among the soldiers. Before Louisa Calderon, the instrument had been introduced into the gaol perhaps about six months. The first person he saw tortured in Trinidad was by direction of the defendant, who said to the gaoler, 'Go and fetch the black man to the picket-guard, and put him to the torture.' After the eight months' confinement, both Carlos and Louisa were discharged.

The order for the application of the torture, in the following words—'Applicase la question a Louisa Calderon' (Apply the torture to Louisa Calderon)—was then proved to be in the handwriting of the defendant; and the suggestion of the alcade Beggerat, before whom the girl had been examined, that slight torture should be applied, was read.

Don Juan Montes then said that he had known the island of

Trinidad since the year 1793, that the torture was never intro duced until after the conquest of the island, and was then practised by order of the defendant. It was first used with the military in 1799, and two years afterwards in the gaol.

Mr Dallas, for the defendant, rested his defence upon the following statements:

First—By the law of Spain, in the present instance, torture was directed; and, being bound to administer that law, he was vindicated in its application.

Secondly—The order for the torture, if not unlawfully, was not maliciously issued.

Thirdly—If it were unlawful, yet, if the order were erroneously or mistakenly issued, it was a complete answer to a criminal charge.

The learned counsel entered at considerable length into these positions, during which he compared the law of Spain as it prevailed in Trinidad, to the law of England as it subsisted in some of our own islands. He contended that the conduct of General Picton was gentleness and humanity, compared to what might be practised with impunity under the authority of the British government.

Mr Gloucester, the Attorney-General of His Majesty in the island, was then called, and he deposed to the authenticity of several books on the laws of the island, among which were the Elisondo, the Curia Philippica, the Bobadilla, the Colom, and the Recopilacion de Leyes.

Various passages in these books were referred to, and translated, for the purpose of showing that torture was not only permitted in certain cases, but in the particular instance before the jury.

Mr Garrow was then allowed to call a witness, to show that, however such a law might at any time have existed, or might still exist, in Spain, it did not prevail in the West Indian colonies of that power. To this end, Don Pedro de Vargass was sworn. He deposed that, during the early part of his life, he had been regularly initiated and admitted to the office of an advocate of the Spanish law-courts in the colonies; that he had practised after his admission, in the regular course, for two years, and had resided at five or six of the West India islands, in the pursuit of his profession; and that, according to his knowledge of the Book of Recapitulation, by which the laws were administered, there was nothing contained in it to justify the infliction of torture, nor was torture, to his knowledge, ever resorted to. There was a law of Old Castile, of the year 1260, which justified the torture in certain cases, but he never understood that it extended to the West Indies, and it was so much abhorred in Spain that it was either repealed or had fallen entirely into disuse.

Mr Dallas and Mr Garrow then severally addressed the jury. Lord Ellenborough, in summing up, recommended them to divest their minds of every feeling which they might have contracted in the course of the present trial, and to throw every part of the case out of their consideration, except that which related to this simple point: What was the law by which the island of Trinidad was governed at the period of its capture by the British? It was for the consideration of the jury whether the law then subsisting authorized personal torture to be inflicted. By the indulgence of the government of this country, the subsisting law was to continue: the question was, What was that subsisting law? The jury would observe that it did not necessarily follow, because Trinidad was a colony of Old Spain, that it must therefore, in every part, have the laws of Old Spain. It did not originally form any part of that country, but had been annexed to it, and on what terms there was no positive evidence. It did not appear that either the schedule peculiar to this island, or the recapitulation, embraced the criminal law or made any mention of torture. So, if torture did subsist in this island, it must be on the authority of law books read to the jury; and it was ascertained by several persons, apparently of competent knowledge, that torture had not, within their recollection, ever been practised in the island. It was, therefore, for the jury to say, in the absence of all positive proof on the subject, and in the face of so much negative evidence, whether the law of Spain was so fully and completely established in Trinidad as to make torture a part of the law of that island. Without going through the authorities, he thought the jury might take it to be the existing law of Old Spain that torture might be inflicted. It was too much to say that a discontinuance of a practice could repeal a law, but they had to determine whether they were convinced that torture had ever been part of the law of Trinidad, and also whether they were convinced that it was part of the law of Trinidad at the time of its capture. If so, they would enter a special verdict: if otherwise they would find the defendant guilty.

The jury found—There was no such law existing in the island of Trinidad, as that of torture, at the time of the surrender of that island to the British.

Lord Ellenborough—'Then, gentlemen, General Picton cannot derive any protection from a supposed law, after you have found that no such law remained in that island at the surrender of it, and when he became its governor; and therefore your verdict should be, that he is guilty.'

By the direction of Lord Ellenborough they therefore found the defendant 'Guilty'.

The trial lasted from nine in the morning till seven at night.

Governor Picton walked the hall of the courts during the whole of the trial. He was a tall man, of a very sallow complexion, apparently about fifty years of age, and was dressed in black. He was accompanied by several of the civil officers of the island.

Mr Dallas moved on the 25th of April for a new trial, upon the following grounds:

First—The infamous character of the girl, who lived in open prostitution with Pedro Ruiz, and who had been privy to a robbery committed upon her paramour by Carlos Gonzalez; and that when a complaint laid against her had been brought before a magistrate, she, refusing to confess, had been ordered to be tortured.

Secondly—That Governor Picton, who condemned her to this torture, did not proceed from any motives of malice, but from a conviction that the right of torture was sanctioned by the laws of Trinidad; and that he was rooted in this opinion by a reference to the legal written authorities in that island.

Thirdly—That whatever his conduct might be, it was certainly neither personal malice, nor disposition to tyranny, but resulted, if it should prove to be wrong, from a misapprehension of the laws of Trinidad.

Fourthly—That one of the principal witnesses in this trial, M. Vargass, had brought forward a book, entitled *Recopilacion des Leyes des Indes*, expressly compiled for the Spanish colonies, which did not authorize torture. But the defendant had no opportunity of ever seeing that book: it had been purchased by the British Institution at the sale of the Marquis of Lansdowne's library, subsequent to his indictment. Having consulted it however, it appeared that when that code was silent upon criminal cases, recourse was always to be had to the laws of Old Spain, and that those laws sanctioned the torture.

The Court, after some consideration, granted the rule to show cause why a new trial should not be had, and as the second trial, which was eventually allowed, was attended with a different result from that of the first, we think it no more than just to the memory of Governor Picton to conclude our notice of this affair with the following apology for his conduct, which is extracted from a respectable monthly publication:

'In an evil hour the governor associated with him, in the government of the island, the British naval commander on the station, and Colonel Fullarton. This was, as might naturally have been expected and as certainly was designed by one of the parties, the origin of disputes and the source of anarchy. It is well known that Fullarton, on his return to England, preferred charges against Picton, which were taken into consideration by the Privy Council and gave rise to a prosecution that lasted for several years. No pains were spared to sully his character, to ruin his fortunes, and to render him an object of public indignation. A little strumpet, by name Louisa Calderon, who cohabited with a petty tradesman in the capital of Trinidad, let another paramour into his house (of which she had the charge) during his absence, who robbed him, with her knowledge and privity, of all he was worth in the world. The girl was taken before the regular judges of the place; who, in the course of their investigation, ascertained the fact that she was privy to the robbery, and therefore sentenced her, in conformity with the laws of Spain, then prevalent in the island, to undergo the punishment of the *picket* (the same as is adopted in our own regiments of horse). But, as it was necessary that this sentence should receive the governor's confirmation before it could be carried into effect, a paper stating the necessity of it was sent to the government-house, and the governor, by his signature, conveyed his assent to the judges. The girl was accordingly picketed, when she acknowledged the facts above stated and discovered her accomplice. That the life of this girl was forfeited by the laws of every civilized country is a fact that will not admit of dispute. Yet clemency was here extended to her, and she was released, having suffered only the punishment above stated, which was so slight, that she walked a considerable distance to the prison, without the least appearance of suffering, immediately after it was inflicted. But what was the return for the lenity of the governor? He was accused by Colonel Fullarton of having put this girl (whom he had never even *seen*) to the *torture*, contrary to law; and the caricaturists of England were enlisted in the service of persecution. After a trial which seemed to have no end, after an expense of *seven thousand pounds* (which must have completed his ruin, had not his venerable uncle, General Picton, defrayed the whole costs of the suit, while the expenses of his prosecutor were all paid *by the government*) his honour and justice were established on the firmest basis, and to the perfect satisfaction of every upright mind.'

At the moment of writing this note, there has been a great deal of public anxiety because of allegations made in the House of Commons that an accused person charged with the murder of a policeman had been ill-treated by the police whilst in custody. It is mentioned here to show how sensitive the public conscience is on a matter of this kind. The freedom of which British people boast is not only a freedom from unlawful arrest, but is also a freedom from oppression of any kind whilst under arrest and awaiting trial. Her Majesty's judges have formulated a set of rules governing the procedure after an accused person has been taken into custody, and any breach of these rules by the police is treated as being of the gravest importance. It is scarcely necessary to say that any violence shown to an accused person when under arrest would be visited with the severest penalties.

Torture, as a means of getting confessions or extracting evidence against the accused or others, was never allowed by law in this country. In a world where torture was in use in many countries as a legalized method of extracting confessions, the example of England received great praise. But it should be remembered that up to 1772 a special form of torture was permitted by law and that was the device known as Peine Forte et Dure. *If any person charged with an offence against the law 'stood mute upon arraignment' and refused to plead to the indictment in order to escape conviction and its consequences, he could be laid upon his back in a dark dungeon, stripped of all his clothing, and pressed with heavy weights of stone or iron upon his body. When accused persons maintained their silence under this awful ordeal they were pressed by further weights until they died. The 'gentle' eighteenth century as it was sometimes called had a great deal to answer for so far as the criminal law was concerned. But in justice to the eighteenth century it ought to be said that the cases where men died after dreadful suffering, rather than leave a stain on their families and forfeit all their property to the Crown, were few in number.*

It ought also to be observed that whilst the English Common Law forbade the use of torture, and whilst Coke in his Institutes had affirmed this to be the law, nevertheless there is no doubt whatever that torture was used on suspects before trial to extort confessions. Warrants of torture never came from common-law judges but from the Queen or Privy Council, in short, from what was called the Prerogative. The manacles, the rack, an instrument known as Skevington's Irons were all used in Elizabethan times: and some 'obstinate fellows' were shut into the cell box called Little Ease. *There is evidence that some were shut in the Tower hole below high water mark, known as 'the low dungeon with the rats'. There is a full discussion of the use of torture in that most scholarly and deeply-interesting book* The Lion and the Throne *by Catherine Drinker Bowen.*

General Picton's case is remarkable for the comparative ease with which the General was brought to trial by a mulatto girl of little reputation, and for the extraordinary strength of the condemnatory language used by the counsel for the Crown, who said amongst other things—'The Governor ought to have been aware that the torture was not known in England; and that it never would be, and that it never could be tolerated in this country.'

JOHN HOLLOWAY and OWEN HAGGERTY, Executed for Murder

THE fatal accident which happened on the spot and at the moment of the execution of these men, will cause their memory, as well as their crimes, to remain a dreadful warning to many generations. Their whole case was attended with singular and awful circumstances. Of their guilt many entertained doubts, which are not yet entirely removed, and as lately as the year 1813, a man named Ward was indicted for the same murder, but acquitted. Their conviction rested, certainly, upon the evidence of a wretch as base as themselves, who stated himself to have been their accomplice, but the public indignation against them was excited to such a pitch, that it is scarcely to be wondered at that a jury pronounced them guilty.

On the 6th of November 1802, Mr John Cole Steele, who kept the Lavender Warehouse in Catherine Street, Strand, was murdered with much barbarity on Hounslow Heath, and his pockets rifled of their contents. The murderers escaped, and, though rewards were offered for their apprehension, no discovery was made.

Every search had been made by the officers of the police, several loose characters had been apprehended on suspicion but discharged on examination, and all hopes had been given up of tracing the murderers, when a circumstance occurred, about four years afterwards, which led to the apprehension of John Holloway and Owen Haggerty. A man of the name of Benjamin Hanfield, who had been convicted at the Old Bailey of grand larceny, in stealing a pair of shoes, was sentenced to seven years' transportation, and was conveyed on board a hulk at Portsmouth, to await his departure for New South Wales. But having been taken with a severe illness, and being tortured in his mind by the apparent recollection of a murder, about which he constantly raved, he said he wished to make a discovery before he died. A messenger was immediately dispatched to the police magistrates at Bow Street, to communicate the circumstance, and an officer was sent to bring Hanfield before them. When he was brought on shore, they were obliged to wait several days, during which his illness would not permit his removal. On his arrival in town, he made a full disclosure of the circumstances attending the murder of Mr Steele, and the magistrates having sent him, in custody of an officer, to Hounslow Heath, he there pointed out the fatal spot where the murder was perpetrated. As his evidence implicated Haggerty and Holloway, measures were taken to apprehend them, and, after a long search, they were taken into custody. Several private examinations of all the parties took place. Hanfield was admitted king's evidence, and the public once more cherished a hope that the murderers would meet the punishment they deserved.

Monday, February 9, 1807, being the day appointed for the final examination of the prisoners, they were brought before Mr Moser, at Worship Street police-office.

There was a great body of evidence adduced, none of which tended materially to criminate the prisoners, except that of Hanfield, the accomplice, who, under the promise of pardon, had turned king's evidence. The prisoners denied having any knowledge whatever of the crime laid to their charge, but the magistrates, after maturely considering the whole of the proofs adduced, thought proper to commit them for trial at the next sessions at the Old Bailey, and bound over no less than twenty-four persons to appear and give evidence on the trial.

Such was the eager curiosity of the public to know the issue of this trial, which came on February 20 before Sir Simon Le Blanc, knight, that the whole Court and area of the Old Bailey were greatly crowded.

When put to the bar, Holloway appeared to be about forty years of age, of great muscular strength, tall and of savage, brutal and ferocious countenance, with large thick lips, depressed nose and high cheek bones. Haggerty was a small man, twenty-four years of age.

Evidence was then adduced to show that Mr Steele, besides his residence in Catherine Street, had a house and grounds at Feltham, where he cultivated lavender and distilled it for sale in London. On the 5th of November 1802, he left Catherine Street, giving his family to understand that he should return on the following evening, and on the same night he arrived at Feltham.

On the next afternoon (Saturday) he quitted Feltham at about seven o'clock, on his way back to London, but he was never seen alive by any member of his family afterwards. His continued absence creating alarm, some persons were employed to search for him, and at length his body was found lying at the bottom of a ditch, near a clump of trees at a short distance from the barracks on Hounslow Heath. From the wounds which appeared about his person, it was evident that his death had been caused by violence, and Mr Frogley, a surgeon, being called in, it was found that his skull was severely fractured, and that he was otherwise wounded in a most dreadful manner. It was found also that he had been robbed of any money which he might have had about him, as well as of his hat and boots, an old pair of shoes and a common felt hat being left in their stead, close to the spot where the body was found. Notwithstanding the most strenuous exertions were subsequently made by the police to discover the perpetrators of this most barbarous murder, no trace was found until the confession of the accomplice Hanfield, in consequence of whose information Holloway was apprehended at Brentford during the election, and Haggerty was taken into custody on board the Shannon frigate, where he was serving as a marine. They were both taken to the police-office and confronted, but they denied all knowledge of each other and of Hanfield, and they both gave accounts of themselves as to their condition and situation at the time of the murder, which, however, turned out to be untrue. While confined in the lock-up attached to the office, Bishop, the officer, secreted himself in the privy adjoining, where he could hear all their conversation, and he heard them make use of expressions, which left no doubt of their being acquainted and of their having been at Hounslow on the night of the murder.

The king's pardon, under the great seal, to Hanfield *alias* Enfield, remitting his sentence of transportation for seven years and restoring him to his competency as a witness, having then been read, that witness was called, and made the following statement on oath: 'I have known Haggerty eight or nine years, and Holloway six or seven. We were accustomed to meet at the Black Horse and Turk's Head public-houses, in Dyot Street. I was in their company in the month of November 1802. Holloway, just before the murder, called me out from the Turk's Head, and asked me if I had any objection to be in a good thing? I replied I had not. He said it was a "*Low Toby*", meaning it was a footpad robbery. I asked when and where, and he said he would let me know. We parted but two days after we met again and Saturday, the 6th of November, was appointed. I asked who was to go with us? He replied that Haggerty had agreed to make one. We all three met on the Saturday at the Black Horse, when Holloway said, "Our business is to *sarve* a gentleman on Hounslow Heath, who, I understand, travels that road with property." We then drank for about three or four hours, and about the middle of the day we set off for Hounslow. We stopped at the Bell public-house, and took some porter. We proceeded from thence upon the road towards Belfont, and expressed our hope that we should get a good booty. We stopped near the eleventh milestone and secreted ourselves in a clump of trees. While there, the moon got up, and Holloway said we had come too soon. After loitering about a considerable time, Holloway said he heard a footstep, and we proceeded towards Belfont. We presently saw a man coming towards us and, on approaching him, we ordered him to stop, which he immediately did. Holloway went round him, and told him to deliver. He said we should have his money and hoped we would not ill-use him. The deceased put his hand in his pocket and gave Haggerty his money. I demanded his pocket-book. He replied that he had none. Holloway insisted that he had a book, and if he did not deliver it he would knock him down. I then laid hold of his legs. Holloway stood at his head, and said if he cried out he would knock out his brains. The deceased again said he hoped we would not ill-use him. Haggerty proceeded to search him, when the deceased made some resistance, and struggled so much that we got across the road. He cried out severely and, as a carriage was coming up, Holloway said, with a terrible oath, "Take care, I will silence him", and immediately struck him several violent blows on the head and body. The deceased heaved a deep groan and stretched himself out lifeless. I felt alarmed, and said, "John, you have killed the man." Holloway replied that it was a lie, for he was only stunned. I said I would stay no longer, and immediately set off towards London, leaving Holloway and Haggerty with the body. I came to Hounslow and stopped at the end of the town for near an hour. Holloway and Haggerty then came up and said they had done the trick, and as a token put the deceased's hat into my hand—the hat Holloway went down in was like a soldier's hat. I told Holloway it was a cruel piece of business and that I was sorry I had any hand in it. We all turned down a lane, and returned to London. As we came along I asked Holloway if he had got the pocket-book. He replied it was no matter, for, as I had refused to share the danger, I should not share the booty. We came to the Black Horse in Dyot Street, had half a pint of gin, and parted. Haggerty went down in shoes but I don't know if he came back in them. The next day I observed Holloway had a hat upon his head which was too small for him. I asked him if it was the same he got the preceding night. He said it was. We met again on the Monday, when I told Holloway that he acted imprudently in wearing the hat, as it might lead to a discovery. He put the hat into my hand, and I observed the name of Steele in it. I repeated my fears. At night Holloway brought the hat in a handkerchief, and we went to Westminster Bridge, filled the hat with stones and, having tied the lining over it, threw it into the Thames.'

The witness, being cross-examined by the counsel for the prisoners, said he had made no other minutes of the transactions he had been detailing than what his conscience took cognisance of. It was accident that led to this disclosure. He was talking with other prisoners in Newgate of particular robberies that had taken place, and the Hounslow robbery and murder being stated amongst others, he inadvertently said that there were only three persons who knew of that transaction. The remark was circulated and a rumour ran through the prison that he was about to turn '*nose*', and he was obliged to hold his tongue, lest he should be ill-used. When at Portsmouth, on board the hulks, the compunctions of conscience came upon him, and he was obliged to dissipate his thoughts by drinking, to prevent him from divulging all he knew. He admitted that he had led a vicious life, that he had been concerned in several robberies, and had entered and deserted from several regiments. He had served in the East and West London Militias, had enlisted into the Ninth and Fourteenth Light Dragoons, and had been in the army of reserve. He added that he was ashamed and sorry at what he had been, and would endeavour to mend his life in future.

Evidence, in corroboration of his statement, with regard to the hat and boots fitting Holloway, was also given by Mr Steele's tradespeople and, the prosecution being closed, the prisoners were called upon to make their defence.

Haggerty protested that he was completely innocent of the charge, and was totally unacquainted with the witness, Hanfield. He denied ever having been at Hounslow, and endeavoured to point out some inconsistencies in the evidence which had been adduced.

Holloway declared that he was equally innocent, but admitted that he had been at Hounslow more than once, and that he might have been in the company of the prisoner Haggerty and Hanfield, although he said that he was not acquainted with either of them.

Mr Justice Le Blanc summed up the evidence in a very clear and perspicuous manner, and the jury, having retired for about a quarter of an hour, returned with a verdict of Guilty against both the prisoners.

The recorder immediately passed sentence in the most solemn and impressive manner, and the unhappy men were ordered for execution on the following Monday morning, February the 23rd, 1807.

They went from the bar reiterating protestations of their innocence, and apparently careless of the miserable and ignominious fate that awaited them.

After conviction Haggerty and Holloway conducted themselves with the most decided indifference. On Saturday, February 21, the cell-door, No 1, in which they were both confined, was opened about half-past two. They were reading in two prayer-books by candle-light, as the cell was very dark. On Sunday, neither of them attended the condemned sermon. Several magistrates interrogated them, but they still persisted in their innocence.

During the whole of Sunday night the convicts were engaged in prayer. They never slept, but broke the awful stillness of midnight by frequent reciprocal protestations of innocence. At five they were called, dressed and shaved, and about seven were brought into the press yard. There was some difficulty in knocking off the irons of Haggerty, and he voluntarily assisted, though he seemed much dejected. A message was then delivered to the sheriffs, that Holloway wanted to speak with them in private. This excited very sanguine expectations of confession, but the sheriffs, on their return, intimated to the gentlemen in the press-yard, that Holloway wanted to address them publicly. He therefore requested they would form themselves into a circle, from the centre of which Holloway delivered, in the most solemn manner, the following energetic address:'Gentlemen, I am quite innocent of this affair. I never was with Hanfield, nor do I know the spot. I will kneel and swear it.' He then knelt down and imprecated curses on his head if he were guilty, and he concluded by saying, 'By God, I am innocent.'

Owen Haggerty first ascended the scaffold. His arms were pinioned, and the halter had been already placed round his neck: he wore a white cap, and a light olive shag great-coat: he looked downwards and was silent. He was attended by a Roman Catholic clergyman, who read to him, and to whom the unfortunate culprit seemed to pay great attention. He made no public acknowledgement of guilt. After the executioner had tied the fatal noose, he brought up Holloway, who wore a smock frock and jacket, as it had been stated by the approver that he did at the time of the murder. He had also a white cap on, was pinioned, and had a halter round his neck: he had his hat in his hand. Mounting the scaffold, he jumped, made an awkward bow, and said, 'I am innocent, innocent, by God!' He then turned round, and, bowing, made use of the same expressions, 'Innocent, innocent, innocent! Gentlemen! No verdict! No verdict! No verdict! Gentlemen! Innocent! Innocent!' At this moment, the executioner proceeded to do his office, by placing the cap over his face, to which he complied, with apparent reluctance, at the same time uttering some words which were not heard. As soon as the rope was fixed round his neck, he became quiet. He was attended in his devotions by an assistant at Rowland Hill's Chapel.

The last that mounted the scaffold was Elizabeth Godfrey. She had been a woman of the town, aged 34, and had been capitally convicted of the wilful murder of Richard Prince, in Mary-le-bone parish, on the 25th of December 1806, by giving him a mortal wound with a pocket-knife in the left eye, of which wound he languished and died.

They were all launched off together, at about a quarter after eight. It was a long time before the body of the poor female seemed to have gone through its last suffering.

The crowd which assembled to witness this execution was unparalleled, being, according to the best calculation, near 40,000; and the fatal catastrophe, which happened in consequence, will cause the day long to be remembered. By eight o'clock, not an inch of ground was unoccupied in view of the platform, and the pressure of the crowd was so great, that before the malefactors appeared, numbers of persons were crying out in vain to escape from it. The attempt only tended to increase the confusion, and several females of low stature, who had been so imprudent as to venture among the mob, were in a dismal situation: their cries were dreadful. Some, who could be no longer supported by the men, were suffered to fall and were trampled to death, and this was also the case with several boys. In all parts there were continual cries of 'Murder! murder!' particularly from the female part of the spectators and children, some of whom were seen expiring without the possibility of obtaining the least assistance, every one being employed in endeavours to preserve his own life. The most affecting scene of distress was seen at Green Arbour Lane, nearly opposite the Debtors'-door. The terrible occurrence which took place near this spot was attributed to the circumstance of two pie-men attending there to dispose of their pies. It appears that one of them having his basket overthrown, which stood upon a sort of stool upon four legs, some of the mob, being severely pressed, fell over the basket and the man, at the moment he was picking it up. Those who fell were never more suffered to rise.

A woman, who was so imprudent as to bring with her a child at the breast, was one of the number killed. Whilst in the act of falling, she forced the child into the arms of the man nearest to her, requesting him, for God's sake, to save its life; but the man, finding it required all his exertions to preserve himself, threw the infant from him. It was fortunately caught at a distance by another man, who, finding it difficult to ensure its safety or his own, got rid of it in a similar way. The child was then again caught by a person, who contrived to struggle with it to a cart, under which he deposited it until the danger was over and the mob had dispersed.

In other parts, the pressure was so great that a horrible scene of confusion ensued, and seven persons lost their lives by suffocation alone. A cart which was overloaded with spectators broke down, and some of the persons falling from the vehicle, were trampled under foot and never recovered.

During the hour for which the malefactors hung, little assistance could be afforded to the unhappy sufferers, but after the bodies were cut down and the gallows removed to the Old Bailey yard, the marshals and constables cleared the street, when shocking to relate, there lay strewed round near one hundred persons dead or in a state of insensibility. Twenty-seven dead bodies were taken to St Bartholomew's Hospital, four to St Sepulchre's church, one to the Swan on Snow Hill, one to a public-house opposite St Andrew's church, Holborn, one, an apprentice, to his master's, Mr Broadwood, pianoforte maker, Golden Square. A mother was seen carrying away the body of her dead boy, and the body of Mr Harrison, a respectable gentleman, was taken to his house at Holloway. There was a sailor-boy killed opposite Newgate by suffocation: he carried a small bag, in which he had some bread and cheese, from which it was concluded that he had come some distance to witness the execution.

After the dead, dying and wounded were carried away, there was a cart-load of shoes, hats, petticoats and other articles of wearing apparel picked up. Until four o'clock in the afternoon, most of the surrounding houses contained some persons in a wounded state, who were afterwards taken away by their friends on shutters or in hackney-coaches. The doors of St Bartholomew's Hospital were closed against the populace, until after the bodies of the dead were stripped and washed. They were ranged round a ward on the first floor, on the women's side, and were placed on the floor with sheets over them and their clothes put as pillows under their heads: their faces were uncovered, and a rail was placed along the centre of the room. The persons who were admitted to see the shocking spectacle went up on one side, and returned on the other. Until two o'clock in the morning, the entrances to the hospital were beset with persons anxiously seeking for their lost relatives and friends.

The next day (Tuesday) a coroner's inquest sat in St Bartholomew's Hospital and other places where the bodies were. Several witnesses were examined with respect to the circumstances of the accident, and on Friday, when the inquest terminated, the verdict was, 'That the several persons came by their death from compression and suffocation.'

This is one of those cases that leaves the reader with an uneasy mind. It does sometimes happen that public indignation is so deep and widespread that it invades the jury-box and possibly results in grave injustice. In our day the warning to the jury by the judge would be such that the risk of a miscarriage of justice would be slight, and of course there is always the Court of Criminal Appeal in the background ready to correct manifest errors. The barbarity of the murder of Mr Steele created a very great wave of resentment but almost five years had passed before the two men were brought to trial and convicted on the word of 'a wretch as base as themselves' according to the text. I do not think any such conviction would be allowed to take place in our modern courts.

But the event which makes the case memorable is the awful disaster which occurred at the public execution of Holloway and Haggerty. It is difficult for modern readers to understand the state of affairs which existed in the eighteenth century concerning the criminal law and its administration. For a long period of time the condemned men and women, some of them condemned to death for the most trivial offences, were driven to Tyburn to be hanged and very large crowds gathered to watch the gruesome ceremony and to indulge in various forms of ignorant superstition. Deterrence was the dominating idea of the criminal law, and as it was felt that the punishment of death was the greatest possible deterrent, it was only logical and natural that the more public the execution, the better it would be for deterrence to have its full and proper effect. When Holloway and Haggerty were hanged the processions to Tyburn had been abandoned and the executions took place in front of Newgate jail. Dr Radzinowicz, whose History of the Criminal Law *bids fair to become a classic, says that when the bodies of Holloway and Haggerty were cut down and the gallows removed, nearly one hundred dead and dying were found scattered over the ground. When Fauntleroy was hanged at Newgate in 1824 more than 100,000 persons assembled and the behaviour of the crowds was no better than it had been at Tyburn. Peers and Members of Parliament and a great number of ladies all thought it quite right and proper to make up parties for the express purpose of attending the horrible and sometimes quite revolting spectacle.*

Mary Bateman, Commonly called the Yorkshire Witch, Executed for Murder

The insidious arts practised by this woman rendered her a pest to the neighbourhood in which she resided, and she richly deserved that fate which eventually befell her.

She was indicted at York on the 18th of March 1809, for the wilful murder of Rebecca Perigo of Bramley in the same county, in the month of May in the previous year.

The examination of the witnesses, who were called to support the case for the prosecution, showed, that Mrs Bateman resided at Leeds, and was well known at that place, as well as in the surrounding districts, as a 'witch', in which capacity she had been frequently employed to work cures of 'evil wishes', and all the other customary imaginary illnesses, to which the credulous lower orders at that time supposed themselves liable. Her name had become much celebrated in the neighbourhood for her successes in the arts of divining and witchcraft, and it may be readily concluded that her efforts in her own behalf were no less profitable.

In the spring of 1806 Mrs Perigo, who lived with her husband at Bramley, a village at a short distance from Leeds, was seized with a 'flacking', or fluttering in her breast whenever she lay down, and applying to a quack doctor of the place, he assured her that it was beyond his cure, for that an 'evil wish' had been laid upon her, and that the arts of sorcery must be resorted to in order to effect her relief. While in this dilemma, she was visited by her niece, a girl named Stead, who at that time filled a situation as a household servant at Leeds, and who had taken advantage of the Whitsuntide holidays to go round to see her friends. Stead expressed her sorrow to find her aunt in so terrible a situation, and recommended an immediate appeal to the prisoner, whose powers she described as fully equal to get rid of any affection of the kind, whether produced by mortal or diabolical charms. An application was at once determined on, and Stead was employed to broach the subject to the diviner. She, in consequence, paid the prisoner a visit at her house in Black Dog

Yard, near the bank at Leeds. Having acquainted her with the nature of the malady by which her aunt was affected, she was informed that the prisoner knew a lady who lived at Scarborough, and that if a flannel petticoat or some article of dress, which was worn next the skin of the patient, was sent to her, she would at once communicate with this lady upon the subject.

On the following Tuesday, William Perigo, the husband of the deceased, proceeded to her house, and having handed over his wife's flannel petticoat, the prisoner said that she would write to Miss Blythe, who was the lady to whom she had alluded at Scarborough, by the same night's post, and that an answer would doubtless be returned by that day week, when he was to call again. On the day mentioned, Perigo was true to his appointment, and the prisoner produced to him a letter, saying that it had arrived from Miss Blythe, and that it contained directions as to what was to be done. After a great deal of circumlocution and mystery the letter was opened and read by the prisoner, and it was found that it contained an order 'that Mary Bateman should go to Perigo's house at Bramley, and should take with her four guinea notes, which were enclosed, and that she should sew them into the four corners of the bed, in which the diseased woman slept.' There they were to remain for eighteen months. Perigo was to give her four other notes of like value, to be returned to Scarborough. Unless all these directions were strictly attended to, the charm would be useless and would not work. On the 4th of August the prisoner went over to Bramley, and having shown the four notes, proceeded apparently to sew them up in silken bags, which she delivered over to Mrs Perigo to be placed in the bed. The four notes desired to be returned were then handed to her by Perigo and she retired, directing her dupes frequently to send to her house, as letters might be expected from Miss Blythe. In about a fortnight, another letter was produced, and it contained directions that two pieces of iron in the form of horse-shoes should be nailed up by the prisoner at Perigo's door, but that the nails should not be driven in with a hammer, but with the back of a pair of pincers, and that the pincers were to be sent to Scarborough, to remain in the custody of Miss Blythe for the eighteen months already mentioned in the charm. The prisoner accordingly again visited

Bramley and, having nailed up the horse-shoes, received and carried off the pincers.

In October the following letter was received by Perigo, bearing the signature of the supposed Miss Blythe.

'My dear Friend—You must go down to Mary Bateman's at Leeds, on Tuesday next, and carry two guinea notes with you and give her them, and she will give you other two that I have sent to her from Scarborough, and you must buy me a small cheese about six or eight pound weight, and it must be of your buying, for it is for a particular use, and it is to be carried down to Mary Bateman's, and she will send it to me by the coach—This letter is to be burned when you have done reading it.'

From this time to the month of March 1807, a great number of letters were received, demanding the transmission of various articles to Miss Blythe through the medium of the prisoner. All these were to be preserved by her until the expiration of the eighteen months. In the course of the same period money to the amount of near seventy pounds was paid over, Perigo, upon each occasion of payment, receiving silk bags, containing what were pretended to be coins or notes of corresponding value, which were to be sewn up in the bed as before. In March 1807, the following letter arrived.

'My dear Friends—I will be obliged to you if you will let me have half-a-dozen of your china, three silver spoons, half-a-pound of tea, two pounds of loaf sugar, and a tea canister to put the tea in, or else it will not do—I durst not drink out of my own china. You must burn this with a candle.'

The china, &c, not having been sent, in the month of April Miss Blythe wrote as follows:

'My dear Friends—*I will be obliged to you if you will buy me a camp bedstead, bed and bedding, a blanket, a pair of sheets, and a long bolster must come from your house.* You need not buy the best feathers, common ones will do. I have laid on the floor for three nights, and I cannot lay on my own bed *owing to the planets being so bad concerning your wife*, and I must have one of your buying or it will not do. You must bring down the china, the sugar, the caddy, the three silver spoons, and the tea at the same time when you buy the bed, and pack them up altogether. My brother's boat will be up in a day or two, and I will order my brother's boatman to call for them all at Mary Bateman's, and you must give Mary Bateman one shilling for the boatman, and I will place it to your account. Your wife must burn this as soon as it is read or it will not do.'

This had the desired effect, and the prisoner having called upon the Perigos, she accompanied them to the shops of a Mr Dobbin and a Mr Musgrave at Leeds, to purchase the various articles named. These were eventually bought at a cost of sixteen pounds, and sent to Mr Sutton's, at the Lion and Lamb Inn, Kirkgate, there to await the arrival of the supposed messenger.

At the end of April, the following letter arrived: 'My dear Friends—I am sorry to tell you you will take an illness in the month of May next, one or both of you, but I think both, but the works of God must have its course. You will escape the chambers of the grave; though you seem to be dead, yet you will live. Your wife must take half-a-pound of honey down from Bramley to Mary Bateman's at Leeds, and it must remain there till you go down yourself, and she will put in such like stuff as I have sent from Scarbro' to her, and she will put it in when you come down, and see her yourself, or it will not do. You must eat pudding for six days, and you must put in such like stuff as I have sent to Mary Bateman from Scarbro', and she will give your wife it, but you must not begin to eat of this pudding while I let you know. If ever you find yourself sickly at any time, you must take each of you a teaspoonful of this honey; I will remit twenty pounds to you on the 20th day of May, and it will pay a little of what you owe. You must bring this down to Mary Bateman's, and burn it at her house, when you come down next time.'

The instructions contained in this letter were complied with, and the prisoner having first mixed a white powder in the honey, handed over six others of the same colour and description to Mrs Perigo, saying that they must be used in the precise manner mentioned upon them, or they would all be killed. On the 5th of May, another letter arrived in the following terms:

'My dear Friends—You must begin to eat pudding on the 11th of May, and you must put one of the powders in every day as they are marked, for six days—and you must see it put in yourself every day or else it will not do. If you find yourself sickly at any time you must not have no doctor, for it will not do, and you must not let the boy that used to eat with you eat of that pudding for six days; and you must make only just as much as you can eat yourselves, if there is any left it will not do. You must keep the door fast as much as possible or you will be overcome by some enemy. Now think on and take my directions or else it will kill us all. About the 25th of May I will come to Leeds and send for your wife to Mary Bateman's; your wife will take me by the hand and say, "God bless you that I ever found you out." It has pleased God to send me into the world that I might destroy the works of darkness; I call them the works of darkness because they are dark to you—now mind what I say whatever you do. This letter must be burned in straw on the hearth by your wife.'

The absurd credulity of Mr and Mrs Perigo even yet favoured the horrid designs of the prisoner; and, in obedience to the directions which they received, they began to eat the puddings on the day named. For five days they had no particular flavour, but upon the sixth powder being mixed, the pudding was found so nauseous that the former could only eat one or two mouthfuls, while his wife managed to swallow three or four. They were both directly seized with violent vomiting and Mrs Perigo, whose faith appears to have been greater than that of her husband, at once had recourse to the honey. Their sickness continued during the whole day, but although Mrs Perigo suffered the most intense torments, she positively refused to hear of a doctor's being sent for, lest, as she said, the charm should be broken by Miss Blythe's directions being opposed. The recovery of the husband, from the illness by which he was affected, slowly progressed; but the wife, who persisted in eating the honey, continued daily to lose strength. She at length expired on the 24th of May, her last words being a request to her husband not to be 'rash' with Mary Bateman, but to await the coming of the appointed time.

Mr Chorley, a surgeon, was subsequently called in to see her body, but although he expressed his firm belief that the death of the deceased was caused by her having taken poison, and although that impression was confirmed by the circumstance of a cat dying immediately after it had eaten some of the pudding, no further steps were taken to ascertain the real cause of death, and Perigo even subsequently continued in communication with the prisoner.

Upon his informing her of the death of his wife, she at once declared that it was attributable to her having eaten all the honey at once. Then in the beginning of June, he received the following letter from Miss Blythe:

'My dear Friend—I am sorry to tell you that your wife should touch of those things which I ordered her not, and for that reason it has caused her death; it had likened to have killed me at Scarborough, and Mary Bateman at Leeds, and you and all, and for this reason, she will rise from the grave, she will stroke your face with her right hand, and you will lose the use of one side, but I will pray for you. I would not have you to go to no doctor, for it will not do. I would have you to eat and drink what you like, and you will be better. Now, my dear friend, take my directions, do and it will be better for you. Pray God bless you. Amen. Amen. You must burn this letter immediately after it is read.'

Letters were also subsequently received by him, purporting to be from the same person, in which new demands for clothing, coals, and other articles were made, but at length, in the month of October 1808, two years having elapsed since the commencement of the charm, he thought that the time had fully arrived when, if any good effects were to be produced from it, they would have been apparent, and that therefore he was entitled to look for his money in the bed. He in consequence commenced a search for the little silk bags in which his notes and money had been, as he supposed, sewn up; but although the bags indeed were in precisely the same positions in which they had been placed by his deceased wife, by some unaccountable conjuration, the notes and gold had turned to rotten cabbage-leaves and bad farthings. The darkness, by which the truth had been so long obscured, now passed away, and having communicated with the prisoner, by a stratagem, meeting her under pretence of receiving from her a bottle of medicine, which was to cure him from the effects of the puddings which still remained, he caused her to be apprehended. Upon her house being searched, nearly all the property sent to the supposed Miss Blythe was found in her possession, and a bottle containing a liquid mixed with two powders, one of which proved to be oatmeal, and the other arsenic, was taken from her pocket when she was taken into custody.

The rest of the evidence against the prisoner went to show that there was no such person as Miss Blythe living at Scarborough, and that all the letters which had been received by Perigo were in her own handwriting, and had been sent by her to Scarborough to be transmitted back again. An attempt was also proved to have been made by her to purchase some arsenic, at the shop of a Mr Clough, in Kirkgate, in the month of April 1807. But the most important testimony was that of Mr Chorley, the surgeon, who distinctly proved that he had analysed what remained of the pudding and of the contents of the honey pot, and that he found them both to contain a deadly poison, called corrosive sublimate of mercury, and that the symptoms exhibited by the deceased and her husband were such as would have arisen from the administration of such a drug.

The prisoner's defence consisted of a simple denial of the charge, and the learned judge then proceeded to address the jury. Having stated the nature of the allegations made in the indictment, he said that in order to come to a conclusion as to the guilt of the prisoner, it was necessary that three points should be clearly made out. 1st. That the deceased died of poison. 2nd. That that poison was administered by the contrivance and knowledge of the prisoner. 3rd. That it was so done for the purpose of occasioning the death of the deceased. A large body of evidence had been laid before them, to prove that the prisoner had engaged in schemes of fraud against the deceased and her husband, which was proved not merely by the evidence of Wm. Perigo, but by the testimony of other witnesses. The inference the prosecutors drew from this fraud was the existence of a powerful motive or temptation to commit a still greater crime, for the purpose of escaping the shame and punishment which must have attended the detection of the fraud—a fraud so gross, that it excited his surprise that any individual in that age and nation could be the dupe of it. But the jury should not go beyond this inference, and presume that, because the prisoner had been guilty of fraud, she was of course likely to have committed the crime of murder. That, if proved, must be shown by other evidence. His Lordship then proceeded to recapitulate the whole of the evidence, as detailed in the preceding pages, and concluded with the following observations. 'It is impossible not to be struck with wonder at the extraordinary credulity of Wm. Perigo, which neither the loss of his property, the death of his wife nor his own severe sufferings, could dispel. It was not until the month of October in the following year, that he ventured to open his hid treasure, and found there what everyone in court must have anticipated that he would find, not a single vestige of his property. His evidence is laid before the jury with the observation which arises from this uncommon want of judgement, but his memory appears to be very retentive and his evidence is confirmed, and that in different parts of the narrative, by other witnesses, while many parts of the case do not rest upon his evidence at all. The illness and peculiar symptoms, which preceded the death of his wife, his own severe sickness, and a variety of other circumstances attending the experiments made upon the pudding, were proved by separate and independent testimony. It is most strange that, in a case of so much suspicion as it appeared to have excited at the time, the interment of the body should have taken place without any inquiry as to the cause of death, an inquiry which then would have been much less difficult, though the fact of the deceased having died of poison is now well established. The main question is, did the prisoner contrive the means to induce the deceased to take it? If she did so contrive the means, the intent could only be to destroy. Poison so deadly could not be administered with any other view. The jury will lay all the facts and circumstances together; and if they feel them press so strongly against the prisoner, as to induce a conviction of the prisoner's having procured the deceased to take poison with an intent to occasion her death, they will find her guilty. If they do not think the evidence conclusive, they will, in that case, find the prisoner not guilty.'

The jury, after conferring for a moment, found the prisoner guilty, and the judge proceeded to pass sentence of death upon her, in nearly the following words:

'Mary Bateman, you have been convicted of wilful murder by a jury who, after having examined your case with caution, have, constrained by the force of evidence, pronounced you guilty. It only remains for me to fulfil my painful duty by passing upon you the awful sentence of the law. After you have been so long in the situation in which you now stand, and harassed as your mind must be by the long detail of your crimes and by listening to the sufferings you have occasioned, I do not wish to add to your distress by saying more than my duty renders necessary. Of your guilt, there cannot remain a particle of doubt in the breast of anyone who has heard your case. You entered into a long and premeditated system of fraud, which you carried on for a length of time which is most astonishing, and by means which one would have supposed could not, in this age and nation, have been practised with success. To prevent a discovery of your complicated fraud, and the punishment which must have resulted therefrom, you deliberately contrived the death of the persons you had so grossly injured, and that by means of poison, a mode of destruction against which there is no sure protection. But your guilty design was not fully accomplished, and, after so extraordinary a lapse of time, you are reserved as a signal example of the justice of that mysterious Providence, which, sooner or later, overtakes guilt like yours. At the very time when you were apprehended, there is the greatest reason to suppose, that if your surviving victim had met you alone, as you wished him to do, you would have administered to him a more deadly dose, which would have completed the diabolical project you had long before formed, but which at that time only partially succeeded; for upon your person, at that moment, was found a phial containing a most deadly poison. For crimes like yours, in this world, the gates of mercy are closed. You afforded your victim no time for preparation, but the law, while it dooms you to death, has, in its mercy, afforded you time for repentance, and the assistance of pious and devout men, whose admonitions, and prayers, and counsels may assist to prepare you for another world, where even your crimes, if sincerely repented of, may find mercy.

'The sentence of the law is, and the court doth award it, That you be taken to the place from whence you came, and from thence, on Monday next, to the place of execution, there to be hanged by the neck until you are dead, and that your body be given to the surgeons to be dissected and anatomized. And may Almighty God have mercy upon your soul.'

The prisoner having intimated that she was pregnant, the clerk of the arraigns said, 'Mary Bateman, what have you to say, why immediate execution should not be awarded against you?' On which the prisoner pleaded that she was twenty-two weeks gone with child. On this plea the judge ordered the sheriff to empanel a jury of matrons: this order created a general consternation among the ladies, who hastened to quit the court, to prevent the execution of so painful an office being imposed upon them. His lordship, in consequence, ordered the doors to be closed, and in about half-an-hour, twelve married women being empanelled, they were sworn in court, and charged to inquire 'whether the prisoner was with quick child?' The jury of matrons then retired with the prisoner, and on their return into court delivered their verdict, which was that Mary Bateman is not with quick child. The execution of course was not respited, and she was remanded back to prison.

During the brief interval between her receiving sentence of death and her execution, the ordinary, the Rev George Brown, took great pains to prevail upon her ingenuously to acknowledge and confess her crimes. Though the prisoner behaved with decorum during the few hours that remained of her existence, and readily joined in the customary offices of devotion, no traits of that deep compunction of mind which, for crimes like hers, must be felt where repentance is sincere, could be observed; but she maintained her caution and mystery to the last. On the day preceding her execution, she wrote a letter to her husband, in which she enclosed her wedding-ring, with a request that it might be given to her daughter. She admitted that she had been guilty of many frauds, but still denied that she had had any intention to produce the death of Mr or Mrs Perigo.

Upon the Monday morning at five o'clock she was called from her cell, to undergo the last sentence of the law. She received the communion with some other prisoners, who were about to be executed on the same day, but all attempts to induce her to acknowledge the justice of her sentence, or the crime of which she had been found guilty, proved vain. She maintained the greatest firmness in her demeanour to the last, which was in no wise interrupted even upon her taking leave of her infant child, which lay sleeping in her cell.

Upon the appearance of the convict upon the platform, the deepest silence prevailed amongst the immense assemblage of persons, which had been collected to witness the execution. As a final duty, the Rev Mr Brown, immediately before the drop fell, again exhorted the unhappy woman to confession, but her only reply was a repetition of the declaration of her innocence, and the next moment terminated her existence.

Her body having remained suspended during the usual time, was cut down, and sent to the General Infirmary at Leeds to be anatomized. Immense crowds of persons assembled to meet the hearse in which it was carried, and so great was the desire of the people to see her remains, that 30*l.* were collected for the use of the infirmary, by the payment of 3*d.* for each person admitted to the apartment in which they were exposed.

A short sketch of the life of this remarkable woman shall conclude this article. Mary Bateman, it appears, was born of reputable parents at Aisenby in the North Riding of Yorkshire, in the year 1768: her father, whose name was Harker, carrying on business as a small farmer. As early as at the age of five years, she exhibited much of that sly knavery, which subsequently so extraordinarily distinguished her character; and many were the frauds and falsehoods, of which she was guilty, and for which she was punished. In the year 1780, she first quitted her father's house, to undertake the duties of a servant in Thirsk, but having been guilty of some peccadilloes, she proceeded to York in 1787. Before she had been in that city more than twelve months, she was detected in pilfering some trifling articles of property belonging to her mistress, and was compelled to run off to Leeds, without waiting either for her wages or her clothes. For a considerable time she remained without employment or friends, but at length, upon the recommendation of an acquaintance of her father, she obtained an engagement in the shop of a mantua-maker, in whose service she remained for more than three years. She then became acquainted with John Bateman, to whom after a three weeks' courtship she was married in the year 1792.

Within two months after her marriage, she was found to have been guilty of many frauds, and she only escaped prosecution by inducing her husband to move frequently from place to place, so as to escape apprehension; and at length poor Bateman, driven almost wild by the tricks of his wife, entered the supplementary militia. Mrs Bateman was now entirely thrown upon her own resources and, unable to follow any reputable trade, she in the year 1799 took up her residence in Marsh Lane, near Timble Bridge, Leeds, and proceeded to deal in fortune-telling and the sale of charms. From a long course of iniquity, carried on chiefly through the medium of the most wily arts, she had acquired a manner and a mode of speech peculiarly adapted to her new profession, and abundance of credulous victims daily presented themselves to her.

It would be useless to follow this wretched woman through the subsequent scenes of her miserable life. Fraud and deceit were the only means by which she was able to carry on the war, and numerous were the impudent and heartless schemes which she put into operation to dupe the unhappy objects of her attacks. Her character was such as to prevent her long pursuing her occupation in one position, and she was repeatedly compelled to change her abode until she at length took up her residence in Black Dog Lane, where she was apprehended. Her husband at this time had returned from the militia several years, and although he followed the trade to which he had been brought up, there can be little doubt that he shared the proceeds of his wife's villainies.

Mary Bateman was neat in her person and dress, and though there was nothing ingenuous in her countenance, it had an air of placidity and composure, not ill adapted to make a favourable impression on those who visited her. Her manner of address was soft and insinuating, with the affectation of sanctity. In her domestic arrangements she was regular, and was mistress of such qualifications in housewifery as, with an honest heart, would have enabled her to fill her station with respectability and usefulness.

This astounding case illustrates the almost unbelievable credulity of certain sections of the public some 150 years ago. The State Trials *contain several cases testifying to a belief in the existence of witches and the practice of witchcraft, the most notable being the trial of the Suffolk witches before Lord Chief Baron Hale in 1661 at the Assizes at Bury St Edmunds. Hale was a deeply religious man and told the jury that 'he made no doubt at all of the existence of witches as proved by the Scriptures, general consent, and Acts of Parliament'. The accused women were two old widows and it was alleged against them that they had caused certain children to be taken with fainting fits, to vomit nails and pins, and to see mysterious mice, ducks and flies invisible to others. A toad ran out of their bed, and on being thrown into the fire exploded with a noise like the crack of a pistol. Hale allowed them to be convicted without commenting on the evidence and sentenced them both to death; and four days later they were both hanged. If so upright and learned a man as Hale could believe in such transparent nonsense, the credulity of a man like Perigo in Mary Bateman's case is at least understandable.*

HARRIET MAGNIS, Tried for Child Stealing

THE offence for which this woman was tried was one which, at the time of its commission, attracted a very considerable degree of attention. The child stolen was the offspring of a respectable couple living in Martin's Lane in the City, named Dellow, and it appears that he was playing with his little sister in the neighbourhood of his mother's house, when he was suddenly missed and all tidings of him were lost. A woman, it was proved, had been seen in the neighbourhood immediately before the child was lost, and suspicion rested upon her; but although the most vigilant search was made, her person could never be identified.

Suspicion first fell upon an innocent lady, the wife of a surgeon in the Navy, and after two examinations of several witnesses, all of whom mistook her person, she was committed for trial at the Old Bailey.

On her trial, however, she was acquitted, as indeed there appeared to be no proof of her identity, and the case was still pervaded by the same uncertainty as before.

At length the mystery began to develop itself. The first information received in London was from a magistrate in Gosport, acquainting Mr and Mrs Dellow of the discovery that their child was safe there and ready to be delivered to its parents. The father instantly set off, and soon after returned home with his son, when he was required to appear before the Lord Mayor of London. There he found William Barber, the keeper of the Gosport prison, ready to give evidence against a woman of that town of the name of Harriet Magnis, in whose possession the child was found.

This man having seen a hand-bill describing the child, got information that it was at Gosport, and went to the lodgings of Mrs Magnis, who lived in a very respectable way. He asked her if she had a child and if it was her own, to which she replied rather faintly that it was. But upon his saying that he doubted it, and desiring to see the child, she took him very readily to the room where it was in bed, and confessed to him that she had found the boy in London.

She afterwards, however, confessed the whole affair, and her motive for the robbery. She said that her husband, who was a gunner on board one of His Majesty's ships and had saved a considerable sum of money for a man in his station of life, was extremely partial to children and had often expressed his most anxious wish to have a little darling, as he used to term it. His wife, not less anxious to gratify him in this respect, wrote to him while at sea, that she was in the family way. The gunner, highly delighted that he had obtained his desired object, sent home the earnings of many a cruise, amounting to three hundred pounds, with a particular charge that the infant should be well rigged and want for nothing—if a boy, so much the better.

The next letter from his hopeful wife announced the happy tidings that his first-born was a son, and that she would name him Richard after his father. The husband expressed his joy at the news, and counted the tedious hours until he should be permitted to come home to his wife and child.

At home he at length arrived, but at an unfortunate time, when the dear Richard was out at nurse at a considerable distance, change of air being necessary to the easy cutting of his teeth. The husband's time being short, he left England with a heavy heart, without being able to see his offspring; but he was assured that on his next trip to Gosport he should have the felicity he had so often pined for, of clasping his darling to his bosom. It was not until November 1810 that he was at liberty to revisit home, when he had again the mortification to find that his son, whom he expected to see a fine boy of three years old, had not yet cut his teeth, or that he was from home on some other pretence. The husband, however, was not to be pacified thus: he would go and see his son, or his son should come to him. Mrs Magnis, finding him determined, thought the latter the much better way, and accordingly set off to fetch the boy. The metropolis occurred to her as the market best calculated to afford her a choice of children and, passing down Martin's Lane, she was struck with the rosy little citizen, Tommy Dellow, and at once determined to make him her prize. He was playing with his sister at the greengrocer's shop door, into which Mrs Magnis went, with the double view of purchasing some apples and carrying off the boy. She made much of the sister, caressed the boy, and gave him an apple. The children being pleased with her attention, she asked the little girl to show her to a pastry-cook's shop to buy some cakes, when she got clear off with the boy and left the girl behind.

Poor Magnis felt a parental affection for the boy, and when the imposition was discovered before the magistrate, he was grieved to the heart at being obliged to part with him under all the circumstances of the transaction.

The woman, upon evidence being produced of these facts, was committed to Winchester jail for trial, but at the assizes she escaped, on account of her being indicted in the wrong county, the felony having been committed in London.

John Clayton and William Jenkins, Executed for Burglary

THE activity, daring and ingenuity of the London 'cracksmen' is well exemplified in the following case:

It appears that Reid, a constable belonging to Perry's party of patrol, received information from a person technically called a 'nose'—that is, an informer or spy—that a set was made at the house of a Mrs Martin, a lady residing at No 4 Bury Street, St James's, by a party of thieves, who had derived sufficient knowledge of the customs of the house from the servant girl, Mary Wakelin, to induce them to suppose that the robbery would be a profitable speculation. Their mode of making themselves acquainted with this circumstance was as follows: The girl, like most others of her condition and years, was vain of her personal charms, and the prisoner Clayton was a young man of pleasing manners and insinuating address. The 'crack' was fixed upon, and Clayton was set to work upon the girl's vanity, and so obtain the necessary information to enable his assistants and associates to complete it cleverly. He addressed her one evening at the public-house to which she was in the habit of going to fetch her mistress's beer and, having passed a few encomiums upon her beauty, was soon admitted into conversation. The impression which he made was not unfavourable, and he was too good a judge to allow an opportunity to pass, by which he might benefit himself.

Day after day he was found at the same place, and each day he was more attentive than the last, till the girl at length looked upon him in the light of a suitor. He informed her that he was a trunk-maker living in Oxford Street, and in return obtained information that her mistress was in the habit of visiting the theatres or some other place of public amusement nearly every night. He did not fail to improve upon his acquaintance at every fresh interview, and at length a Monday evening was fixed upon, when the lover was to be admitted to spend an hour with the girl in the kitchen during her mistress's absence.

It was at this period that the officers gained information of the intended robbery, and they in consequence obtained permission to occupy a room opposite to Mrs Martin's house, from which they could witness all that passed. Half-past eight o'clock was the time appointed by Mary to see her swain, and the constables took care to be as punctual as he. A few minutes before the time, they saw four men and two women arrive at the spot, from whom Clayton separated himself and went and knocked at the door. He was, however, doomed to be disappointed. The mistress was unwell and could not go out, and therefore, with a kiss or two and an affectionate hug, the sweethearts were obliged to part, not, however, without fixing the next Tuesday to carry out their design. Tuesday night came, and the officers were again at their post; but the loving pair separated after taking a little gin together. Wednesday evening passed in the same manner, Mrs Martin being still too unwell to go out; and notwithstanding the most praiseworthy attention on the part of the supposed trunk-maker to his inamorata, every evening until the following Tuesday passed in the same way, the professions of inviolable attachment made by the tender-hearted youth growing each night more strong, and his anxiety to enter the house increasing at every meeting. On the Tuesday night, however, the girl told Clayton that her mistress was so much recovered that she expected she would be well enough to go the following night to the play, and on Wednesday night, about eight o'clock, Mrs Martin, accompanied by a male and female friend, went in a coach to the theatre. A few minutes after, the servant girl came out, and returned shortly with Clayton, arm in arm together. They talked together several minutes at the door, and then went in. In about a quarter of an hour, Clayton came out, and returned in about five minutes, accompanied by another man. Clayton knocked at the door, and the girl opened it. She appeared to refuse to let the other man in; but Clayton forced open the door, and the other man rushed in.

The officers, who had been upon the close watch every night, then went over to the house and heard all three talking very loud in the kitchen. From the noise, and what they saw through a keyhole, they ascertained that the two men were dragging the girl upstairs against her will, and she was exclaiming, 'Lord have mercy upon me! what shall I do?' One of the men told her if she made such a noise he would blow her brains out, and presented a pistol to her head and kept it there. They forced her upstairs, and the officers heard doors being broken open, &c. A few minutes after, the second man came downstairs, and returned with the kitchen poker. They then heard other doors break open, but not hearing the noise of the girl continued, the officers were afraid she was being murdered, and were proceeding to force the street-door with an iron crow, when the girl exclaimed it was her mistress, gave a sudden spring, released herself from her assailants, and ran downstairs, with the robbers after her. They got into the passage just as the officers had entered. Clayton and Jenkins appeared as if nothing had happened, and wanted to get out; but Perry and Reid seized them. The villains made a most desperate resistance, which they were enabled to do, being very tall, stout, powerful men; but they were eventually secured. On searching Clayton, a large clasp knife and a bad dollar were found. On Jenkins were found a pistol, two bad dollars, &c. On examining the house, the officers discovered that a large quantity of property had been packed up, ready to be carried off. Several rooms and closets were broken open, and the thieves were in the act of breaking open a chest when they were disturbed.

The trial of these desperadoes came on at the Old Bailey, on the 15th of January, when Mary Wakelin, before named, deposed that she first became acquainted with the prisoner Clayton about eight or ten days before the 1st of January. He then came to her mistress's house, when she answered the door, and told her his name was Wilson and that he had a letter for Mrs Martin, which was the name her mistress went by. A night or two afterwards he threw things down the area. Her mistress sent her out with a message, and she then saw Clayton, who asked her to take something to drink, which she at first refused; but upon his insisting they went and had something to drink. She saw him a night or two afterwards in the streets, as she went out on an errand, and frequently after that; but she never saw the prisoner Jenkins till the night of the 1st of January.

The jury found both the prisoners guilty, and they were sentenced to death.

The fearful sentence was carried into effect on the scaffold before the Debtors' door, Newgate, on the 19th February 1812, at the usual hour, and with the accustomed solemnity. Clayton was twenty-eight years of age, and Jenkins thirty-five.

After the culprits had been divested of their irons, Clayton observed to Jenkins it was an awful moment, and he exhorted him to cheer his spirits, and die with manly fortitude—adding that the sentence was just, and trusting their example would warn others against keeping bad company.

When the reader finds that persons convicted of burglary or forgery were sentenced to death, it should be remembered that down to the year 1826 this was the penalty for all felonies.

The sentence of death for the most trivial of offences seems to us to be heartless and cruel, but it is hard for us to realize the state of the country at the time these capital statutes were in force. There was a terrible feeling of insecurity in every part of the land, due in part at least to the absence of a proper police force. Horace Walpole, writing in 1752, spoke of the necessity of being armed when travelling even in daylight, and Smollett, too, spoke of the 'robbers, assassins and incendiaries' with which the country was infested. Henry Fielding confirmed this view and put forward many proposals to combat it.

It should also be remembered that when a society is threatened with grave evils it resorts to Emergency Laws and because of the circumstances in which they come into being they are usually of a very severe and sometimes ferocious kind. The tendency is for these emergency laws to become permanent, and the dreadful Waltham Black Act to which reference was made in the earlier Newgate Calendar *is a good example. It was passed in 1722 for a period of three years and was renewed from time to time and made a permanent part of the criminal law in 1757, that is, some thirty-five years from its original passing. The result of incorporating very severe emergency laws into the general framework of the criminal law is to make the whole code a severe one, and as there was no system of secondary punishments, such as exist today, the death penalty sometimes in a most aggravated form remained the standard penalty for what we now regard as perfectly petty offences. But the truth remains that the criminal law of any age must be considered in the light of the conditions then prevailing and the dangers it was designed to meet.*

JOHN BELLINGHAM, Executed for the Murder of the Right Honourable SPENCER PERCEVAL

ON the 11th of May, in the year 1812, an event occurred which excited universal dismay and regret in the minds of the whole of the British public—the death of the Right Honourable Spencer Perceval, then Chancellor of the Exchequer, by the hand of an assassin.

John Bellingham, the author of this crime, was brought up in a counting-house in London, and afterwards went to Archangel, where he lived during a period of three years in the service of a Russian merchant. Having returned to England, he was married to a Miss Nevill, the daughter of a respectable merchant and ship-broker, who at that time resided at Newry, but who subsequently removed to Dublin. Bellingham, being a person of active habits and of considerable intelligence, was subsequently employed by some merchants in the Russian trade, by whom he was induced again to visit Archangel, and he in consequence proceeded thither, accompanied by his wife, in the year 1804. His principal dealings were with the firm of Dorbecker and Co; but before twelve months had expired, a misunderstanding arose between them, and each party made pecuniary claims upon the other. The subject was referred by the Governor-General to the decision of four merchants, two of whom Bellingham was allowed to select from his countrymen resident on the spot, and by the award of these arbitrators Bellingham was found to be indebted to the house of Dorbecker and Co in the sum of two thousand roubles; but this sum he refused to pay, and appealed to the senate against the decision.

In the meantime, a criminal suit had been instituted against him by the owners of a Russian ship which had been lost in the White Sea. They accused him of having written an anonymous letter to the underwriters in London, stating that the insurances of that ship were fraudulent transactions, in consequence of which the payment for her loss was resisted. No satisfactory proof being adduced, Bellingham was acquitted: but before the termination of the suit, he attempted to quit Archangel, and being stopped by the police whom he resisted, he was taken to prison, but was soon after liberated, through the influence of the British consul, Sir Stephen Shairp, to whom he had made application, requesting to be protected from what he considered the injustice of the Russian authorities.

Soon after this the senate confirmed the award of the arbitrators, and Bellingham was delivered over to the College of Commerce, a tribunal established, and acknowledged by treaty, for taking cognizance of commercial matters relating to British subjects. He was to remain in custody till he discharged the debt of the two thousand roubles, but his confinement was by no means severe, for he had permission to walk wherever he pleased, attended by an officer belonging to the college. Lord Granville Leveson Gower being at this time ambassador at the Russian Court, Bellingham made frequent application to him and, at various times, received from his secretary small sums of money to support him during his confinement. One night, in particular, he rushed into his lordship's house at St Petersburgh, and requested permission to remain all night, to avoid being secured by the police, whom he had escaped. This was granted, although Lord Gower had no authority to protect him from a legal arrest; but it appears he was afterwards retaken, and being confined by the authorities of the country, the British ambassador could have no pretence to solicit his release. His lordship, however, in a conversation with the minister for foreign affairs, expressed a personal wish that the Russian Government, seeing no prospect of recovering the money from Bellingham, would liberate him on condition of his immediately returning to England: but we are not told what effect was produced, as Lord Gower soon after quitted the Russian Court.

Bellingham having, by some means or other, procured his liberation, in the year 1809 returned to England, and at Liverpool commenced the business of an insurance broker. It appears, however, that from a constant recital of the circumstances which had occurred in Russia, his complaints were aggravated in his own mind into grievances, and he at length began to talk of demanding redress from the Government for what he termed and appeared to consider the culpable misconduct of their officer,

Lord Gower, and his secretary, in omitting to defend his rights as a British subject. He eventually wrote to the Marquis Wellesley, setting forth the nature of his case, and the grounds upon which he expected that some compensation would be made. By the noble marquis he was referred to the Privy Council, and by that body to the Treasury; but his efforts being unattended with success in either quarter, he determined to proceed to the Chancellor of the Exchequer (Mr Perceval), with a view to obtain his sanction and support for his demand. Mr Perceval, however, having made himself master of the case submitted to him, declined to interfere, and Mr Bellingham was then advised by his friends that the only resource left to him was a petition to parliament. As an inhabitant of Liverpool, he applied to General Gascoyne, then member for that city, to present a petition to the House of Commons, but that honourable gentleman having ascertained upon inquiry that the case was unsupported by the Chancellor of the Exchequer, he refused to have anything to do with it. Driven now to pursue a course quite unusual in such cases, he petitioned the Prince Regent, but from him he was referred again to the Treasury, and again received an intimation that all applications from him must be futile. Three years had now been spent in these constant and fruitless attacks upon the Government, but the unfortunate and misguided gentleman appeared even yet to cherish hopes that his case would be attended to. On one occasion, it is reported that he carried his wife, who had in vain striven to wean him from what she considered to be his malady, and another lady, to the Secretary of State's office for the purpose of showing them the success with which his exertions were attended. Although he then, as before, received a flat denial of his claims, yet he continued to assure them that he did not in the least doubt that ere long all his hopes would be made good, and he would receive compensation for his sufferings.

He now adopted a new and certainly an unprecedented mode of attack. He wrote to the police magistrates of Bow Street in the following terms:

'SIRS—I much regret its being my lot to have to apply to your worships under most peculiar and novel circumstances. For the particulars of the case, I refer to the enclosed letter of Mr

Secretary Ryder, the notification from Mr Perceval, and my petition to parliament, together with the printed papers herewith. The affair requires no further remark, than that I consider his majesty's government to have completely endeavoured to close the door of justice, in declining to have, or even to permit, my grievances to be brought before parliament, for redress, which privilege is the birthright of every individual. The purport of the present is, therefore, once more to solicit his majesty's ministers, through your medium, to let what is right and proper be done in my instance, which is all I require. Should this reasonable request be finally denied, I shall then feel justified in executing justice myself—in which case I shall be ready to argue the merits of so reluctant a measure with his majesty's attorney-general, wherever and whenever I may be called upon so to do. In the hopes of averting so abhorrent, but compulsive an alternative, I have the honour to be, Sirs, your very humble and obedient servant,

'JOHN BELLINGHAM.'

This letter was at once conveyed to the members of the government, but it was treated by them as a mere threat, and no further notice was taken of it, than on Mr Bellingham's again presenting himself, by a fresh refusal being given to him by Mr Read. Once more he applied to the Treasury: again he was told that he had nothing to expect, and according to his statement, Mr Hill, whom he now saw, told him that he might 'resort to whatever measures he thought fit.' This he declared he considered 'a *carte blanche* to take justice into his own hands', and he accordingly determined to take such measures of revenge as he madly supposed would effectually secure that attention and consideration for his case, which he deemed it had not received.

This unhappy determination being made, he began to make the necessary preparations for the foul deed which he contemplated. His first step was to make himself acquainted with the persons of those ministers who had seats in the House of Commons. For this purpose he nightly visited the House and there usually took his seat in the gallery appropriated to strangers, and having obtained a general knowledge of their persons, afterwards posted himself in the lobby of the House, in order to be able to identify them. He then purchased a pair of pistols, with powder and ball, and had an additional pocket made in his coat for carrying them the more conveniently.

On the evening of the 11th of May 1812, he took his station behind the folding-doors leading into the body of the House, and at five o'clock, as Mr Perceval advanced up the lobby, he presented one of his pistols and fired. His aim was true, and the ball entered the left breast of his victim and passed through his heart. Mr Perceval reeled a short distance, and exclaiming 'Murder!' in a low tone of voice, fell to the ground. He was instantly picked up by Mr Smith, the member for Norwich, and another gentleman, and carried into the office of the Speaker's secretary, where he expired almost immediately. Loud cries of 'Shut the door—let no one out', were heard immediately after the shot was fired, and several persons exclaimed, 'Where's the murderer?' Bellingham, who still held the pistol in his hand, answered, 'I am the unfortunate man', and he was immediately seized and searched. Mr V. G. Dowling was among the first who went up to him, and on his examining his person, he found in his left-hand trousers pocket a pistol loaded with ball and primed. There were also found upon him an opera-glass, with which he had been accustomed to examine the persons of the members of the House while sitting in the gallery, and a number of papers. Upon his being interrogated as to his motives for committing such an act, he replied, 'Want of redress, and denial of justice.'

During the momentary confusion which followed the firing of the pistol, he made no attempt to escape; and though when taken into custody he betrayed some agitation, he soon recovered his self-possession, and with great calmness answered every question put to him.

During his examination before the magistrates upstairs in the House of Commons, he still retained his self-possession, and even corrected a witness as to an omission in his evidence. He persisted in denying any personal enmity to Mr Perceval, for whose death he expressed the greatest sorrow, separating, by a confusion of ideas, the man from the minister.

This event excited the greatest sensation in the country. A cabinet council was called, and the mails were stopped until instructions were prepared to secure tranquillity in the districts.

For at first it was apprehended that the assassin was instigated by political motives, and that he was connected with some treasonable association.

Measures being provided for securing order through the country and the metropolis, Bellingham was removed, under a strong military escort, about one o'clock in the morning, to Newgate, and conducted to a room adjoining the chapel. One of the head turnkeys, and two other persons, sat up with him all night. He retired to bed soon after his arrival at the jail; but he was disturbed during the night, and had no sound sleep. He rose soon after seven o'clock, and requested some tea for breakfast, of which, however, he took but little. No private persons were admitted to see him, but he was visited in the course of the day by the sheriffs and some other public functionaries. He conversed very cheerfully with the sheriffs and others who were in his room, and expressed no regret for the deed which he had perpetrated, conceiving himself, as he stated, justified in what he had done, which he did not seem to view in a criminal light. He stated that the question would soon be tried, when it would be seen how far he was justified. He considered the whole as 'a private matter between him and the Government, who gave him a *carte blanche* to do his worst, which he had done.'

Alderman Combe, as one of the committing magistrates, was very active in his endeavours to trace Bellingham's connexions and habits, and for that purpose went to the house of a respectable woman where he lodged in New Millman Street, but could learn from her nothing that indicated any conspiracy with others. His landlady represented him as a quiet inoffensive man, though at times rather eccentric, which she instanced by observing that when he had lodged there only three weeks, at 10*s* 6*d* per week, she was surprised to find that he had given her servant-maid half-a-guinea for herself. On being told the deed which he had perpetrated, she said that was impossible, for that she had met him a few minutes before the stated time, when he told her that he had just been to buy a prayer-book. She represented him as of a religious turn of mind.

In jail the prisoner requested to have pen, ink and paper, to write some letters to his friends, and he accordingly wrote one to his family at Liverpool, which was delivered open to Mr

Newman. The following was sent to Mrs Roberts, No 9 New Millman Street, the lady at whose house he lodged. It will serve to show the state of his mind in the miserable situation to which he had reduced himself:

'Tuesday morning, Old Bailey

'DEAR MADAM—Yesterday midnight I was escorted to this neighbourhood by a noble troop of Light Horse, and delivered into the care of Mr Newman (by Mr Taylor, the magistrate and M.P.) as a state prisoner of the first class. For eight years I have never found my mind so tranquil as since this melancholy but necessary catastrophe, as the merits or demerits of my peculiar case must be regularly unfolded in a criminal court of justice to ascertain the guilty party, by a jury of my country. I have to request the favour of you to send me three or four shirts, some cravats, handkerchiefs, night-caps, stockings, &c, out of my drawers, together with comb, soap, tooth-brush, with any other trifle that presents itself which you think I may have occasion for, and inclose them in my leather trunk, and the key please to send sealed, per bearer; also my great-coat, flannel gown, and black waistcoat: which will much oblige,

'Dear madam, your very obedient servant,

'JOHN BELLINGHAM.

'To the above please to add the prayer-books.'

Soon after two o'clock the wretched prisoner ate a hearty dinner, and requested that in future he might dine at about the same hour, and after passing the rest of the day in a tranquil manner, he retired to bed at twelve and slept until seven the next morning, being attended by two persons during the night. He breakfasted at about nine o'clock, and appeared perfectly composed, and on the sheriffs revisiting him, accompanied by several gentlemen, he was found to be unaltered in his demeanour. On his being spoken to on the subject of his trial, he conversed with apparent indifference, but on the melancholy fact of Mr Perceval's murder being alluded to, he became less tranquil, persisted in vindicating the act, and said that when his trial came on before a jury of his countrymen, it would be for them to determine how far a minister of the crown was justified in refusing justice to an injured individual. He declared that if he had a thousand lives to lose, he would have risked them in pursuit of justice in the same way. He spoke of the result of his trial with the utmost confidence, and on his being asked whether he had any commands to his wife at Liverpool, he declared that he had not, and that in a day or two he should join her in that city.

On the 15th of May 1812, four days after the death of Mr Perceval, the trial of the prisoner came on at the Old Bailey. At ten o'clock, the judges took their seats on each side of the Lord Mayor, and the Recorder, the Duke of Clarence, the Marquis Wellesley, and almost all the aldermen of the city of London, occupied the bench. The court was crowded to excess, and no distinction of rank was observed, so that members of the House of Commons were forced to mingle in the throng. There were also present a great number of ladies, all led by the most intense curiosity to behold the assassin and to hear what he might urge in defence or in palliation of his atrocious act.

At length Bellingham appeared, and advanced to the bar with a firm step and quite undismayed. He bowed to the court most respectfully and even gracefully, and it is impossible to describe the impression which his appearance, accompanied by this unexpected fortitude, produced. He was dressed in a light brown surtout coat, and striped yellow waistcoat; his hair plainly dressed, and without powder.

Before the prisoner was called on regularly to plead, Mr Alley, his counsel, made application to have the trial postponed, for the purpose of procuring proofs of his client's insanity, which was alleged in two affidavits he held: he said that he had no doubt, if time were allowed, that the prisoner could be proved to be insane. Mr Alley was here interrupted by the court, who refused to hear him until the prisoner had first pleaded.

The indictment was then read, and the usual question, 'Guilty, or not guilty?' was put to Bellingham, when he addressed the court: 'My lords—Before I can plead to this indictment, I must state, in justice to myself, that by hurrying on my trial I am placed in a most remarkable situation. It so happens that my prosecutors are actually the witnesses against me. All the documents on which alone I could rest my defence have been taken from me and are now in possession of the Crown. It is only two days since I was told to prepare for my defence, and when I asked for my papers, I was told they could not be given up. It is therefore, my lords, rendered utterly impossible for me to go into my justification, and under the circumstances in which I find myself, a trial is absolutely useless. The papers are to be given to me after the trial, but how can that avail me for my defence? I am, therefore, not ready for my trial.'

The Attorney-General was proceeding to explain to the court what had been done with reference to the prisoner's papers, when—

Chief Justice Mansfield interrupted him, observing, it was necessary the prisoner should first plead.

The prisoner was again interrogated, when he pleaded 'Not guilty' to both counts of the indictment.

The Attorney-General—'I will now answer what has fallen from the prisoner. He says that he has been denied access to his papers. It is true that Government, for the purposes of justice, has retained them—but it is also true that he has been informed that if he asked for them at the time of his trial they should be ready, and any of them, which he might think useful to his defence, should be given to him: and in the meantime, if he considered it necessary, he might have copies of them. This we are ready to verify on oath.'

The clerk of the arraigns, Mr Shelton, then read the indictment, which charged the prisoner in the usual way with the murder of the Right Hon Spencer Perceval, with which he was also charged on the coroner's inquisition.

Mr Abbott having opened the case,

The Attorney-General addressed the jury. He said that a lamentable and painful task devolved upon him to state to the jury the circumstances of this horrid murder—a crime perpetrated on a man whose whole life, he should have thought, would have guarded and protected him against such an attack, who, he was sure, if enough of life had been left him to see by whose hand he had fallen, would have spent his last moment in uttering a prayer for the forgiveness of his murderer. But it was not a time for him to dwell on the public loss, which had been sustained—its brightest ornament had been torn from the country, but the country had done justice to his memory. These were not considerations, however, by which they must be swayed. It was not revenge, nor was it resentment, that ought to have any influence on their consideration of the question. They were to satisfy public justice—to take care, by their verdict, that the public should not be exposed to such horrid crimes. With respect to the prisoner, he knew nothing, nor did he know how his life had been spent, except so far as related to the circumstances of the case. He had been in business and had acted as a merchant, in the course of which he had shown himself a man of sound understanding in every act which he performed; and he had not only conducted his own affairs with understanding, but he had been selected by other persons to manage theirs.

Having stated the main facts of the case as we have already detailed them, he entreated the jury to consider it not as the murder of so eminent a person, but as the murder of a common individual—to suppose the meanest subject to have suffered as Mr Perceval had suffered, and to return their verdict as they would upon that case. Was he or was he not guilty? To that point they must direct their attention, and he knew of no reason to cause even a doubt. But what remained? This only—the attempt which had been made that day to put off the trial of the prisoner, on the ground of his being fit for this or any other crime, as he was afflicted with insanity. Let them consider this a little. The prisoner was a man conducting himself like others in all the ordinary circumstances of life—who carried on business, none of his family or friends interfering—no pretence being suggested that he was unable to superintend his own affairs. What clearer proofs, then, could be given to show, contrary to the defence set up, that he was not what the law called *non compos mentis*—that he was an accountable being?

He knew the cases where the plea of insanity would be received—where for instance a murder was committed by a person whose mental infirmity might be considered as very nearly the absence of all mind. Against their defence there was no argument. But he was this day to learn whether the wickedness of the act which the prisoner was called on to answer was to be considered an excuse for its perpetration. Travelling through his whole life, what ground could they adduce for such a plea? His every act appeared rational except one, and that was only irrational, because it was so horrid that the imagination of man could not fancy to itself the existence of so atrocious a deed. But how far must this argument go? It must arrive at this conclusion —that every act of gross and unusual atrocity would carry its defence along with it, that every act of peculiar horror would have within itself a certain defence, for the barbarity of the deed would be considered as a proof that the mind which directed it was not in a state of sufficient security to judge whether the action was right or wrong. If the mind possessed the power of forming that judgement, the prisoner was criminally accountable for the act. A man might be infirm in mind, insufficient to dispose of his property or to judge of the claims of his respective relatives, and if he were in that situation, the management of his affairs might be taken from him and vested in trustees: but such a man was not discharged from criminal acts because he could not transact civil business. Many cases had occurred within his memory in courts of law, in which it was proved that a person in many respects had evinced symptoms of insanity up to a certain time; but the question then was, whether that insanity was of such a description as precluded or permitted the knowledge of right or wrong? In every one of the cases which recurred to his memory, though a certain degree of madness was proved, still as the parties seemed to have sufficient sense to distinguish right from wrong at the time of the perpetration of the acts charged against them, they were held to be criminally accountable. Here there was no deficiency of understanding whatever. No opinion of others to that effect was adduced: on the contrary, he was entrusted with the management of his own and others' affairs. The question was, whether at the time the murder was perpetrated he possessed sufficient sense to distinguish between right and wrong? What conclusion could they draw in favour of the idea which had been suggested? Let them take from their recollection the frightful nature of the act with the commission of which he was charged, let them take from it its accumulated horrors, and the prisoner stood before them in a state of sanity, and fully accountable for the act, of which, he thought, little doubt could be entertained he had been guilty.

The learned gentleman concluded by expressing his satisfaction at the fact that the prisoner stood alone on that occasion, that he was unconnected with, and unaided and uninfluenced by, any other person or party in the country, and that this deed could not therefore be attributed to any but the personal feelings which he entertained towards His Majesty's Government. On him, and on him only, did the disgrace which he had excited rest, and the character of the country was entirely free from any participation in it.

The first witness called on the part of the Crown was:

Mr William Smith (M.P. for Norwich) who, being sworn, deposed as follows:

He was on his way to attend the House of Commons on the evening of Monday the 11th of May, and was going through the lobby towards the door of the house, when he heard the report of a pistol, which appeared to have been fired close to the entrance door of the lobby. Immediately on the report, he turned towards the place from whence the noise appeared to proceed, and observed a tumult and probably a dozen or more persons about the spot. Almost in the same instant he saw a person rush hastily from among the crowd, and heard several voices cry out, 'Shut the doors—let no one escape.' The person came towards him from the crowd, looking first one way, then another, rather like one seeking for shelter than a person wounded. But taking two or three steps towards the witness, he reeled by him and almost instantaneously fell on the floor with his face downward. Before he fell, witness heard him cry, though not very distinctly, and in what he uttered, he heard the word 'murder!' or something very like it. When he first fell, witness thought that he might have been slightly wounded, and expected to see him make an effort to rise. But gazing on him for a few moments, he observed that he did not stir at all, and he, therefore, immediately stooped down to raise him from the ground, requesting the assistance of a gentleman close by him for the purpose. As soon as they had turned his face upwards, and not till then, he found that it was Mr Perceval. They then took him into their arms, and carried him into the office of the Speaker's secretary, where they seated themselves on the table, with Mr Perceval between them, also sitting on the table, and resting on their arms. His face was now perfectly pale, the blood issuing in small quantities from each corner of his mouth, and probably in two or three minutes from the firing of the pistol all signs of life had ceased. The eyes of the unfortunate gentleman were open, but he did not appear to know witness, nor to take any notice of any person about him, nor did he utter the least articulate sound from the moment he fell. A few convulsive sobs, which lasted perhaps three or four moments, together with a scarcely perceptible pulse, were the only signs of life which appeared then, and those continued but a very short time longer. When witness felt Mr Perceval's pulse for the last time, just before Mr Lynn, the surgeon, arrived, it appeared to him that he was quite dead. Witness remained supporting the body until it was conveyed into the Speaker's house, but he was unable to give any account of what passed in the lobby.

Mr William Lynn, a surgeon in Great George Street, deposed that he was called to the deceased, but on his arrival he was quite dead. There was blood upon his white waistcoat and shirt, and upon his examining the body, he found that there was an opening in the skin. He probed the wound three inches downwards, and entertained no doubt that the pistol-ball passed into the heart, and was the cause of death.

Mr Henry Burgess, a solicitor who was in the lobby, stated, that after having seen Mr Perceval fall, as had been already described, he heard someone exclaim, 'That's the man!' and saw a hand pointing towards the bench by the fire-place which is on one side of the lobby. He immediately went over to the bench and saw the prisoner at the bar sitting on it in great agitation. There were one or two persons by him. He looked at his hands, and saw his left hand on the bench; and near or under his other hand he saw a pistol, which he took, and asked the prisoner what had induced him to do such a deed? He replied, 'Want of redress of grievances and refusal by government', or words to that effect. Witness then said to the prisoner, 'You have another pistol?' He replied, 'Yes.' Witness asked if it was loaded, to which he answered in the affirmative. Witness then saw some person take the other pistol from his person. The pistol which witness took from the prisoner was warm, and appeared as if it had been recently discharged. The lock was down and the pan open. (Here the pistol was produced, and recognized by the witness.) He then stated, that he put his hand into the right waistcoat-pocket of the prisoner, from which he took a small penknife and a pencil, and from his left-hand waistcoat-pocket he took a bunch of keys and some money. The prisoner was detained in custody, and examined shortly afterwards above stairs in the House of Commons before the magistrates. Witness related in the presence of the prisoner, on that occasion, the facts which he had now detailed. When he had concluded, the prisoner made an observation to this effect, as well as he could recollect. 'I wish to correct Mr Burgess' statement in one point; but I believe he is perfectly correct in every other. Instead of my hand being, as Mr Burgess stated, upon or near the pistol, I think he took it from my hand or upon it.'

James Taylor, a tailor, at No 11 North Place, Gray's Inn Lane, deposed that he had been employed by the prisoner to repair some clothes. He was afterwards in Guildford Street, when the prisoner called him, and took him to his lodgings in Millman Street, and there directed him to put a side-pocket into a coat, which he gave him, of a particular length which he pointed out. He completed the job on the same night, and carried the coat home.

Mr John Morris stated that he often attended in the gallery appropriated for strangers, and went down to the House on Monday, the 11th of May, for that purpose. He passed into the lobby about the hour of five in the afternoon. He observed the prisoner at the bar standing in the lobby near the outer door: he was standing beside that part of the door which is generally closed. It was a double door, and one half was usually closed, within which half the prisoner was standing, and any one to have entered the lobby must have passed him at arm's length. He observed the prisoner as if watching for somebody coming, and he appeared to look anxiously towards the door. As well as the witness recollected, the prisoner had his right hand within the left breast of his coat. Witness passed on to the staircase of the gallery, and almost immediately after he got into the upper lobby, he heard the report of a pistol, and found soon after that it was connected with the fatal event which occurred on that evening. He had frequently seen the prisoner before in the gallery, where gentlemen who report the parliamentary proceedings resorted, and about the passages of the House of Commons.

John Vickery, a Bow Street officer, said that he went on

Monday afternoon to New Millman Street, to the lodgings of the prisoner, which he searched, and found, in the bedroom upstairs, a pair of pistol-bags, and in the same drawer a small powder-flask and some powder in a small paper, a box with some bullets, and some small flints wrapped in paper. There was also a pistol-key to unscrew the pistol for the purpose of loading, and some sand-paper and a pistol-mould. The witness on comparing the bullet found in the loaded pistol with the mould, and the screw with the pistols, found them all to correspond.

Mr Vincent George Dowling was next called. He stated that he was in the gallery on the afternoon in question, and ran down into the lobby on hearing the report of a pistol. He saw the prisoner at the bar sitting on a stool, and going to him, he seized him and began to search his person. He took from his left-hand small-clothes pocket a small pistol, which he produced and which, on his examining it, he found to be loaded with powder and ball. It was primed as well as loaded. The pistol which had been discharged and that which he took from the prisoner were in his belief a brace: they were of the same size and bore, and were marked with the same maker's name. The witness had seen the prisoner several times before in the gallery and in the avenues of the house, and to the best of his recollection the last time he saw him was six or seven days before the death of Mr Perceval. He was frequently in the gallery during the debates, and upon several occasions entered into conversation with the witness. He had often asked for information as to the names of the gentlemen speaking, and also as to the persons of the members of His Majesty's Government.

Other witnesses from Newgate produced the coat worn by the prisoner at the time of his apprehension, and it was identified by Taylor as the same into which he had put the side-pocket.

Lord Chief Justice Mansfield then addressed the prisoner, and told him, that the case on the part of the Crown being now gone through, the period was come for him to make any defence he might wish to offer.

The prisoner asked whether his counsel had nothing to urge in his defence?

Mr Alley informed him that his counsel were not entitled to speak.

The prisoner then said that the documents and papers necessary to his defence had been taken out of his pocket, and had not since been restored to him.

Mr Garrow said that it was the intention of the counsel for the Crown to restore him his papers, having first proved them to be the same which were taken from him, and that they had not suffered any subtraction: his solicitor already had copies of them.

General Gascoigne and Mr Hume (M.P. for Weymouth) proved that the papers were those which had been taken from the person of the prisoner, and that they had been in their custody ever since, and had suffered no subtraction.

The papers were then handed to the prisoner, who proceeded to arrange and examine them.

The prisoner, who had been hitherto sitting, now rose and, bowing respectfully to the court and jury, went into his defence, in a firm tone of voice, and without any appearance of embarrassment. He spoke nearly to the following effect:

'I feel great personal obligation to the Attorney-General for the objection which he has made to the plea of insanity. I think it is far more fortunate that such a plea as that should have been unfounded, than that it should have existed in fact. I am obliged to my counsel, however, for having thus endeavoured to consult my interest, as I am convinced the attempt has arisen from the kindest motives. That I am or have been insane is a circumstance of which I am not apprised, except in the single instance of my having been confined in Russia: how far that may be considered as affecting my present situation, it is not for me to determine. This is the first time that I have ever spoken in public in this way. I feel my own incompetency, but I trust you will attend to the substance, rather than to the manner, of my investigating the truth of an affair which has occasioned my presence at this bar.

'I beg to assure you that the crime which I have committed has arisen from compulsion rather than from any hostility to the man whom it has been my fate to destroy. Considering the amiable character and universally admitted virtues of Mr Perceval, I feel, if I could murder him in a cool and unjustifiable manner, I should not deserve to live another moment in this world. Conscious, however, that I shall be able to justify everything which

I have done, I feel some degree of confidence in meeting the storm which assails me, and shall now proceed to unfold a catalogue of circumstances which, while they harrow up my own soul, will, I am sure, tend to the extenuation of my conduct in this honourable court. This, as has already been candidly stated by the Attorney-General, is the first instance in which the slightest imputation has been cast upon my moral character. Until this fatal catastrophe, which no one can more heartily regret than I do, not excepting even the family of Mr Perceval himself, I have stood alike pure in the minds of those who have known me, and in the judgement of my own heart. I hope I see this affair in the true light.

'For eight years, gentlemen of the jury, have I been exposed to all the miseries which it is possible for human nature to endure. Driven almost to despair, I sought for redress in vain. For this affair I had the *carte blanche* of government, as I will prove by the most incontestible evidence, namely, the writing of the Secretary of State himself. I come before you under peculiar disadvantages. Many of my most material papers are now at Liverpool, for which I have written; but I have been called upon my trial before it was possible to obtain an answer to my letter. Without witnesses, therefore, and in the absence of many papers necessary to my justification, I am sure you will admit I have just grounds for claiming some indulgence. I must state that after my voyage to Archangel, I transmitted a petition to his royal highness the Prince Regent, through Mr Windle, my solicitor, and in consequence of there being no reply I came to London to see the result. Surprised at the delay, and conceiving that the interests of my country were at stake, I considered this step as essential, as well for the assertion of my own right as for the vindication of the national honour. I waited upon Colonel MacMahon, who stated that my petition had been received, but, owing to some accident, had been mislaid. Under these circumstances, I drew out another account of the particulars of the Russian affair, and this may be considered the commencement of that train of events which led to the afflicting and unhappy fate of Mr Perceval.'

The prisoner then read various documents containing the statement of the whole of his affairs in Russia. In the course of narrating these hardships, he took occasion to explain several points, adverting with great feeling to the unhappy situation in which he was placed, from the circumstance of his having been lately married to his wife, then about twenty years of age, with an infant at her breast, and who had been waiting for him at St Petersburgh, in order that she might accompany him to England, a prey to all those anxieties which the unexpected and cruel incarceration of her husband, without any just grounds, was calculated to excite. (He was here much affected.) He also described his feelings at a subsequent period, when his wife, from an anxiety to reach her native country (England) when in a state of pregnancy, and looking to the improbability of his liberation, was obliged to quit Petersburgh unprotected, and undertake the voyage at the peril of her life, while Lord L. Gower and Sir S. Shairp suffered him to remain in a situation worse than death. 'My God! my God!' he exclaimed, 'what heart could bear such excruciating tortures, without bursting with indignation at conduct so diametrically opposite to justice and to humanity. I appeal to you, gentlemen of the jury, as men—I appeal to you as brothers—I appeal to you as Christians—whether, under such circumstances of persecution, it was possible to regard the actions of the ambassador and consul of my own country with any other feelings but those of detestation and horror! In using language thus strong, I feel that I commit an error; yet does my heart tell me, that towards men who lent themselves thus to bolster up the basest acts of persecution, there are no observations, however strong, which the strict justice of the case would not excuse my using. Had I been so fortunate as to have met Lord Leveson Gower instead of that truly amiable and highly-lamented individual, Mr Perceval, he is the man who should have received the ball!'

[Bellingham then went on to recount at great length the history of his various attempts to obtain satisfaction from the Government, which have already been described, ending with his letter to the Bow Street magistrates quoted on pp. 57–8.]

'In the course of two days,' he continued, 'I called again at Bow Street for an answer to this letter, when I received a little memorandum, in Mr Reid's writing, in which he states that he cannot interfere in my affairs, and that he had felt it his duty to communicate the contents of my packet to the Secretary of State. Had he done otherwise he would have been extremely reprehensible, as events have turned out so calamitously—events which go to my heart to allude to. (Much affected.) At last, in reply to a letter of the 13th of April, I received a final and direct answer, which at once convinced me that I had no reason to expect any adjustment whatever of those claims which I had on His Majesty's government, for my criminal detention in Russia.

'After this, on personal application at the office of the Secretary of State, and intimating my intention to take justice in my own hand, I was told, by the mouth of Mr Hill, that I was at liberty to take such measures as I thought proper. Who then is to be reprobated in this case—those who were regardless of every feeling of honour and of justice, or him who, spurred on by injury and neglect, and with a due notice of his intentions, pursued the only course likely to lead to a satisfactory termination of calamities which had weighed him down to the lowest ebb of misery? I will now only mention a few observations by way of defence. You have before you all the particulars of this melancholy transaction. Believe me, gentlemen, the rashness of which I have been guilty has not been dictated by any personal animosity to Mr Perceval, rather than injure whom from private or malicious motives I would suffer my limbs to be cut from my body. (Here the prisoner seemed again much agitated.)

'If, whenever I am called before the tribunal of God, I can appear with as clear a conscience as I now possess in regard to the alleged charge of the wilful murder of the unfortunate gentleman, the investigation of whose death has occupied your attention, it would be happy for me, as essentially securing to me eternal salvation; but that is impossible. That my arm has been the means of his melancholy and lamented exit, I am ready to allow. But to constitute murder, it must clearly and absolutely be proved to have arisen from malice prepense and with a malicious design, as I have no doubt the learned judge will shortly lay down, in explaining the law on the subject. If such is the case, I am guilty: if not, I look forward with confidence to your acquittal.

'That the contrary is the case has been most clearly and irrefutably proved. No doubt can rest upon your minds, as my uniform and undeviating object has been an endeavour to obtain justice, according to law, for a series of the most long-continued and unmerited sufferings that were ever submitted to a court of law, without having been guilty of any other crime than an appeal for redress for a most flagrant injury offered to my sovereign and my country, wherein my liberty and property have fallen a sacrifice for the continued period of eight years, to the total ruin of myself and family (with authenticated documents of the truth of the allegations), merely because it was Mr Perceval's pleasure that justice should not be granted, sheltering himself with the idea of there being no alternative remaining, as my petition to parliament for redress could not be brought (as having a pecuniary tendency) without the sanction of His Majesty's ministers, and that he was determined to oppose my claim, by trampling both on law and right.

'Gentlemen, where a man has so strong and serious a criminal case to bring forward as mine has been, the nature of which was purely national, it is the bounden duty of Government to attend to it; for justice is a matter of right and not of valour. And when a minister is so unprincipled and presumptuous at any time, but especially in a case of such urgent necessity, to set himself above both the sovereign and the laws, as has been the case with Mr Perceval, he must do it at his personal risk; for by the law he cannot be protected.

'Gentlemen, if this is not fact, the mere will of a minister would be law: it would be this thing today and the other thing tomorrow, as either interest or caprice might dictate. What would become of our liberties? Where would be the purity and the impartiality of the justice we so much boast of? To Government's non-attendance to the dictates of justice is solely to be attributed the melancholy catastrophe of the unfortunate gentleman, as any malicious intention to his injury was the most remote from my heart. Justice, and justice only, was my object, which Government uniformly objected to grant. The distress it reduced me to, drove me to despair in consequence, and, purely for the purpose of having this singular affair legally investigated, I gave notice at the public office, Bow Street, requesting the magistrates to acquaint His Majesty's ministers, that if they persisted in refusing justice, or even to permit me to bring my just petition into parliament for redress, I should be under the imperious necessity of executing justice myself, solely for the purpose of ascertaining, through a criminal court, whether His Majesty's ministers have the power to refuse justice to a well-authenticated and irrefutable act of oppression, committed by the consul and ambassador abroad, whereby my sovereign's and country's honour were materially tarnished, by my person endeavouring to be made the stalking-horse of justification, to one of the greatest insults that could be offered to the crown. But in order to avoid so reluctant and abhorrent an alternative, I hoped to be allowed to bring my petition to the House of Commons—or that they would do what was right and proper themselves. On my return from Russia, I brought most serious charges to the privy council, both against Sir Stephen Shairp and Lord Granville Leveson Gower, when the affair was determined to be purely national, and consequently it was the duty of His Majesty's ministers to arrange it by acting on the resolution of the council. Suppose, for instance, the charge I brought could have been proved to be erroneous, should not I have been called to a severe account for my conduct? But, being true, ought not I to have been redressed?

'It is a melancholy fact, that the warping of justice, including all the various ramifications in which it operates, occasions more misery in the world, in a moral sense, than all the acts of God in a physical one, with which he punishes mankind for their transgressions—a confirmation of which, the single, but strong, instance before you is one remarkable proof.

'If a poor unfortunate man stops another upon the highway, and robs him of but a few shillings, he may be called upon to forfeit his life. But I have been robbed of my liberty for years, ill-treated beyond precedent, torn from my wife and family, bereaved of all my property to make good the consequences of such irregularities, deprived and bereaved of everything that makes life valuable, and then called upon to forfeit it, because Mr Perceval has been pleased to patronize iniquity that ought to have been punished, for the sake of a vote or two in the House of Commons, with, perhaps, a similar good turn elsewhere.

'Is there, gentlemen, any comparison between the enormity of these two offenders? No more than a mite to a mountain. Yet the one is carried to the gallows, while the other stalks in security, fancying himself beyond the reach of law or justice: the most honest man suffers, while the other goes forward in triumph to new and more extended enormities.

'We have had a recent and striking instance of some unfortunate men who have been called upon to pay their lives as the forfeit of their allegiance, in endeavouring to mitigate the rigours of a prison. But, gentlemen, where is the proportion between the crimes for which they suffered, and what the Government has been guilty of, in withholding its protection from me? Even in a Crown case, after the years of sufferings, I have been called upon to sacrifice all my property and the welfare of my family, to bolster up the iniquities of the Crown. And then am prosecuted for my life, because I have taken the only possible alternative to bring the affair to a public investigation, for the purpose of being enabled to return to the bosom of my family with some degree of comfort and honour. Every man within the sound of my voice must feel for my situation; but by you, gentlemen of the jury, it must be felt in a peculiar degree, who are husbands and fathers, and can fancy yourselves in my situation. I trust that this serious lesson will operate as a warning to all future ministers, and lead them to do the thing that is right, as an unerring rule of conduct, for, if the superior classes were more correct in their proceedings, the extensive ramifications of evil would, in a great measure, be hemmed up. A notable proof of the fact is, that this court would never have been troubled with the case before it, had their conduct been guided by these principles.

'I have now occupied the attention of the court for a period much longer than I intended, yet I trust they will consider the awfulness of my situation to be a sufficient ground for a trespass which, under other circumstances, would be inexcusable. Sooner than suffer what I have suffered for the last eight years, however, I should consider five hundred deaths, if it were possible for human nature to endure them, a fate far more preferable. Lost so long to all the endearments of my family, bereaved of all the blessings of life, and deprived of its greatest sweet, liberty, as the weary traveller, who has long been pelted by the pitiless storm, welcomes the much desired inn, I shall receive death as the relief of all my sorrows. I shall not occupy your attention longer, but, relying on the justice of God, and submitting myself to the dictates of your conscience, I submit to the *fiat* of my fate, firmly anticipating an acquittal from a charge so abhorrent to every feeling of my soul.'

Here the prisoner bowed, and his counsel immediately proceeded to call the witnesses for the defence.

Anne Billet, who appeared under the strongest impressions of grief, being sworn, deposed that she lived in the county of Southampton: she came to London in consequence of having read in the newspapers of the prisoner having been apprehended for the murder of Mr Perceval. She was induced to come to town, from a conviction that she knew more of him than any other friend. She knew him from a child. He resided latterly at Liverpool, from whence he came at Christmas last. She knew him to be a merchant. His father died insane in Titchfield Street, Oxford Road. She firmly believed that for the last three or four years the prisoner was in a state of derangement, respecting the business which he had been pursuing. She had not seen him for twelve months until the present moment. She always thought him deranged when his Russian affairs were the subject of conversation.

When cross-examined by Mr Garrow, she deposed that, when in London with the prisoner about twelve months since, he was going to different government offices to seek redress of his grievances. He was then in a state of derangement, as he had been ever since his return from Russia. There was one instance which occurred at the period to which she was alluding, which strongly confirmed her in the opinion of his insanity. About Christmas he told his wife and witness, that now he was come from Russia he had realized more than 100,000*l*, with which he intended to buy an estate in the west of England and to have a house in London. He admitted that he had not got the money, but said it was the same as if he had, for he had gained his cause in Russia and our government would make good all the loss he had sustained. He repeatedly said to her and to his wife that this was assuredly the fact. Upon one occasion he took Mrs Bellingham and the witness to the Secretary of State's office, where they saw Mr Smith, who said if he had not ladies with him he would not have come to him at all. The prisoner told Mr Smith, that the reason why he brought them was to convince them that his claims were just, and that he would very shortly receive the money. Mr Smith told him he could say nothing upon this subject: he had already sent him a letter alleging that he had nothing to expect. The prisoner then requested Mr Smith would answer him one question—'My friends say I am out of my senses. Is it your opinion that I am so?' Mr Smith said it was a very delicate question, and one he did not wish to answer. Having then departed, when they got into the carriage which waited for them, he took hold of his wife's hand and said, 'I hope, now, my dear, you are convinced all will now end as we wish.' Since that period she knew that he had been pursuing his object *alone*, his wife remaining at Liverpool.

Other witnesses were called, who deposed to like facts and to their belief in the insanity of the prisoner, but Lord Chief Justice Mansfield having summed up the case, the jury, after a consultation of two minutes and a half in the box, expressed a wish to retire, and an officer of the court being sworn, accompanied them to the jury-room. As they passed out, the prisoner regarded them separately with a look of mingled confidence and complacency. They were absent fourteen minutes, and, on their return into court, their countenances, acting as indices to their minds, at once unfolded the determination to which they had come. The prisoner again directed his attention to them in the same manner as before.

The names being called over, and the verdict asked for in the usual form, the foreman in a faltering voice, announced the fatal decision of—Guilty.

The prisoner's countenance here indicated surprise, unmixed, however, with any demonstrations of that concern which the awfulness of his situation was calculated to produce.

The Recorder then passed the awful sentence of death on the prisoner in the most feeling manner, and he was ordered for execution on the following Monday, his body to be anatomized. He received the sentence without any emotion.

From the time of his condemnation, the unfortunate convict was fed upon bread and water. All means of suicide were removed, and he was not allowed to be shaved—a prohibition which gave him much concern, as he feared he should not appear as a gentleman. He was visited by the ordinary on Saturday, and some religious gentlemen called on him on Sunday, with whose conversation he seemed greatly pleased. He appeared naturally depressed by his situation, but persisted in a resolute denial of his guilt. He frequently said that he had prepared himself to go to his Father, and that he should be pleased when the hour came.

Being informed by Mr Newman that two gentlemen from Liverpool had called and left word that his wife and children would be provided for, he seemed but little affected, but, having requested pen, ink, and paper, he wrote the following letter to his wife:

'MY BLESSED MARY—It rejoiced me beyond measure to hear you are likely to be well provided for. I am sure the public at large will participate in, and mitigate, your sorrows. I assure you, my love, my sincerest endeavours have ever been directed to your welfare.—As we shall not meet any more in this world, I sincerely hope we shall do so in the world to come. My blessing to the boys, with kind remembrance to Miss Stephens, for whom I have the greatest regard, in consequence of her uniform affection for them. With the purest intentions, it has always been my misfortune to be thwarted, misrepresented and ill-used in life but, however, we feel a happy prospect of compensation in a speedy translation to life eternal. It's not possible to be more calm or placid than I feel, and nine hours more will waft me to those happy shores where bliss is without alloy. Yours ever affectionate, JOHN BELLINGHAM.'

That the unfortunate man was afflicted with a strange malady, which occasionally rendered him incapable of correct conclusions, must be evident from the following note, which he wrote the night preceding his execution: 'I lost my suit solely through the improper conduct of my attorney and counsel, Mr Alley, in not bringing my witnesses forward (of whom there were more than twenty): in consequence, the judge took advantage of the circumstance, and I went of [on] the defence without having brought forward a single friend—otherwise I must inevitably have been acquitted.'

On the Monday morning at about six o'clock he rose, dressed himself with great composure, and read for half an hour in the prayer-book. Dr Ford being then announced, the prisoner shook him most cordially by the hand, and left his cell for the room allotted for the condemned criminals. He repeated the declaration which he had frequently before made, that his mind was perfectly calm and composed and that he was fully prepared to meet his fate with resignation. After a few minutes spent in prayer, the sacrament was administered to him, and during the whole of the ceremony he seemed to be deeply impressed with the truths of the Christian religion, and repeatedly uttered some pious ejaculations. After the religious ceremony was ended, the prisoner was informed that the sheriffs were ready. He answered in a firm tone of voice, 'I am perfectly ready also.'

The executioner then proceeded to fasten his wrists together, and the prisoner turned up the sleeves of his coat, and clasped his hands together, presenting them to the man who held the cord, and said, 'So.' When they were fastened, he desired his attendants to pull down his sleeves so as to cover the cord. The officer then proceeded to secure his arms behind him. When the man had finished, he moved his hand upwards, as if to ascertain whether he could reach his neck, and asked whether they thought his arms were sufficiently fastened, saying that he might struggle, and that he wished to be so secured as to prevent any inconvenience arising from it. He was answered that the cord was quite secure, but he requested that it might be tightened a little, which was accordingly done. During the whole of the awful scene he appeared perfectly composed and collected: his voice never faltered, but just before he left the room to proceed to the place of execution, he stooped down his head and appeared to wipe away a tear. He was then conducted by the Lord Mayor, sheriffs, under-sheriffs and officers (Dr Ford walking with him) from the room, in which he had remained from the time his irons were taken off, through the press-yard and the prison to the fatal spot, before the Debtors' door at Newgate.

He ascended the scaffold with rather a light step, a cheerful countenance, and a confident, a calm, but not an exulting air. He looked about him a little, lightly and rapidly, which seems to have been his usual manner and gesture, but made no remark.

Before the cap was put over his face, Dr Ford asked if he had any last communication to make, or anything particular to say. He was again proceeding to talk about Russia and his family, when Dr Ford stopped him, calling his attention to the eternity into which he was entering, and praying. Bellingham prayed also. The clergyman then asked him how he felt, and he answered calmly and collectedly, that 'he thanked God for having enabled him to meet his fate with so much fortitude and resignation'. When the executioner proceeded to put the cap over his face, Bellingham objected to it, and expressed a strong wish that the business could be done without it; but Dr Ford said that was not to be dispensed with. While the cap was being fastened on, it being tied round the lower part of the face by the prisoner's neckerchief, and just when he was tied up, about a score of persons in the mob set up a loud and reiterated cry of 'God bless you!' 'God save you!' This cry lasted while the cap was fastening on, and, though those who raised it were loud and daring, it was joined in by but very few. The ordinary asked Bellingham if he heard what the mob were saying. He said he heard them crying out something, but he did not understand what it was, and inquired what. The cry having by this time ceased, the clergyman did not inform him what it was. The fastening on of the cap being accomplished, the executioner retired and a perfect silence ensued. Dr Ford continued praying for about a minute, while the executioner went below the scaffold, and preparations were made to strike away its supporters. The clock struck eight, and while it was striking the seventh time, the clergyman and Bellingham both fervently praying, the supporters of the internal part of the scaffold were struck away, and Bellingham dropped out of sight down as far as the knees, his body being in full view. The most perfect and awful silence prevailed; not even the slightest attempt at a huzza or noise of any kind whatever was made.

The body was afterwards carried in a cart, followed by a crowd of the lower class, to St Bartholomew's Hospital, and privately dissected.

The greatest precautions were adopted to prevent accidents among the crowd. A large bill was placarded at all the avenues to the Old Bailey, and carried about on a pole, to this effect: 'Beware of entering the crowd! Remember thirty poor creatures were pressed to death by the crowd when Haggerty and Holloway were executed.' But no accident of any moment occurred.

To prevent any disposition to tumult, a military force was

stationed near Islington and to the south of Blackfriars Bridge, and all the volunteer corps of the metropolis received instructions to be under arms during the whole of the day.

It will be observed that at the outset of the trial the learned counsel for Bellingham applied before plea pleaded (which is the proper time) for an adjournment, indicating that the defence would be one of insanity. It does not appear that Mr Alley submitted that Bellingham was unfit to plead. Where such a submission is made the tests are whether the accused is of sufficient intellect to comprehend the course of the proceedings of the trial, so as to make a proper defence, to challenge a juror to whom he might wish to object, and to understand the details of the evidence; and those questions are determined before plea pleaded.

It is also to be observed that the Attorney-General in opening the case to the jury spent a long time in rebutting in advance the defence of insanity, and when Bellingham addressed the jury he thanked the Attorney-General for rejecting the idea of insanity.

The defence of insanity since 1843 rests upon what are called the M'Naughten rules which are the answers given by the judges in the House of Lords to a series of questions addressed to them in the case of Daniel M'Naughten. M'Naughten (to give him the name which appears in all the accounts of the trial) in January 1843 fired at and wounded Mr Drummond, Sir Robert Peel's private secretary. Mr Drummond died, and M'Naughten was indicted for murder. At the trial, medical witnesses were called to prove M'Naughten's insanity, and Chief Justice Tindal, who presided over the trial, finding that the Crown were not prepared with witnesses to rebut this evidence, stopped the case and directed the jury to return a verdict of not guilty on the ground of insanity. This created so much dissatisfaction in high places, that the House of Lords decided to take the opinion of the judges on the law governing such cases. A full account of the trial and of the answers made by the judges may be seen in the State Trials *(New Series) Vol. 4, pages 848 to 934. Quite shortly the law of insanity since 1843 has been:*

> *. . . every man is presumed to be sane until the contrary is shown; and that to establish a defence on the ground of insanity, it must be clearly proved that, at the time of the committing of the act, the party accused was labouring under such a defect of reason,*

from disease of the mind, as not to know the nature and quality of the act he was doing, or, if he did know it, that he did not know he was doing what was wrong.

This is a question of fact for the jury and the onus of proving insanity is upon the defence.

In Bellingham's case in 1812 Lord Chief Mansfield said to the jury:

It must, in fact, be proved beyond all doubt that, at the time he committed the atrocious act with which he stood charged, he did not consider that murder was a crime against the laws of God and of Nature.

Lord Lyndhurst in Offord's case approved this direction, but Lord Campbell later expressed some doubts 'as to the mode in which that case had been conducted', referring apparently to Lord Mansfield's refusal of an adjournment to allow the defence of insanity to be presented properly.

The M'Naughten rules are still the law today, but a great change was made in the Homicide Act of 1957. If an accused person is shown to be suffering from such abnormality of mind . . . as substantially impaired his mental responsibility for his acts and omissions in doing or being a party to any killing he shall not be convicted of murder, but if he would have been guilty of murder but for this new provision, he shall be liable to be convicted of manslaughter. It is for the defence to prove that the accused ought not to be convicted of murder because he is within the new provision.

It will be noticed no doubt with some surprise that, when the case for the Crown had been concluded and Lord Mansfield had informed Bellingham that he might now make any defence he wished to offer, Mr Alley told Bellingham that counsel was not allowed to address the jury, Bellingham having actually asked whether his counsel had nothing to urge in his defence. Mr Alley could examine and cross-examine witnesses but he could not address the jury. This state of affairs lasted until 1836 when 6 and 7 Will. IV, cap. 114 was passed. The preamble to that Statute recited:

Whereas it is just and reasonable that persons accused of offences against the Law should be enabled to make their full Answer and Defence to all that is alleged against them . . .

and it was then enacted that all persons tried for felony should, after the close of the prosecution, be able to make full answer and defence by counsel learned in the law, or by solicitors in courts where solicitors practise as counsel, e.g. at Courts of Quarter Sessions where less than four counsel attend. In trials for misdemeanours the accused has always been entitled to be defended by counsel.

One other thing is to be noticed. Bellingham was allowed to make a long speech in his defence but he was not allowed to go into the witness box to give evidence. When he finished his speech to the jury Mr Alley then stepped in and called evidence for the defence but not Bellingham himself. It was only in 1898 that it was enacted that 'every person charged with an offence, and the wife or husband, as the case may be, of the person so charged, shall be a competent witness for the defence at every stage of the proceedings'. Whilst this provision is very helpful to some accused persons, it can be very difficult for others, because the problem so frequently is: Shall I go into the witness box and be cross-examined, or shall I stay outside and risk the jury thinking that I was afraid to face the cross-examination? It is fairly clear, I think, that many an accused person might have been acquitted if he had not gone into the witness box to give evidence. I sometimes think that Rouse, the blazing car murderer, and Seddon might have had a chance of acquittal but for their appearance and behaviour in the witness box. The Act of 1898 is very helpful to those who have a good defence: but it is a handicap, rather than a help, to those who have not.

In a fascinating biography of Edward Marsh by Christopher Hassall published in 1959, there is a most interesting account of the shooting of Spencer Perceval by Bellingham and a history of the subsequent events. Parliament voted a considerable sum of money for the widow and children, and over a century later, Edward Marsh, the Private Secretary to Sir Winston Churchill, found himself in possession of one-sixth of the money granted, which he was accustomed to refer to as 'the murder money' and which he devoted to the advancement of the arts and to aid young poets and painters. Never was 'murder money' put to better uses.

THOMAS BROCK, JOHN PELHAM, and MICHAEL POWER, Convicted of Coining

IN the year 1816, when Sir Matthew Wood was lord mayor of London, several conspiracies of a most diabolical nature were detected, and some of the conspirators punished. The conduct of the chief magistrate was such as to do honour not only to his understanding and ability, but to his disinterestedness and humanity.

The legislature, with the intention of stimulating the exertions of police officers, and inducing others to give information, had awarded certain rewards to the parties who should contribute to the conviction of offenders against the laws. The object was laudable, but it was capable of great perversion, and was liable to many objections; it gave the prosecutor an interest in the conviction of the accused, and on that account tended to impress the public with the belief that the condemnation, and not the acquittal of the prisoner, was the object of our criminal laws. It was too true that 'blood money', as this species of remuneration was emphatically denominated, did contribute in reality to the evil we allude to. But had not a development of unparalleled villany put scepticism to flight, we could not have brought ourselves to believe that those who were paid to detect crime should be found the most active in seducing innocence and youth to its commission. Yet it is an indubitable fact that, for ten years preceding 1816, victims were brought up, session after session, to be convicted of crimes to which they were seduced by the very men who gave evidence against them, that they might revel on the 'blood money', or make use of it to provide other victims for the law.

The discovery of this diabolical system took place in the course of the trial of three men named Quin, Riorton, and Connolly; it appears that these unfortunate beings were detected in fabricating base shillings and bank tokens, and being brought to trial, they were convicted. During the examination of the witnesses for the prosecution, however, whose names appear at the head of this article, some circumstances came out, which induced a suspicion in the mind of the Lord Mayor that the prosecutors were in some way mixed up with the guilt of the prisoners. An investigation in consequence took place; but the convicts, on being confronted with their accusers, refused to say anything against them, saying that they were 'under an oath'. They were Irishmen and Catholics, and the rigid observance which they pay to an oath is well known; but a priest having at length persuaded them that they were not bound by such an oath administered unlawfully, they disclosed the whole particulars of the plot, and their accusers were in consequence secured.

The three new prisoners were then indicted for participation in the crime of their dupes, which amounted to high treason; and at the session held on the 25th of September 1816, were brought to trial at the Old Bailey.

A man named Barry then swore that Pelham had applied to him to get some men to make bad shillings, which Power, it was said, could colour. Barry said they must go to the market for them, which was in Cheapside, at the corner of King Street, where poor Irishmen were waiting for employment. Some days after, he went with Brock and Power to the market, when Quin and Riorton were engaged by them. Being told they could not be employed unless they would be sworn to secrecy, they took an oath on a piece of paper. A room was hired and tools procured by the prisoners, and the poor Irishmen were set to work to cut brass into the form of shillings, &c under the superintendence of Power. Connolly was sent for to assist. He said to Barry, in Irish, 'We are doing a job that will hang us all', to which the latter replied that if he thought so he would not work another day at it. The Irishmen were then employed in colouring the metal, and everything being in readiness, notice was given, the officers entered, and the Irishmen were seized, tried, and found guilty.

Pelham's landlady proved that the scissors used by the Irishmen in cutting through brass had been procured by her at Pelham's request. Another woman also swore that the hammer and files taken in the coining room had been sold by her to Brock and Pelham.

Brock, in his defence, declared his innocence. Power denied either going to the market or the room; and Pelham said the

Barrys were noted perjurers, and the women were false witnesses.

The jury, without hesitation, however, brought in a verdict of Guilty, and the prisoners were transported.

The three Irishmen were then pardoned; and the Lord Mayor having interested himself in their behalf, a subscription was opened, and they were enabled to return to their own country and there to purchase small farms.

Although at this time the principle had been revived, the statutes under which rewards were paid to informers had been passed between the reigns of William and Mary and George II. The rewards varied between £10 for information leading to the conviction of a sheep-stealer to £40 in cases of treason, robbery and counterfeiting.

It is interesting to note in this connexion that in 1699 an Act was passed 'for the better apprehending, prosecuting and punishing of Felons that commit Burglary, House-Breaking or Robbery . . . or that steal horses'. This introduced what was known as 'The Tyburn Ticket', the purpose of which was to encourage people to bring offenders to justice. This statute provided that anybody who apprehended a person accused of any of the offences set out in the Statute would be entitled on the conviction of the offender to a Tyburn Ticket exempting him from holding any office of the parish or ward where the crime was committed. These tickets were being issued throughout the eighteenth century and the holder of the ticket could sell it to another person for any price he wished, if he had not made previous use of it himself. Sometimes when several persons took part in apprehending a prisoner the tickets were divided into shares, and sometimes very high prices were obtained for a share or for a ticket, but the usual price ranged from £12 to £40, and it was not until 1818 that Tyburn Tickets were abolished by a statute of George III. Dr Radzinowicz records that as late as 1856 a man claimed exemption from jury service because he possessed a Tyburn Ticket and he was exempted (it is said, though it is difficult to believe) because the judge had overlooked the fact that the old statute had been repealed thirty-eight years before.

ABRAHAM THORNTON, Tried for Murder

THIS case is remarkable, not only for the lamentable atrocity of the offence imputed to the unfortunate prisoner, but from the fact also of the brother of the deceased person having lodged an appeal, upon which the prisoner demanded 'wager of battle'. The consequence of this was the repeal of the old law, by which the wager was allowed in former ages, and which had already grown into disuse although it still remained in existence.

Thornton was a well-made young man, the son of a respectable builder, and was by trade a bricklayer. He was indicted at the Warwick assizes in August 1817, for the murder of Mary Ashford, a lovely and interesting girl, whose character was perfectly unsullied up to the time at which she was most barbarously ravished and murdered by the prisoner.

From the evidence adduced, it appeared that the poor girl went to a dance at Tyburn, a few miles from Birmingham, on the evening of the 26th of May 1817, where she met the prisoner, who professed to admire her figure and general appearance, and who was heard to say, 'I have been intimate, and I will have connexion with her, though it cost me my life.' He danced with her, and accompanied her from the room, at about three o'clock in the morning. At four o'clock she called at a friend's at a place called Erdington, and the offence alleged against the prisoner was committed immediately afterwards. The circumstances proved in evidence were that the footsteps of a man and woman were traced from the path through a harrowed field, by which her way lay home to Langley. The marks were at first regular, but afterwards exhibited proofs of the persons whose footfalls they represented running and struggling. At length they led to a spot where a distinct impression of a human figure and a large quantity of coagulated blood were discovered, and on this spot the marks of a man's knees and toes were also distinguishable. From thence the man's footfalls only were seen, and accompanying them blood marks were distinctly traced for a considerable space towards a pit; and it appeared plainly as if a man had walked along the footway carrying a body, from which the blood dropped. At the edge of the pit, the shoes, bonnet, and bundle of the deceased were found; but only one footstep could be seen there, and that was a man's. It was deeply impressed, and seemed to be that of a man who thrust one foot forward to heave something into the pit; and the body of the deceased was discovered lying at the bottom. There were marks of laceration upon the body; and both her arms had the marks of hands, as if they had pressed them with violence to the ground.

By his own admission Thornton was with her at four o'clock, and the marks of the man's shoes in the running corresponded exactly to his. By his own admission, also, he was intimate with her; and this admission was made not before the magistrate, nor till the evident proofs were discovered on his clothes. Her clothes, too, afforded most powerful evidence: at four in the morning she called at a friend's, Hannah Cox, and changed her dancing-dress for that in which she had gone from Birmingham. The clothes she put on there, and which she had on at the time of her death, were all over blood and dirt.

The case, therefore, appeared to be that Thornton had paid attention to her during the night, had shown, perhaps, those attentions which she might naturally have been pleased with; and later waited for her on her return from Erdington, and after forcibly violating her, threw her body into the pit.

The prisoner declined saying anything in his defence, stating that he would leave everything to his counsel, who called several witnesses to the fact of his having returned home at an hour which rendered it very improbable, if not impossible, that he could have committed the murder, and have traversed the distance from the fatal spot to the places in which he was seen, in the very short time that appeared to have elapsed. But it was acknowledged that there was considerable variation in the different village clocks, and the case was involved in so much difficulty from the nature of the defence, that although the case for the prosecution appeared unanswerable, the judge's charge to the jury occupied no less than two hours. 'It were better,' he said in conclusion, 'that the murderer, with all the weight of his crime upon his head, should escape punishment, than that another person should suffer death without being guilty.' This consideration weighed so powerfully with the jury, that, to the surprise of all who had taken an interest in this awful case, they returned a verdict of Not Guilty, which the prisoner received with a smile of silent approbation, and an unsuccessful attempt at concealment of the violent apprehensions as to his fate by which he had been inwardly agitated.

He was then arraigned *pro forma*, for the rape, but the counsel for the prosecution declined offering evidence on this indictment and he was accordingly discharged.

Thus ended, for the present, the proceedings on this most brutal and ferocious violation and murder; but the public at large, and more particularly the inhabitants of the neighbourhood in which it had been committed, were far from considering Thornton innocent, and subscriptions to defray the expense of a new prosecution were entered into.

The circumstances of the case having been investigated by the Secretary of State, he granted his warrant to the sheriff of Warwick to take the defendant into custody on an appeal of murder, to be prosecuted by William Ashford, the brother and heir-at-law of the deceased. Thornton was in consequence lodged in Warwick jail, and from thence he was subsequently removed by a writ of *habeas corpus* to London, the proceedings on the appeal being had in the Court of King's Bench, in Westminster Hall. On the 6th of November, the appellant, attended by four counsel, appeared in court, when the proceedings were adjourned to the 17th, by the desire of the prisoner's counsel; and on that day the prisoner demanded trial by *wager of battle*. The revival of this obsolete law gave rise to much argument on both sides; and it was not until the 16th of April 1818, that the decision of the Court was given upon the question. The learned judges gave their opinions seriatim, and the substance of the judgement was, that the law must be administered as it stood, and that therefore the prisoner was entitled to claim trial by battle; but the Court added that the trial should be granted only 'in case the appellant should show cause why the defendant should not depart without delay'. On the 20th the arguments were resumed by the appellant's counsel; but the defendant was ordered to 'be discharged from the appeal, and to be allowed to go forth without bail'.

Though the rigid application of the letter of the law thus, a second time, saved this unfortunate man from punishment, nothing could remove the conviction of his guilt from the public mind.

Shunned by all who knew him, his very name became an object of terror, and he soon afterwards attempted to proceed to America; but the sailors of the vessel in which he was about to embark refused to go to sea with a character on board who, according to their fancy, was likely to produce so much ill-luck to the voyage, and he was compelled to conceal himself until another opportunity was afforded him to make good his escape.

The Shire Hall at Warwick is a building which stands on a site long hallowed by traditions and local history. It was in this building, which still stands, that the famous case of Thornton was tried. He was acquitted on the charge of murder, and no evidence was offered against him on the charge of rape: he was consequently acquitted on that charge too. In our day that would have been the end of the matter, for once acquitted a man cannot be convicted on the same charge. If arraigned on the charge on which he has been acquitted the accused would make the special plea of Autrefois Acquit *and the provisions of the Criminal Procedure Act of 1851 would apply. By that Act it is enough for any defendant to say that he has been lawfully acquitted of the offence charged in the indictment, but the plea must be made before a plea of Not Guilty to the indictment. Otherwise the plea of* Autrefois Acquit *would be bad in law, for once a plea of Not Guilty is accepted, a jury is sworn to try the issue and the verdict which they give cannot be set aside and a new trial had even if it is given without evidence and against the opinion of the judge.*

In 1817 there existed a procedure that was known as an Appeal of Murder. The Secretary of State issued his warrant to the Sheriff of Warwick and Thornton was re-arrested: the brother of Mary Ashford was to prosecute the appeal. The proceedings on the trial took place in Westminster Hall and the defendant claimed trial by Wager of Battle. The court, after great argument, allowed the claim, for the existing law permitted it; but they added 'only in case the appellant should show cause why the defendant should not depart without day'. In fact, those advising Ashford had never contemplated that the Defendant would demand trial by Wager of Battle, which even at that time was considered to be obsolete in law. When he did so, Ashford's advisers fought the Defendant's claim with great vigour, but the court, after prolonged argument, was compelled to say that the law as it stood permitted the Defendant to make the claim, and they could not do other than grant it. But they gave Ashford the opportunity to withdraw the appeal and Ashford did so. The Crown then presented the Appeal of Murder to which the Defendant pleaded the Defence of Autrefois Acquit *and put in evidence the proceedings at the former trial at Warwick when he was acquitted.*

This plea was successful, Thornton was discharged, and shortly afterwards both the Appeal of Murder and Trial by Wager of Battle were abolished.

When wager of battle was actually carried out, it was a most solemn and imposing ceremony though quite fantastic and barbarous to our way of thinking. A piece of land, sixty feet square, was set apart and a court was erected at the side where the judges in scarlet and ermine attended with a special bar for the predecessors of the modern Queen's Counsel, the Serjeants at Law. The parties were armed with a staff tipped with horn and with a leather target for defence. The defendant pleaded Not Guilty and threw down his glove and declared that he would defend the same with his body. The appellant took up the glove and declared that he was ready to make good the appeal body for body. Then solemn oaths were sworn including an oath against sorcery and enchantment 'whereby the law of God may be abased, or the law of the Devil exalted'. The battle having begun the combatants were forced to fight until the stars appeared in the evening. If the defendant was vanquished or too exhausted to fight more he was adjudged to be hanged immediately, Providence having determined this end in favour of the truth. But if he killed the appellant or maintained the fight from the rising of the sun until the stars appeared, he was acquitted.

It is curious that wager by battle survived until the nineteenth century, in the sense that it was part of the law, although regarded as obsolete, until the case of Thornton revived it; for other forms of trial which rested on the immediate judgement of the Deity were abolished in the early thirteenth century. Trial by Ordeal, for example, which consisted of the accused person being subjected to some physical test such as plunging the hand into boiling water, or walking blindfold and barefoot between red hot ploughshares whereby the judgement of God was made manifest, was in force for nearly 150 years after the Norman Conquest but was then abolished entirely.

Arthur Thistlewood, Richard Tidd, James Ings, William Davidson, and John Thomas Brunt, Executed for High Treason

THE plot in which these notorious criminals were involved, and which was to cost them their lives, had for its object neither more nor less than the assassination of the whole of His Majesty's ministers, and the consequent overthrow of the Government.

It would appear that it had been long known to the members of the Government, that a plan was in meditation by which they would all be murdered, and that Thistlewood was one of the originators of and prime movers in the horrid design; but in accordance with the system which then existed, of waiting until the crime should be all but matured, in order to secure a conviction of the offenders, they determined to make no effort to crush the scheme until a period should have arrived, when their own safety rendered it necessary. The conspirators meanwhile having weighed various plans and projects for the accomplishment of their object, eventually determined to select the evening of Wednesday the 23rd February 1820 as that on which they would carry out their plot, and it was deemed advisable that this night should be fixed upon, because it became known to them by an announcement in the newspapers, that a cabinet dinner would then be held at the house of Lord Harrowby in Grosvenor Square. Contemptible as the means possessed by the conspirators were to carry their design fully into execution, it is certain, from the confession of one of them, that the first part of their project was planned with so much circumstantial exactness, that the assassination of all the ministers would have been secured. It would appear that it was arranged that one of the party should proceed to Lord Harrowby's house with a parcel addressed to his lordship, and that when the door opened his companions should rush in, bind, or, in the case of resistance, kill the servants, and occupy all the avenues of the house, while a select band proceeded to the chamber where the ministers were at dinner and massacred the whole of them indiscriminately. To increase the confusion hand-grenades were prepared, which it was intended should be thrown lighted into the several rooms; and one of the party engaged to bring away the heads of lords Castlereagh and Sidmouth in a bag which he had provided for that purpose.

Thus far the conspirators might probably have carried their plans into effect; but of the scheme for a general revolution, which these men, whose number never exceeded thirty, appear to have considered themselves capable of accomplishing, we cannot seriously speak. Among other arrangements the Mansion House, selected we suppose for its proximity to the Bank, was fixed upon for the 'palace of the provisional government'.

The place chosen for the final organization of their proceedings, and for collecting their force previous to immediate action, was a half-dilapidated tenement in an obscure street called Cato Street, near the Edgware Road. The premises were composed of a stable, with a loft above, and had been for some time unoccupied. The people in the neighbourhood were ignorant that the stable was let, till the day fixed upon for the perpetration of their atrocious purpose, when several persons, some of whom carried sacks and other packages, were seen to go in and out and carefully to lock the door after them.

The information upon which ministers proceeded, in frustrating the schemes of the conspirators, was derived from a man named Edwards, who pretended to enter into their views, for the purpose of betraying them.

Thus accurately informed of the intentions of the gang, measures were taken for their apprehension. A strong body of constables and police-officers, supported by a detachment of the guards, was ordered to proceed to Cato Street, under the direction of Mr (afterwards Sir Richard) Birnie, the magistrate. On arriving at the spot they found that the conspirators had taken the precaution to place a sentinel below, and that the only approach to the loft was by passing up a ladder and through a trapdoor so narrow as not to admit more than one at a time. Ruthven led the way, followed by Ellis, Smithers and others of the Bow Street patrol, and on the door being opened they discovered the

John Bellingham assassinating the Right Honourable Spencer Perceval (*page 59*)

whole gang, in number between twenty and thirty, hastily arming themselves. There was a carpenter's bench in the room, on which lay a number of cutlasses, bayonets, pistols, sword-belts, and a considerable quantity of ammunition. Ruthven, upon bursting into the loft, announced himself as a peace officer, and called upon them to lay down their arms. Thistlewood stood near the door with a drawn sword, and Smithers advanced upon him, when the former made a lunge, and the unfortunate officer received the blade in his breast and almost immediately expired.

About this time the guards, who had been delayed in consequence of their having entered the street at the wrong end, arrived under the command of Captain (Lord Adolphus) Fitzclarence, and mounted the ladder; but as the conspirators had extinguished the lights, fourteen or fifteen of them succeeded in making their escape, and Thistlewood, the chief of the gang, was among the number. A desperate conflict now took place, and at length nine persons were made prisoners; namely Ings, Wilson, Bradburn, Gilchrist, Cooper, Tidd, Monument, Shaw, and Davidson. The whole of them were immediately conveyed to Bow Street, together with a large quantity of arms, consisting of pistols, guns, swords and pikes, and a large sack full of hand-grenades, besides other ammunition, which had been found in the loft. The same means, by which the conspiracy had been discovered, were now adopted in order to procure the discovery of the hiding-place of Thistlewood, and it was found that instead of returning to his own lodgings in Stanhope Street, Clare Market, on the apprehension of his fellows, he had gone to an obscure house, No 8 White Street, Moorfields. On the morning of the 24th February, at nine o'clock, Lavender and others of the Bow Street patrol were dispatched to secure his apprehension; and after planting a guard round the house, so as to prevent the possibility of his escaping, they entered a room on the ground-floor, where they found the object of their inquiry in bed, with his stockings and breeches on. In his pockets were found some ball-cartridges and flints, a black girdle or belt, which he was seen to wear at Cato Street, and a military sash.

He was first conveyed to Bow Street, and there shortly examined by Sir R. Birnie, by whom he was subsequently conducted to Whitehall, where he was introduced to the presence of the Privy Council. He was still handcuffed, but he mounted the stairs leading to the council-chamber with great alacrity. On his being informed by the Lord Chancellor of the nature of the charges made against him, he declined saying anything and was remanded to prison. In the course of the week several other persons were apprehended as being accessories to the plot, and on the 3rd March, Thistlewood, Monument, Brunt, Ings, Wilson, Harrison, Tidd, and Davidson, were committed to the Tower as state prisoners, the rest of the persons charged being again sent to Coldbath-fields prison, where they had been previously confined.

The case of the parties to this most diabolical conspiracy immediately received the attention of the law officers of the crown, and on the 15th April 1820, a special commission having issued, the prisoners were arraigned at the bar of the Old Bailey on the charge of high treason, and also of murder, in having caused the death of the unfortunate Smithers. There were eleven prisoners, Arthur Thistlewood, William Davidson (a man of colour), James Ings, John Thomas Brunt, Richard Tidd, James Wilson, John Harrison, Richard Bradburn, John Shaw Strange, James Gilchrist, and Charles Cooper, and they all pleaded Not Guilty to the charges preferred against them.

Counsel having been assigned to the prisoners, and the necessary forms having been gone through, Thistlewood received an intimation that his case would be taken on Monday morning the 17th of the same month, and the prisoners were remanded to that day.

At the appointed time, accordingly, Arthur Thistlewood was placed at the bar. He looked pale, but evinced his usual firmness. The jury having been sworn, and the indictment read, the Attorney-General stated the case at great length, and twenty-five witnesses were examined in support of the prosecution, among whom were several accomplices, whose testimony was satisfactorily corroborated. Some of those who appeared to give evidence had been apprehended on the fatal night in Cato Street, but were now admitted witnesses for the crown. After a trial which occupied the court four days, Thistlewood was found Guilty of high treason. He heard the verdict with his wonted composure, seeming to have anticipated it, for when it was pronounced he appeared quite indifferent to what so fatally concerned him.

The evidence against Tidd, Ings, Davidson, and Brunt, whose trials came on next in succession, differed little from that upon which Thistlewood was convicted, and they were also found Guilty. Their trials being separate, occupied the court six days. On the evening of the tenth day the six remaining prisoners, at the suggestion of their counsel, pleaded Guilty, having been permitted to withdraw their former plea, by which they eventually escaped capital punishment.

On Friday, April the 28th, the eleven prisoners were brought up to receive sentence. When the usual question was put to Thistlewood by the clerk of arraigns, why he should not receive sentence to die, he pulled a paper from his pocket, and read as follows:

'I am asked, my lord, what I have to say that judgement of death should not be passed upon me according to law. This to me is mockery—for were the reasons I could offer incontrovertible, and were they enforced even by the eloquence of a Cicero, still would the vengeance of my lords Castlereagh and Sidmouth be satiated only in the purple stream which circulates through a heart more enthusiastically vibrating to every impulse of patriotism and honour, than that of any of those privileged traitors to their country, who lord it over the lives and property of the sovereign people with barefaced impunity. The reasons which I have, however, I will now state—not that I entertain the slightest hope from your sense of justice or from your pity. The former is swallowed up in your ambition, or rather by the servility you descend to, to obtain the object of that ambition, the latter I despise. Justice I demand; if I am denied it, your pity is no equivalent. In the first place, I protest against the proceedings upon my trial, which I conceive to be grossly partial, and contrary to the very spirit of justice; but, alas! the judges, who have heretofore been considered the counsel of the accused, are now, without exception, in all cases between the Crown and the people, the most implacable enemies of the latter. In every instance, the judges charge the jury to find the subject guilty; nay, in one instance, the jury received a reprimand, and that not in the genteelest terms, for not strictly obeying the imperious mandate from the bench.

'The court decided upon my trial to commit murder rather than depart in the slightest degree from its usual forms; nay, it is with me a question if the form is usual, which precluded me from examining witnesses to prove the infamy of Adams, of Hieden and of Dwyer. Ere the Solicitor-General replied to the address of my counsel, I applied to the court to hear my witnesses: the court inhumanly refused, and I am in consequence to be consigned to the scaffold. Numerous have been the instances in which this rule of court has been infringed; but to have infringed it in my case would have been to incur the displeasure of the Crown, and to forfeit every aspiring hope of promotion.

'A few hours hence I shall be no more, but the nightly breeze which shall whistle over the silent grave that shall protect me from its keenness, will bear to your restless pillow the memory of one who lived but for his country, and died when liberty and justice had been driven from its confines by a set of villains, whose thirst for blood is only to be equalled by their activity in plunder. For life, as it respects myself, I care not—but while yet I may, I would rescue my memory from the calumny, which I doubt not will be industriously heaped upon it, when it will be no longer in my power to protect it. I would explain the motives which induced me to conspire against the ministers of His Majesty, and I would contrast them with those which those very ministers have acted upon in leading me to my ruin. To do this, it will be necessary to take a short review of my life for a few months prior to my arrest for the offence for which I am to be executed, without a trial, or at least without an impartial one, by a jury of my peers. 'Tis true the form, the etiquette of a trial, has been gone through; but I challenge any of the judges on the bench to tell me, to tell my country, that justice was not denied me in the very place where justice only should be administered. I challenge them to say that I was fairly tried; I challenge them to say if I am not murdered, according to the etiquette of a court, falsely called of justice? I had witnesses in court to prove that Dwyer was a villain beyond all example of atrocity. I had witnesses in court to prove that Adams was a notorious swindler and that Hieden was no better; these were the three witnesses—indeed almost the only ones against me—but the form and rules of court must not be infringed upon to save an unfortunate individual from the scaffold. I called those witnesses at the close of Mr Adolphus' address to the jury, and before the Solicitor-General commenced his reply, but the court decided that they could not be heard. Some good men have thought, and I have thought so too, that before the jury retired, all evidence was in time for either the prosecutor or the accused, and more particularly for the latter; nay, even before the verdict was given, that evidence could not be considered too late. Alas! such people drew their conclusion from principles of justice only; they never canvassed the rules of court, which have finally sealed my unhappy doom.

'Many people, who are acquainted with the barefaced manner in which I was plundered by my lord Sidmouth, will, perhaps, imagine that personal motives instigated me to the deed, but I disclaim them. My every principle was for the prosperity of my country—my every feeling, the height of my ambition, was the securing the welfare of my starving brother Englishmen. I keenly felt for their miseries; and when their miseries were laughed at, when because they dared to express those miseries, they were cut down by hundreds, inhumanly massacred and trampled upon, when infant babes were sabred in their mothers' arms, nay, when the breast from whence they drew the tide of life was severed from the body which supplied that life, my feelings became too intense, too excessive for endurance, and I resolved on vengeance. I resolved that the lives of the instigators should be the requiem to the souls of the murdered innocents.

'In this mood I met with George Edwards, and if any doubt should remain upon the minds of the public whether the deed I meditated was virtuous or contrary, the tale I will now relate will convince them, that in attempting to exercise a power which the law had ceased to have, I was only wreaking national vengeance on a set of wretches unworthy of the name or character of men.

'This Edwards, poor and penniless, lived near Pickett Street in the Strand, some time ago, without a bed to lie upon, or a chair to sit in. Straw was his resting-place, his only covering a blanket. Owing to his bad character, and his swindling conduct, he was driven from thence by his landlord. It is not my intention to trace him through his immorality: suffice to say that he was in every sense of the word a villain of the deepest atrocity. His landlord refused to give him a character. Some short time after this, he called upon his landlord again, but mark the change in his appearance—dressed like a lord, in all the folly of the reigning fashion. He now described himself as the right heir to a German baron, who had been some time dead; that lords Castlereagh and Sidmouth had acknowledged his claims to the title and property, had interfered in his behalf with the German government, and supplied him with money to support his rank in society. From this period I date his career as a government spy.

'He got himself an introduction to the Spenceans, by what means I am not aware of; and thus he became acquainted with the reformers in general. When I met with Edwards, after the massacre at Manchester, he described himself as very poor; and after several interviews, he proposed a plan for blowing up the House of Commons. This was not my view. I wished to punish the guilty only, and therefore I declined it. He next proposed that we should attack the ministers at the fête given by the Spanish ambassador. This I resolutely opposed, because the innocent would perish with the guilty: besides, there were ladies invited to the entertainment and I, who am shortly to ascend the scaffold, shuddered with horror at the idea of that, a sample of which had previously been given by the agents of government at Manchester, and which the ministers of His Majesty applauded. Edwards was ever ready at invention; and at length he proposed attacking them at a cabinet dinner. I asked where were the means to carry his project into effect? He replied, if I would accede, we should not want for means. He was as good as his word: from him, notwithstanding his apparent penury, the money was provided for purchasing the stores which your lordships have seen produced in court upon my trial. He who was never possessed of money to pay for a pint of beer, had always plenty to purchase arms or ammunition. Amongst the conspirators, he was ever the most active, inducing people to join him up to the last hour ere the undertaking was discovered.

'I had witnesses in court, who could prove they went to Cato Street by appointment with Edwards, with no other knowledge or motive than that of passing an evening amongst his friends. I could also have proved that subsequent to the fatal transaction, when we met in Holborn, he endeavoured to induce two or three of my companions to set fire to houses and buildings in various parts of the metropolis. I could prove that, subsequent to that again, he endeavoured to induce men to throw hand-grenades into the carriages of the ministers, as they passed through the streets. Yet this man, the contriver, the instigator, the entrapper, is secured from justice and from exposure, by those very men, who seek vengeance against the victims of his and their villainy. To the Attorney and Solicitor Generals I cannot impute the clearest motives: their object seems to me to have been rather to secure a verdict against me, than to obtain a full and fair exposition of the whole affair since its commencement. If their object was justice alone, why not bring Edwards as a witness, if not as an accomplice? But no, they knew that by keeping him in the background, my proofs, ay my incontrovertible proofs, of his being a hired spy, the suggester and promoter, must, according to the rules of court, also be excluded. Edwards and his accomplices arranged matters in such a manner that his services might be dispensed with on the trial, and thus were the jury cut off from every chance of ascertaining the real truth. Adams, Hieden and Dwyer were the agents of Edwards, and truly he made a most admirable choice, for their invention seems to be inexhaustible.

'With respect to the immorality of our project, I will just observe that the assassination of a tyrant has always been deemed a meritorious action. Brutus and Cassius were lauded to the very skies for slaying Caesar; indeed, when any man, or any set of men, place themselves above the laws of their country, there is no other means of bringing them to justice than through the arm of a private individual. If the laws are not strong enough to prevent them from murdering the community, it becomes the duty of every member of that community to rid the country of its oppressors. High treason was committed against the people at Manchester, but justice was closed against the mutilated, the maimed, and the friends of those, who were upon that occasion indiscriminately massacred. The Prince, by the advice of his ministers, thanked the murderers, still reeking in the gore of their hapless victims. If one spark of honour, if one spark of independence still glimmered in the breasts of Englishmen, they would have risen to a man. Insurrection then became a public duty; and the blood of the victims should have been the watch-word to vengeance on their murderers. The banner of independence should have floated in the gale that brought their wrongs and their sufferings to the metropolis. Such, however, was not the case; Albion is still in the chains of slavery. I quit it without regret—I shall soon be consigned to the grave, my body will be immured beneath the soil whereon I first drew breath—my only sorrow is that that soil should be a theatre for slaves, for cowards, for despots. My motives, I doubt not, will hereafter be justly appreciated. I will now conclude, therefore, by stating that I shall consider myself as murdered, if I am to be executed on the verdict obtained against me, by the refusal of the court to hear my evidence.

'I could have proved Dwyer to be a villain of the blackest dye, for since my trial, an accomplice of his, named Arnold, has been capitally convicted at this very bar, for obtaining money under circumstances of an infamous nature. I seek not pity; I demand but justice. I have not had a fair trial, and upon that ground I protest that judgement ought not to be passed against me.'

The Lord Chief Justice, during the reading of this address, more than once interposed, to prevent the prisoner from either seeking to justify assassination, or slandering the characters of witnesses who had appeared to give evidence in that court. The prisoner, however, proceeded to read till he had finished what had been written on the paper in his hand. His manner was rapid and confused; and the mode in which he pronounced several words, gave abundant evidence that this paper was not his own composition.

Mr Shelton then put the same question to Davidson, who spoke with great vehemence, and much gesticulation, nearly as follows:

'My lords, you ask me what I have to say why I should not receive judgement to die for what has been said against me. I answer, that I protest against the proceedings in this trial *in toto*. In the first place, I always thought that in a court of justice, the balance of justice was held with an even hand. But this has not been the case with me; I stand here helpless and friendless. I endeavoured to show that the evidence against me was contradictory and incredible, and I hoped I had made an impression on the gentlemen in the box; but the moment I was done, the Attorney-General got up and told them, that the evidence was pure and uncontaminated, and to this I may add, that Baron Garrow almost insisted that they should pronounce me guilty. I would ask, has any person identified me but the officers who, everyone knows, have at all times been instrumental in the death of innocent persons? I do not now plead for my life; I know I must fall a victim to the vengeance of my enemies. But in what manner have I been guilty of high treason? It would seem I was a silent spectator; none of the witnesses impute to me a single observation. Now is this probable? I had always got a great deal to say for myself, consequently I was not the person who would stand by without uttering a word; and yet such has been the testimony of Adams. Then, with regard to the blunderbuss, I have already explained that this was not mine, and that I acted in that affair entirely as the agent of Edwards. I have also declared how I came by the sword, and I now declare upon my soul, which will shortly appear before its Maker, that I never made any blow at any man, or discharged any carbine. As for Munday, the man who swore that I had a long sword, with a pair of pistols in my girdle, who is he? He is a poor labouring man, who comes here for his day's pay and his victuals, to swear away the life of a fellow-creature, and to support the unfounded charge against me that I meant to assassinate His Majesty's ministers. I appeal to any man, whether it is upon such evidence that the life of an innocent man is to be sacrificed? But even supposing, for the sake of argument, that the lives of His Majesty's ministers were threatened, it did not follow that this was to extend to the king himself. In a passage of Magna Carta, it was ordained that twenty-five barons should be nominated to see that the terms of the charter were not infringed; and if it was found His Majesty's ministers were guilty of such infringement, then four barons were to call upon them for redress. If this were not granted, then the four barons were to return to their brethren, by whom the people were to be called together to take up arms, and assert their rights. Such an act was not considered, in old times, as an act of treason towards the king, however hostile it might be towards his ministers. But this does not apply to me. I had no intention of joining in any scheme whatever, either to put down my king, or to murder his ministers. I was entrapped by Goldsworthy and Edwards, in order, for some private purposes of their own, that they might have my life sworn away. I have no objection to tender my life in the service of my country; but let me at least, for the sake of my children, save my character from the disgrace of dying a traitor. For my children only do I feel, and when I think of them, I am deprived of utterance—— I can say no more.'

Ings, on being called upon, said, 'I have very little to say, for my abilities will not allow me to speak. If Mr Edwards had not got acquainted with me, I should not be here; he came to me, unfortunately, when I had no business, nor any means of getting a living for my family. I entered into the conspiracy only through him, and it was only necessity and the want of means to support my wife and family that brought me here. It is only through Edwards that I shall lose my life. I do not mind dying, if you will let that man come forward and die with me on the scaffold; for it was through him that I was going to do that which, I must allow, was of a most disgraceful and inhuman nature. On the other hand, His Majesty's ministers conspire together, and impose laws to starve me and my family and my fellow countrymen; and if I were going to assassinate these ministers, I do not see that it is so bad as starvation. There is another thing, a meeting was called at Manchester, under the protection of the law of England, for which our forefathers died, and which King John signed in the open air. This meeting was called under the protection of that law, for the people to petition parliament to give them their rights; but previous to the business of the meeting, the Manchester yeomanry rode in among them, and cut down men, women, and children, in a manner that was a disgrace to the very name of Englishmen. Those yeomen had their swords ground beforehand, and I had a sword ground also, but I do not see any harm in that. I shall suffer, no doubt; but I hope my children will live to see justice done to their bleeding country: I would rather die like a man, than live like a slave. I am sorry I have not power to say more; I shall therefore withdraw.'

John Thomas Brunt next addressed the court in the following terms: 'I am precluded from saying much: I had intended to have committed to writing my defence, but I have been denied pen, ink, and paper—as such, what I have to state will be very short. In the first place, whatever impression I made on the jury yesterday, was knocked down by the Solicitor-General, who appears to me, by his sophistical eloquence, to be capable of making the worst of crimes appear a virtue. And next, with regard to Edwards, to whose machinations I have at last fallen a dupe: he once before nearly entrapped me, when a cabinet dinner was given, I believe, at the Earl of Westmoreland's. He said he had part of the men mustered, but there was not sufficient. He had like to have hooked me in then, but I happened not to go to the house. No doubt that Hieden was in that plot for me; it was held at the Scotch Arms. Of all the infamous characters on earth, Edwards is the worst; and yet he has been kept altogether out of the view of the court. I protest against the verdict which has been pronounced against me. For my life, if it was sacrificed in the cause of liberty, I care not a farthing; but it is galling to have it sworn away by a set of villains who thirst after blood, merely for the sake of personal gain. Edwards is far more worthy of punishment than any of us. He it was that furnished the arms—and he it was that goaded us on to our own ruin. He always spoke well of me, and said, if he had a hundred such men as me, he would be satisfied. He knew I was not a shuttlecock, to be bandied about at pleasure. He knew he could put confidence in my word, and that I would perish before I shrunk from what I undertook.' The prisoner then went on in a strain of strong invective against the witness Adams. After which he referred to the two Monuments. These two persons had been described by the Solicitor-General, as having had no communication with each other, and yet having agreed in all respects in their testimony. Was this the fact? No, for three weeks previous to the trials, they met twice a day at the Tower, rehearsed their story, and thus were enabled to come forward quite perfect in their respective parts. He next adverted to the character of his apprentice Hale, and was casting strong reflections on his conduct—when

The chief justice said he could not suffer such observations to be made under such circumstances.

Brunt begged pardon, but said he stated nothing but facts. He next adverted to the conduct of lords Castlereagh and

Sidmouth; 'They,' he said, 'had been the cause of the death of millions, and although he admitted he had conspired to put such men out of the world, still he did not think that amounted to high treason. He was one of those who would have been satisfied with taking off the cabinet ministers; but the verdict against him, of intending to depose His Majesty, he contended, was utterly at variance with truth and justice. He had never contemplated any such consequence. He was neither a traitor to his king nor to his country; nor would he suffer any man in his presence to speak irreverently of his soverign. In undertaking to kill Lord Castlereagh, Lord Sidmouth, and their fellow ministers, he did not expect to save his life—he was determined to die a martyr in his country's cause, and to avenge the innocent blood shed at Manchester.' In conclusion, he said he was willing to suffer for the acts which he had contemplated, but it grieved him to think that he was to suffer for a crime of which he was innocent, namely, High Treason. On these grounds, he protested against the verdict of the jury, as contrary to law and justice.

Richard Tidd was the next called upon. He spoke as follows:

'My lords and gentlemen, being only found guilty so late last night, I have not had an opportunity to make up any defence. All I can say is, and I positively swear it, that the evidence that has come before you, with the exception of that of Captain Fitzclarence, is utterly false.'

James Wilson said, 'I am not gifted with the power of talking much, but I mean to say, that I was certainly drawn into this by this Edwards.'

John Harrison, and John Shaw Strange, contented themselves with declaring that they had been brought into the matter by Edwards.

James Gilchrist addressed the court in the following terms. 'What I shall say in the presence of my God and you is, that till the Wednesday evening at four o'clock, I knew nothing about this business. I was going to look for work, and I had neither money nor bread, so I went to what I was told was to be a supper of the radicals. At six o'clock I met Charles Cooper, who was the only man I knew, and I borrowed a halfpenny of him, which with another enabled me to get a pennyworth of bread, and this I eat very sweet. I wish I may never come out of this place if I tell false. We then went into the stable and upstairs, where there was some bread and cheese. I took an old sword and hewed down the loaf, of which others who were as hungry as me partook. I then asked what all these arms were about, and when I heard, I was so shocked that I determined to get away as fast as I could. Soon after the officers and soldiers came, and I thought it my duty to surrender. I now stand here convicted of high treason, after I served my king and country for twelve years, and this is the recompense. Oh, God! I have nothing more to say.'

Charles Cooper said, he had much to say, but his friends thought it would be imprudent. He said, 'he could only declare that he was not guilty of the crime imputed to him'.

The crier of the court now proclaimed silence in the usual manner, while sentence of death was passing upon the prisoners, and the Lord Chief Justice then proceeded to address the prisoners severally by their respective names.

After a most admirable and affecting speech, he passed sentence in the usual form upon them, directing that after they should have been hanged, their heads should be severed from their bodies, and their bodies divided into four quarters, which should be at the disposal of His Majesty.

The execution of Thistlewood, Ings, Brunt, Davidson, and Tidd, took place on the following Monday, at Newgate. Davidson was the only prisoner who did not reject religious consolation, and Thistlewood, when on the scaffold, turned away from the ordinary, with an expression of indifference and contempt.

Thistlewood having been first called upon to ascend the gallows, he did so with much alacrity, and he was immediately followed by Tidd, who shook hands with all his companions, except Davidson, who was standing apart from the rest. At the moment he was going out Ings seized him by the hand, exclaiming with a shout of laughter, 'Come, give us your hand; goodbye,' but the remark was coldly received by the unfortunate convict, who dropped a tear, at the same time making some observation with regard to his 'wife and daughter'. Ings, however, with the most astonishing degree of levity, cried out, 'Come, my old cock-o'-wax, keep up your spirits, it will be all over soon', and Tidd appeared to squeeze his hand, and then attempted to run up the steps to the scaffold. In his haste and agitation he stumbled, but he quickly recovered himself, and, with a species of hysterical action, jumped upon the stage, and there stamped his feet as if anxious for the executioner to perform his dreadful office. He was received by the gazing multitude with loud cheers, which he acknowledged by repeated bows. While the executioner was fixing the fatal noose he appeared to recognize a friend at an opposite window, and he nodded to him with much ease and familiarity of manner. He repeatedly turned round and surveyed the assembled mob, and catching sight of the coffins, which were ranged behind the gallows, he smiled upon them with affected indifference and contempt. While waiting for the completion of the preparations for the execution of those whom he had left behind him in the press-room, he, as well as Thistlewood, was observed repeatedly to refresh himself by sucking an orange; but upon Mr Cotton's approaching him, like that prisoner, he rejected his proffered services.

Ings was the next who was summoned, and while on the scaffold he exhibited the same indecent levity of manner which he had shown in the press-room. He laughed while he sucked an orange, and on his being called, he screamed with a sort of mad effort,

'Oh! Give me Death or Liberty!'

to which Brunt, who stood near him, rejoined, 'Ay, to be sure: it is better to die free than to live like slaves.'

On being earnestly and charitably desired to turn their attention to more serious subjects, and to recollect the existence of a God, into whose presence they would soon be ushered, Brunt said, 'I know there is a God'; and Ings, agreeing to this, added 'that he hoped he would be more merciful to them than they were then'.

Just as the hatch was opening to admit him to the steps of the scaffold, he turned round to Brunt, and smiling, shook him by the hand, and then with a loud voice, cried out, 'Remember me to King George the Fourth; God bless him, and may he have a long reign!' Then recollecting that he had left off the suit of clothes in which he had been tried, but which after his conviction he had exchanged for his old slaughtering jacket, because, as he said, he was resolved that Jack Ketch should have no coat of his, he desired his wife might have what clothes he had thrown off. He then said to Mr Davies, one of the turnkeys, 'Well, Mr Davies, I am going to find out this great secret.'

He was again proceeding to sing

'Oh! Give me Death or Liberty!'

when he was called to the platform, upon which he leaped and bounded in the most frantic manner. Then turning himself round towards Smithfield, and facing the very coffin that was soon to receive his mutilated body he raised his pinioned hands, as well as he could, and leaning forward with savage energy, roared out three distinct cheers to the people, in a voice of the most frightful and discordant hoarseness. But it was pleasing to remark, that these unnatural yells of desperation, which were evidently nothing more than the ravings of a disordered mind, or the ebullitions of an assumed courage, were not returned by the motley mass of people who heard them.

Turning his face towards Ludgate Hill, he bowed, and cried out, 'Here's the last remains of James Ings!' and again sung aloud, preserving the well-known tune of that song as much as possible,

'Oh! Give me Death or Liberty!
Oh! Give me Death or Liberty!'

Observing some persons near him, and amongst them one who was taking notes, he said, 'Mind, I die an enemy to all tyrants. Mind, and put that down!' Upon viewing the coffins, he laughed, and said, 'I will turn my back on death. Those coffins are for us I suppose.'

At this time Tidd, who had been just spoken to by Thistlewood, was heard to remonstrate with Ings, and to tell him not to make such a noise, adding, 'We can die without making a noise.' Upon this Ings for a moment was silent but soon burst out afresh, asking the executioner not to cover his eyes, as he wished to see as long as he could. At another time he said, 'Mind you do it well—pull it tight'; or, as some heard it, 'Do it tidy.' He also requested to have a greater length of rope to fall and that at last his eyes should be tightly bandaged round with a handkerchief, which he held in his hand.

Upon the approach of Mr Cotton, he rejected his pious services, but cried out, as if sarcastically, 'I hope you'll give me a good character, won't you, Mr Cotton?'

Davidson was the next summoned; and it is truly gratifying to state the difference that marked the character and conduct of him who had derived his fortitude to face death, and all its awful preparations, from other principles and sources than those from which the others appear to have borrowed their wild determination. He had paid earnest and devoted attention to the consolatory offices bestowed upon him by the ordinary of the jail; and when he was called upon to ascend the scaffold, he did so with a firm and steady step, but with that respectful humiliation which might well be derived from his firm reliance in his Creator's goodness. His lips moved in prayer, and he gently bowed to the people before him: he continued fervently praying with Mr Cotton until the last duty of the executioner was performed.

The last summoned to the fatal platform was Brunt, whose conduct presented nothing particularly worthy of remark. The whole of the necessary arrangements were completed within a very few minutes after he had ascended the drop and, the fatal signal being given, the bolt was withdrawn and the whole of the men almost instantly died. When their bodies had hung for half an hour, a new character entered upon the scaffold—the person who was to perform that part of the sentence which required the deceased men to be decapitated. He was masked; and from the ready and skilful manner in which he performed his office, it was supposed by many that he was a surgeon. The heads were exhibited successively at the corners of the stage and, the whole ceremony having now been completed, the bodies were carried into the interior of the jail in the coffins which had been prepared for them.

It will be observed that there were six prisoners remaining, upon whom sentence was not executed. Of these, Gilchrist, who in reality turned out to be no party to the plot, received His Majesty's pardon, and the other five were transported for life.

The following particulars with regard to Edwards, whose name so frequently occurs during the preceding narrative, will enable the reader to form a just estimate of his character.

It appears that he had been originally a modeller, and kept a

William Corder shooting Maria Marten (page 144)

little shop in Fleet Street, where he sold plaster-of-Paris images. His poverty had been always apparent until a few months previous to the Cato Street plot, when there is no doubt he accepted the wages of Government and became a spy. For this office he appears to have been admirably adapted, as he was shrewd, artful and unprincipled. His former acquaintance with the Spenceans procured him the confidence of some of its deluded members, and through them he got acquainted with Thistlewood and the others.

There is little doubt that the Cato Street plot was 'got up' by him, although he found the unfortunate men who were hanged willing instruments in his hands. He furnished the means of providing the destructive weapons which were found in their possession, and he actually made the grenades himself; and when Thistlewood had escaped from Cato Street, he conducted him to the lodgings where he was next day apprehended.

Immediately after the execution of the traitors, several persons made depositions before Alderman Wood, stating the numerous attempts of Edwards to seduce them from their allegiance, and the worthy alderman applied to the Secretary of State to have the villain apprehended, but he refused to interfere. A motion was made in the House of Commons a few nights afterwards by the same alderman, but, although some debate took place upon the subject, no effect was produced other than the exposition of the system which had been resorted to. An indictment was next preferred before the grand jury of the county of Middlesex, upon which a true bill was found; but although a reward of 100*l* was offered for the apprehension of Edwards, he was nowhere to be found. It was eventually discovered that he had gone to New Brunswick, to avoid the unpleasant consequences to which his conduct might have subjected him.

This much abbreviated account of the trial of the Cato Street conspirators contains many points of great interest.

By the Treason Act of 1695 it was provided that in cases of treason counsel must be assigned to the person charged, on request, to the number of two. Thistlewood was defended by Mr Curwood and Mr Adolphus. Mr Curwood opened the case for the defence in a most eloquent and moving speech which is set out in full in the 33rd volume of the State Trials *and Mr Adolphus made an equally eloquent speech after certain evidence had been called.*

In the State Trials *the account of the trials of the conspirators occupies no less than 884 pages of small print and the speech of Thistlewood is much fuller than the report here printed. The Clerk of Arraigns put the familiar but dreadful question to Thistlewood:*

> *'What have you to say for yourself, why the Court should not pass upon you sentence to die, according to law?'*

Thistlewood had prepared his speech and he complained that he had not had a fair trial and specified certain matters of complaint. Some of his references may sound a little obscure, and a brief note upon a few of them may make them more easily understood.

Thistlewood had wanted to call witnesses to prove what he called 'the infamy' of some of the witnesses for the prosecution. Lord Chief Justice Abbot dealt with this in his summing-up to the jury, but the procedure is that if a witness is examined as to improper conduct and denies it, his denial is conclusive if the question is merely collateral to the point in issue, and it is not permissible to call witnesses to contradict him. But if the question is relevant to the point at issue and the witness denies the thing imputed, he may be contradicted. Thus for example where a witness denied that he had said he would be revenged on his master and would fix him in jail, witnesses were allowed to be called to contradict him and there are many cases in the books to the like effect. On this point it is clear that Thistlewood had no real grievance as the fuller report shows.

Thistlewood also complained that he had not been tried by an impartial jury of his peers but there was no foundation for the complaint in fact. The True Bills were first found by the Grand Jury which has now been abolished, and the petty jury was called into the jury box in the ordinary way, and showed themselves anxious to do justice in all their interventions that are recorded in the account of the trial. There was certainly no attempt to pack the jury and it must be remembered at all times that the learned counsel for Thistlewood were watching his interests with exceptional keenness.

The 'massacre at Manchester' to which reference is made, resulted from a meeting in St Peter's Fields at Manchester on August the 6th 1819. The occasion has become known as 'Peterloo'. The purpose of the meeting was to demand the return of Parliament, and some 60,000 persons attended including a great number of women and children. Nobody was armed and their behaviour was quite peaceable. The magistrates ordered the yeomanry, who were Manchester businessmen, to seize the speakers just after the meeting had begun. The yeomanry not only did this but attacked the audience with their sabres. Thereupon a fresh order was given by the chairman of the magistrates to the 15th Hussars and the Cheshire Yeomanry to charge the crowd and, when they did so, many hundreds were either killed or wounded. The tremendous indignation aroused by this wanton behaviour of the yeomanry and the support given to their action by the Government immensely assisted the growing movement for reform. The non-existence of a civilian police was a principal cause of the shocking events of Peterloo, and the Reform Bill of 1832 made it certain that there would be no more magistrates of the type that issued the disgraceful orders.

Thistlewood was clearly a man of some education and his speech as recorded in the State Trials *is well worth reading. There seems little justification for the suggestion that it was not his own work. He had to be stopped by the Lord Chief Justice when he was advocating and justifying assassination and murder as reprisals for the Manchester 'massacres'.*

Thistlewood, who has merited over five columns in the Dictionary of National Biography, *was brought up as a land surveyor but never practised. He was much influenced by the works of Tom Paine and by visits to America and to France shortly before the fall of Robespierre. Alison in his history says that Thistlewood returned to England in 1794 'firmly persuaded that the first duty of a patriot was to massacre the Government and overturn all existing institutions'. In 1816, he organized a great meeting at Spa Fields to inaugurate a revolution but informers kept the Government aware of all that was being plotted and at the appropriate moment Thistlewood was arrested. Acquitted of a charge of high treason on the direction of the judge, he promptly challenged the Home Secretary to a duel for which he was sentenced to six months' imprisonment. His allusion to 'the bare-faced manner in which I was plundered by my Lord Sidmouth' refers to this incident.*

Henry Fauntleroy, Executed for Forgery

THE station in society which was occupied by this unfortunate gentleman, together with the long established respectability of the banking-house in which he was a most active partner, and the vast extent of the heartless forgeries which he committed, gave to his case an intensity of interest, which has rarely been exceeded.

The apprehension of Mr Fauntleroy took place on the 10th of September 1824, when he was taken into custody on a warrant, issued in consequence of information being lodged at Marlborough Street police office, that it had been discovered that in the month of September 1820, stock in the three per cents to the extent of 10,000*l*, which stood in the name of himself, J. D. Hulme and John Goodchild, as trustees for Francis William Bellis, had been sold out under a power of attorney, to which the names of Mr Fauntleroy's co-trustees and of one of the subscribing witnesses had been forged. The name of the firm with which Mr Fauntleroy was connected was Marsh, Stracey, Fauntleroy, and Graham, and their banking-house was situated in Berners Street, where they enjoyed no inconsiderable portion of public patronage. The apprehension of Mr Fauntleroy, on one charge, no sooner became generally known, than, on inquiries being made, it was found that, since 1814 he had, under similar circumstances, sold out stock to the enormous amount of 170,000*l*, the whole of which he had converted to his own use. The most extraordinary degree of interest was, in consequence, exhibited, and the public, unconscious of the degree of mischief which might be apprehended, became so alarmed that a run on the banking-house took place, which was checked by a suspension of payments, and eventually by a commission of bankruptcy.

Meanwhile Mr Fauntleroy's private character and conduct became the subject of general comment in the newspapers, and exaggerated accounts of his depravity of habit were published. He was described as a licentious libertine, and as a deep and determined gamester, and it was alleged that his extravagance knew no bounds. His private life was also inquired into, and it was found that he had been married to a young lady of respectable family named Young, by whom he had previously had a child, but that after his marriage, he had never lived with his wife. It is not a little remarkable, that it was for a forgery, by means of which his wife's family was defrauded, that he underwent the final dreadful sentence of the law.

His trial took place at the Old Bailey, on the 30th of October 1824, when he was indicted for forging a power of attorney for the transfer of stock in the three per cent consols, to the amount of 5,000*l*, with intent to defraud Frances Young. As early as seven o'clock in the morning the doors leading to the courthouse were thronged with persons anxious to obtain a glimpse of the prisoner and, on the arrival of the judges before whom the unfortunate gentleman was tried, every corner of the court was filled with spectators. The Attorney-General was employed to conduct the case for the prosecution, and in his opening address to the jury, he described the prisoner as the acting partner in the house of Messrs Marsh and Co. Mr Fauntleroy, the father of the prisoner, had become a partner in that firm, at the period of its establishment, and had continued so up to the time of his death, which took place in the year 1807. The prisoner was then admitted into the concern, and became a most active member in carrying on its extensive transactions. In the year 1815, Frances Young of Chichester, a customer of the house, lodged in their hands a power of attorney, to receive the dividends on 5,450*l* stock, invested in her name in the three per cent consols. The dividends were regularly handed over by the banking-house; but it was found that, soon after the period mentioned, another power of attorney, authorizing the prisoner to sell the stock, was presented to the bank, and the sale was effected by him. To this power the prisoner had forged the names of Frances Young, and of two witnesses to it. But the most extraordinary part of the case was, that among the prisoner's private papers, contained in a tin box, there had been found one in which he acknowledged his guilt, and adduced a reason for his conduct. The Attorney-General then read the paper, which presented the following items:—De la Place, 11,150*l* three per cent consols;

E. W. Young, 5,000*l* consols; General Young, 6,000*l* consols; Frances Young, 5,000*l* consols; H. Kelly, 6,000*l* consols; Lady Nelson, 11,995*l* consols; Earl of Ossory, 7,000*l* four per cents; W. Bowen, 9,400*l* four per cents;—Parkins, 4,000*l* consols. Sums were also placed to the names of Mrs Pelham, Lady Aboyne, W. R. and H. Fauntleroy, and Elizabeth Fauntleroy; and the learned gentleman observed, that all the sums were added together, and the sum total, 120,000*l*, appeared at the foot of this list in the prisoner's hand-writing. The statement was followed by this declaration:

'In order to keep up the credit of our house, I have forged powers of attorney for the above sums and parties, and sold out to the amount here stated, and without the knowledge of my partners. I kept up the payment of the dividends, but made no entries of such payments in our books. The Bank began first to refuse to discount our acceptances and to destroy the credit of our house: the Bank shall smart for it.'

The Attorney-General then called his witnesses, who confirmed in every point his statement of the case.

On being asked what he had to say in his defence, the prisoner read from a paper the following address:

'My lord and gentlemen of the jury—Overwhelmed as I am by the situation in which I am placed, and being uninformed in what manner I should answer the charges which have been alleged against me, I will endeavour to explain, so well as the poignancy of my feelings will enable me, the embarrassments of the banking-house in which I have been for many years the active and only responsible partner, and which have alone led to the present investigation. Although I am aware I cannot expect to free myself from the obloquy brought upon me by my anxiety to preserve the credit and respectability of the firm, still I trust that an impartial narrative of the occurrences will obtain for me the commiseration of the well-disposed part of the community.

'Anticipating the Court will extend its indulgence to me, I will respectfully submit such observations as I think will tend to remove from influenced minds those impressions, which, with sorrow I say, must have been made upon them by the cruel and illiberal manner in which the public prints have untruly detailed a history of my life and conduct; hoping therefrom I may deserve your compassion, and although I may be unable to justify my proceedings, and secure my liberation, by a verdict of the jury, yet they may be considered, in the mercy of the court and a discerning public, as some extenuation of the crimes with which I stand arraigned.

'My father established the banking-house in 1792, in conjunction with Mr Marsh, and other gentlemen. Some of the partners retired in 1794, about which time a loss of 20,000*l* was sustained. Here commenced the difficulties of the house. In 1796, Mr Stracey and another gentleman came into the house with little or no augmentation of capital. In 1800 I became a clerk in the house, and continued so six years; and although during that time I received no salary, the firm were so well satisfied with my attention and zeal for the interest and welfare of the establishment, that I was handsomely rewarded by them. In 1807 my father died; I then succeeded him. At this time I was only twenty-two years of age, and the whole weight of an extensive, but needy, banking establishment devolved upon me. I found the concern deeply involved in advances to builders and others, which had rendered a system of discounting necessary, and this we were obliged to continue in consequence of the scarcity of money at that time, and the necessity of making further advances to those persons, to secure the sums in which they already stood indebted. In this perplexed state the house continued until 1810, when its embarrassments were greatly increased owing to the bankruptcies of Brickwood and others, which brought upon it a sudden demand for no less a sum than 170,000*l*, the greater part being for the amount of bills, which our house had either accepted or discounted for those parties said to have become bankrupts. About 1814, 1815, and 1816, from the speculations with builders, brickmakers, &c in which the house was engaged, it was called upon to provide funds to the extent of near 100,000*l* to avert the losses which would otherwise have visited it from those speculations. In 1819 the most responsible of our partners died, and we were called upon to pay over the amount of his capital, although the substantial resources of the house were wholly inadequate to meet so large a payment. During these numerous and trying difficulties, the house was nearly without resources, and the whole burden of management falling upon me,

I was driven to a state of distraction, in which I could meet with no relief from my partners. Almost heart-broken, I sought resources where I could, and so long as they were provided, and the credit of the house supported, no inquiries were made, either as to the manner in which they were procured, or as to the sources from which they were derived. In the midst of these calamities, which were not unknown to Mr Stracey, he quitted England and continued in France on his own private business for two years, leaving me to struggle as well as I could with difficulties almost insurmountable. Having thus exposed all the necessities of the house, I declare that all the moneys temporarily raised by me were applied, not in one instance for my own separate purposes or expenses, but in every case were immediately placed to the credit of the house in Berners Street, and applied to the payment of the pressing demands upon it. This fact does not rest on my assertion, as the transactions referred to are entered in the books now in the possession of the assignees, and to which I have had no access since my apprehension. These books, I understand, are now in court, and will confirm the truth of my statement; and to whatever account all the sums may be entered, whether to that of stock, or of Exchequer bills, or to my own private account, the whole went to the general funds of the banking-house. I alone have been doomed to suffer the stigma of all the transactions. But tortured as I have been, it now becomes an imperative duty to explain to you, gentlemen, and through you to the world at large, that the vile accusations heaped upon me, known to be utterly false by all those who are best acquainted with my private life and habits, have been so heaped upon me for the purpose of loading me with the whole obloquy of those transactions, from which, and from which alone, my partners were preserved from bankruptcy. I have been accused of crimes I never even contemplated, and of acts of profligacy I never committed; and I appear at this bar with every prejudice against me, and almost prejudged. To suit the purposes of the persons to whom I allude, I have been represented as a man of prodigal extravagance—prodigal indeed I must have been, had I expended those large sums which will hereafter be proved to have gone exclusively to support the credit of a tottering firm, the miseries of which were greatly accelerated by the drafts of two of its members to the amount of near 100,000*l*. I maintained but two establishments, one at Brighton, where my mother and sister resided in the season—the expenses of which to me, exclusive of my wine, were within 400*l* per annum—and one at Lambeth, where my two children lived, from its very nature private and inexpensive, to which I resorted for retirement, after many a day passed in devising means to avert the embarrassments of the banking-house. The dwelling-house in Berners Street belonged solely to my mother, with the exception of a library and single bedroom. This was the extent of my expenditure, so far as domestic expenditure is concerned. I am next accused of being an habitual gambler, an accusation which, if true, might easily account for the diffusion of the property. I am, indeed, a member of two clubs, the Albion and the Stratford, but never in my life did I play in either, at cards or dice, or any game of chance; this is well known to the gentlemen of these clubs—and my private friends, with whom I more intimately associated, can equally assert my freedom from all habit or disposition to play. It has been as cruelly asserted, that I fraudulently invested money in the funds to answer the payment of annuities, amounting to 2,200*l*, settled upon females. I never did make any such investment; neither at home or abroad, in any funds whatever, have I any investment; nor is there one shilling secretly deposited by me in the hands of any human being. Equally ungenerous, and equally untrue it is, to charge me with having lent to loose and disorderly persons large sums which never have, and never will be repaid. I lent no sums but to a very trifling amount, and those were advanced to valued friends. I can, therefore, at this solemn moment declare, most fervently, that I never had any advantage beyond that in which all my partners participated in any of the transactions which are now questioned. They indeed have considered themselves as partners only in the profits, and I am to be burdened with the whole of the opprobrium, that others may consider them as the victims of my extravagance. I make this statement not with a view to criminate others, or to exculpate myself; but borne down as I am by calamity, I will not consent to be held out to the world as a cold-blooded and abandoned profligate, ruining all around me for the selfish gratification of vice and sensuality, and involving even my confiding partners in the general destruction. Gentlemen, I have frailties and errors enough to account for. I have sufferings enough, past, present and in prospect; and if my life were all that was required of me, I might endure in silence, though I will not endure the odium on my memory, of having sinned to pamper delinquencies to which I never was addicted. Thus much has been extorted from me by the fabrications which have been cruelly spread amongst the public, that very public from whom the arbiters of my fate were to be selected. Perhaps, however, I ought to thank the enemy who besieged the prisoner with his slanders, that he did so whilst my life was spared to refute them, and that he waited not until the grave, to which he would hurry me, had closed at once on my answer and my forgiveness. There is one subject more connected with these charges to which I am compelled to advert, and I do so with great reluctance. It has added to the other charges made against me, lest the world should think there was any vice in which I was not an adept. I have been accused of acting treacherously towards the female who now bears my name, having refused to make reparation until threatened by her brother, and of having deserted her at a moment when she had the greatest claim on my protection. Delicacy forbids me entering into an explanation on this subject further than to declare that the conduct I adopted on that occasion was uninfluenced by the interference of any individual, and arose, as I then considered and do still consider, from a laudable and honourable feeling on my part; and the lady's brother, so far from coming forward at the time alluded to, was on service in the West Indies. Could all the circumstances be exposed, I feel convinced that every liberal-minded man would applaud my determination; and I feel satisfaction in saying, that the lady in question has always been, and still is actuated by the best feelings towards me. I have now to apologize to the court for having entered so much at length into the statement of my unfortunate case and, in conclusion, I have to express my perfect confidence that it will receive every favourable consideration at your hands. I fully rely that you, gentlemen of the jury, will give an impartial and merciful decision.'

The unfortunate gentleman having completed the reading of this document, sat down, and wept with much agitation. Seventeen gentlemen of the highest respectability were then called, and they all attested their high opinion of his honour, integrity, and goodness of disposition, and that he was the person whom, of all others, they would have supposed incapable of a dishonourable action. During their examination the prisoner buried his face in his handkerchief, apparently anxious to conceal his features from their view.

In summing up, the judge told the jury that, as the evidence did not show the forgery to have been committed within their jurisdiction, they, being a London jury, would have to decide on the count for uttering; and after twenty minutes' consideration they returned a verdict—Guilty of uttering—Death.

Every exertion was used by Mr Fauntleroy's counsel, his case being twice argued before the judges upon points of law; but both decisions were against him, and on the 30th of November 1824, his execution took place. The number of persons assembled on the fatal day was estimated at nearly one hundred thousand! Every window and roof which could command a view of the dreadful ceremony was occupied, and places from which it was impossible to catch a glimpse of the scaffold were blocked up by those who were prevented by the dense crowd before them from advancing farther.

At a quarter before eight o'clock, the sheriffs arrived at Newgate and proceeded immediately to the prisoner's room. The prisoner gently bowed to them on perceiving that they were present, but made no observation. Besides the ordinary of Newgate, the Rev Mr Cotton, there were the Rev Mr Springett and Mr Baker with the prisoner, the former of whom had remained all night.

Mr Fauntleroy was dressed in a black coat, waistcoat, and trousers, with silk stockings and shoes. The demeanour of the unhappy man was perfectly composed. His eyes continued closed, and no emotion was visible in his countenance. His appearance had undergone little or no change since the trial. The necessary arrangements having been completed, the sheriffs moved forward, and Mr Springett and Mr Baker each took hold of one of the prisoner's arms; and thus accompanied, he followed the sheriffs and the ordinary. He never turned his head to the right nor the left till he reached the foot of the steps leading to the scaffold, and the moment he appeared the vast crowd took off their hats. In less than two minutes after the criminal ascended the platform, everything was prepared for his execution. Mr Cotton now placed himself before the prisoner, who stood with his face towards Ludgate Hill, and commenced reading the passage—'Yet, O Lord God, most Holy! O Lord, most mighty! O holy and most merciful Saviour! deliver us not into the bitter pains of eternal death. Thou knowest, Lord, the secrets of our hearts'; towards the conclusion of which the trap-door fell, and the unhappy man died without a struggle.

An almost universal sympathy was excited in his favour, in consequence of the melancholy termination of his career; but many, even to the present day, have but too powerful reasons to mourn the crimes of which he was guilty, depriving them as they did, in many instances, of every shilling of what otherwise would have been comfortable competencies, sufficient to maintain them in respectability through life.

George Alexander Wood, and Alexander Wellesley Leith, Indicted for Manslaughter

The scene of the melancholy event by which one youth, a member of a noble family, was hurried into an untimely grave, and two others were brought to the bar of a public court of justice upon a charge of manslaughter, was at Eton College, and it occurred on Monday the 28th February 1825.

On the 9th of March 1825 George Alexander Wood, son of Colonel Wood and nephew of the Marquis of Londonderry, and Alexander Wellesley Leith, were placed at the bar at the Aylesbury Assizes, charged with killing and slaying the Hon F. Ashley Cooper, son of the Earl of Shaftesbury. The circumstances will be best explained as they appeared in evidence before the coroner.

On Sunday, the 27th of February, about two o'clock, two young gentlemen, scholars at Eton, the Hon F. A. Cooper and Mr Wood, were in the play-ground, when some words arose between them. From words they proceeded to blows; and they had fought for several minutes, when the captain came up and separated them. It was subsequently determined that they should meet on the following afternoon, and terminate their differences by a pugilistic contest. Many of the scholars were present to witness the battle: the combatants stripped at four o'clock on Monday afternoon, and commenced fighting. Mr Cooper was under fifteen years, and his opponent, who was half a head taller, was near seventeen. Mr Wood had the advantage in point of strength, but the quickness and precision of Mr Cooper were remarkable for one so young, and he declared that he would never give in. In the eight, ninth, and tenth rounds, he became weak and exhausted, and it was then evident he was not a match for Mr Wood. Some of the 'backers' had brought a quantity of brandy in bottles into the field, and the second of Mr Cooper having, in the eleventh round, poured a portion of it down Mr C.'s throat, he recovered his wind and strength. The young men continued fighting from four till nearly six o'clock, and when they were in a state of exhaustion, they were plied between the rounds with brandy. They fought about sixty rounds and, at the end of the last round, Mr Cooper fell very heavily upon his head and never spoke afterwards. He was carried off the ground to his lodgings, at the house of the Reverend Mr Knapp, by his brothers, who were present at the fight. He was put to bed, but no medical assistance was sent for till four hours had elapsed: shortly afterwards he expired.

At two o'clock on Tuesday, a jury assembled to hold an inquest on the body. The jury and coroner proceeded to the house of the Reverend Mr Knapp, and viewed the body. The temples, eyes, and upper part of the cheek-bones were very black, and there were other external marks of violence about the ribs, breast, &c. The following evidence as to the circumstances attending the battle was then taken:

Christopher Teasdale. 'I am a student at Eton College. I knew the deceased—he was the son of Lord Shaftesbury; and I know his antagonist Mr Wood, the son of Colonel Wood. I saw them set-to about the hour of four o'clock on Monday afternoon. I saw repeated blows, during the fight, given to Cooper on different parts of the head. I remember, in one period of the fight, a severe blow being given on his temple; the deceased instantly fell, and lay on the ground about half a minute. There were loud shouts from Wood's party, in consequence of his being the best. It was a fair fight; I saw no unfair advantage taken. A young gentleman named Leith seconded the deceased. The fight lasted about an hour; the deceased's spirits were kept up in a most extraordinary manner by Leith giving him brandy in the eleventh and subsequent rounds. I remember that before the last round, Wood said he wanted to go to his tutor, Mr Ottery, to attend his private business (studies), and he would make it up afterwards. Mr Leith, the second, said that as Wood wanted to go, he would appeal to the deceased's party, and hear what they had to say. The deceased's party exclaimed, "We will have another round; we are in no hurry." The parties fought another round, and the deceased at the conclusion fell from a severe blow; Wood fell heavily on him. After the round, Wood said, "he must go, and he would make it up". Leith advised it to be made up on the spot, and directly the proposition was made the deceased fell back senseless. Wood walked up to the deceased and lifted his head, but I did not hear him say anything.'

Other witnesses proved that the deceased was taken home to Mr Knapp's, where he remained for some time under the care of his brother, and that after the lapse of some hours surgical aid was procured. It was then too late, however, and he died. On his body being opened, it was found that he had died from the rupture of the blood-vessels on the brain.

Upon the arraignment of the defendants they pleaded Not Guilty, and the witnesses for the prosecution did not answer. Mr Justice Gasalee having ordered their recognizances to be estreated, a verdict of Not Guilty was returned, and the defendants left the bar attended by Lord Nugent, Colonel Brown, Sir John Dashwood King, and other persons of distinction.

Edward Gibbon Wakefield, William Wakefield, and Frances Wakefield, Convicted of the Abduction of Miss Turner

No case of a similar nature ever excited one quarter of the degree of interest which was produced by the extraordinary abduction of Miss Turner, a wealthy heiress, and the daughter of Mr Turner, a gentleman of the highest respectability living at Shrigley in the county of Cheshire.

It would appear that Miss Turner, at the time of this affair, had just entered her fifteenth year. Her father was a man of large property, and was high sheriff of Cheshire; and with a view to the proper education of his daughter, who was a young lady of lively disposition, of quick perception, and of great personal beauty besides, he placed her at the school of a Mrs Daulby, at Liverpool. She had continued there during a considerable time when, in the month of February 1827, Mr E. G. Wakefield and his brother William went to Macclesfield on a visit, where they learned the situation, the wealth and the beauty of Miss Turner. A design was soon formed, by means of which they proposed to secure possession of her person, and they quitted Macclesfield on the evening of the 5th March, with the professed object of proceeding to the metropolis on their route to Paris. But instead of taking the road to London, at seven o'clock on the morning of the 6th of the same month they presented themselves at the Albion Hotel, Manchester, in a Wilmslow post chaise. Having purchased a carriage in this place, they went on towards Liverpool. At eight o'clock on the morning of Tuesday the 7th March, the newly bought carriage was driven up to the house of Mrs Daulby, and a servant alighting from it presented a letter in the following terms, which he professed to have brought with him from Shrigley. It was addressed to Miss Daulby, and was as follows:

'Shrigley, Monday night, half-past Twelve

'MADAM—I write to you by the desire of Mrs Turner, of Shrigley, who has been seized with a sudden and dangerous attack of paralysis. Mr Turner is unfortunately from home but has been sent for, and Mrs Turner wishes to see her daughter immediately. A steady servant will take this letter and my carriage to you to fetch Miss Turner, and I beg that no time may be lost in her departure, as, though I do not think Mrs Turner in immediate danger, it is possible she may soon become incapable of recognizing anyone. Mrs Turner particularly wishes that her daughter may not be informed of the extent of her danger as, without this precaution, Miss Turner might be very anxious on the journey; and this house is so crowded, and in such confusion and alarm, that Mrs Turner does not wish any one to accompany her daughter. The servant is instructed not to let the boys drive too fast, as Miss T. is rather fearful in a carriage. I am, madam, your obedient servant,

'JOHN AINSWORTH, M.D.

'The best thing to say to Miss T. is, that Mrs T. wishes to have her daughter home rather sooner, for the approaching removal to the new house, and the servant is instructed to give no other reason in case Miss Turner should ask any questions. Mrs Turner is very anxious that her daughter should not be frightened, and trusts to your judgement to prevent it. She also desires me to add that her sister, or niece, or myself, should they continue unable, will not fail to write to you by post.'

The allusion to the indisposition of the young lady to ride quickly, gave the letter an air of authenticity, and its contents were immediately communicated to Miss Turner. On her seeing the servant, however, she expressed her surprise at his being strange to her, but the fellow, whose name was Thévenot, and who was in the service of Wakefield, answered, with great readiness, that in consequence of Mr Turner's having taken a new mansion, he had made some alteration in his establishment, and that he had engaged him as butler, in lieu of the person who had before filled that situation. He added that the carriage would return by way of Manchester, where it would take up Dr Hull, who, it was known, had previously attended Mrs Turner, and that then it would immediately proceed to Shrigley. The extreme plausibility of the man's manner and story left no room for suspicion, and the young lady was in a few minutes handed into the carriage and driven off. The vehicle reached Manchester in due course, but instead of going to Dr Hull's residence, it stopped at the door of the Albion Hotel, and there the young lady was directed to alight. She was shown into a private room, but she had scarcely been there five minutes when Mr E. G. Wakefield presented himself. Miss Turner was at this time completely unacquainted with him, and she was about to leave the room; but on his stating to her that he came from her papa, she remained. She proceeded immediately to make inquiries of him as to the state of her mother's health, but the necessity of some reason being given why she was not taken to Shrigley, Mr Wakefield told her, that the real cause of her removal from the school was the state of her father's affairs, and that the only reason why this was not at once communicated to her was a desire on the part of her parents to keep the circumstance secret from her schoolmistress and companions. He then introduced his brother William to her and, telling her that they were directed immediately to conduct her to Mr Turner, they ordered post-horses to be instantly got ready.

They then proceeded on the road to Huddersfield, and Miss Turner, buoyed up with the assurance of seeing her father at almost every stage, travelled all night until they arrived at Kendal, where she was assured that her parent would be in waiting for them. Here, however, a fresh disappointment awaited the unhappy young lady and Wakefield, perceiving that she began to exhibit great anxiety, now found it necessary to become 'more explicit' upon the subject of the state of her father's affairs. He stated to her that the bank of Messrs Daintry and Kyle at Macclesfield had failed, and that an uncle of his, who was a banker at Kendal, had lent her father 60,000*l.* This had partially relieved him but the Blackburn bank having also failed, everything was now worse and worse. Her father was completely ruined, but he (Wakefield) was his greatest friend. His uncle could turn Mr Turner out of doors, but Mr Grimsditch, the legal adviser of the latter, had hit upon a plan which, if it were followed out, would make all right. Some settlements were to be drawn up and made, and some property transferred to her, so that her estate would belong to her husband, whoever he might be. Mr Grimsditch had proposed that he (Mr Wakefield) should marry her, but as he had never seen her, he had laughed at the proposition; but his uncle, the Kendal banker, had insisted upon his seeing her, and it now remained for her to determine whether she would accede to this proposition, or whether her father should be turned out of doors. He added, that she might come to a determination when she saw her father who was then on his way to Scotland pursued by sheriffs' officers.

Imposed upon by these representations, Miss Turner permitted herself to be carried to Carlisle on the way to Gretna Green, and on their arrival, the younger Wakefield quitted the party for a short time. When he returned, he said that he had seen Mr Turner and Mr Grimsditch at an inn close by, but that in consequence of their dread of sheriffs' officers, the former was afraid to show himself. Mr Grimsditch, in his fear, had thrust him from the house, declaring his anxious desire that the marriage should take place immediately, for as soon as the certificate arrived at Carlisle, Mr Turner would be released. He also added, that Mr Turner had desired him to inform his daughter, that he entreated she would not hesitate; for if she did, there would be an execution at Shrigley, and they would all be ruined.

At such an injunction, Miss Turner, with a degree of filial solicitude which did her honour, hesitated no longer, but at once proceeded to Gretna with Mr Wakefield, where the ceremony of marriage was performed by the far-famed blacksmith in the customary manner. This done, she returned with Mr Wakefield to Carlisle, and there expressed her anxious solicitude with regard to her father's situation, desiring at once to see him, in order that she might be assured of his safety. A new subterfuge was adopted, however, and she was informed that her father, having now secured his liberty and intelligence of her marriage having already reached him, had gone on to Shrigley, whither they were to follow him. Leeds was the point to which they next proceeded; and on their arrival there, Wakefield recollected that he had an appointment at Paris, which he must keep in the ensuing week. He declared it impossible therefore that they could then go to Shrigley, and he pretended to dispatch his brother to Cheshire, with directions to conduct Miss Turner to London, where they would all meet. Wakefield and Miss Turner arrived at Blake's Hotel, in Prince's Street, Hanover Square, at half-past eleven o'clock, on the night of Friday the 19th of March, but there a person who was waiting having declared that Mr Turner and Mr W. Wakefield had proceeded to France, a chaise was directly ordered, and they started for Dover and from thence by the first packet to Calais.

For several days the circumstance of the abduction remained totally unknown to the friends of the young lady; but the fact of her not having arrived at Shrigley having been discovered by Mrs Daulby, some members of the family were dispatched in pursuit of her, and she was traced to Manchester, and thence to Huddersfield. There all trace of her and her companion was lost. The dreadful anxiety entertained by the unhappy parents of the young lady was soon still further excited by the receipt of a letter from Mr Wakefield, dated Carlisle, begging that Mr and Mrs Turner would render themselves quite easy, for that the writer had married their daughter. In a state of mind bordering on distraction, Mr Turner instantly proceeded to London, for the purpose of procuring such aid as could be afforded by the police of the metropolis. His inquiries soon taught him that Mr Wakefield had carried his daughter to the Continent, and thither he dispatched the paternal uncle of the young lady, accompanied by his solicitor and Ellis, an active and prudent officer, attached to Bow Street, and armed with a letter from Mr Canning to the British Ambassador in France. In the meantime, a letter was received by Mrs Turner from Mr Wakefield, dated Calais, in which the writer repeated the declaration that he had married Miss Turner, and taking all the blame of the transaction on himself, as far as 'over-persuasion' went, he added, 'Miss Turner is fondly attached to me, and I do assure you, my dear madam, that it shall be the anxious endeavour of my life to promote her happiness by every means in my power.'

Upon the landing of Mr Turner and his companions at Calais, the first persons whom they saw were the young lady whom they sought, and Mr Wakefield, who were walking on the pier. The exclamation of Miss Turner afforded a convincing proof that she remained with Mr Wakefield unwillingly, for crying out 'Good God! here's my uncle', she rushed from her companion, and was soon locked in the embrace of her relation, declaring how rejoiced she was that he had come to convey her home. Mr

Wakefield, on finding matters take this turn, declared that the young lady could not be taken from him by force, and appealed to the civil authorities of the town, whether any person could be hurried from the country against her consent? The mayor immediately interfered; but upon his applying to the young lady to ascertain her feeling upon the subject, she clung to the protecting arm of her uncle, exclaiming that 'she would freely go with him, to avoid the sight of that man' (Mr Wakefield). Mr Wakefield still urged his right to the possession of the young lady, as she was his wife; but Miss Turner cried out, 'No, no, I am not his wife: he carried me away by fraud and stratagem, forced me to accompany him to Gretna Green, and there, in the presence of a third person, I was compelled to acknowledge him as my husband and to be called his wife. By the same forcible means I was compelled to quit England and to trust myself to the protection of this person, whom I never saw until I was taken from Liverpool, and now never wish to see again.' Wakefield finding his plans completely frustrated, on this said to the uncle, 'Then, sir, you may dispose of your niece as you think proper, but you receive her at my hands as a pure and spotless virgin.' Mr Wakefield also drew up an acknowledgment, declaring that no familiarities whatever had passed between him and the young lady, and having signed it, he put it into the hands of Mr Turner.

Mr Turner and his niece then forthwith returned to England; while Mr Wakefield proceeded to his hotel, and, having packed up his luggage, started directly for Paris.

A question now arose as to the proper mode of proceeding in the courts of law against the offending parties in this extraordinary transaction. Warrants were, however, issued against the Wakefields, upon one of which Mr William Wakefield was apprehended at Dover within a few days after his brother's flight to Paris. He was instantly conveyed before the magistrates of Cheshire, where an examination of great length took place, and after a long argument upon the nature of the offence, he was committed to Lancaster Castle to await his trial, the magistrates refusing to take bail for his appearance at the assizes. Under a writ of *habeas corpus*, Mr Wakefield was brought before the Court of King's Bench on the first day of the following Easter

Term, and the depositions in the case being produced on the succeeding day, he was admitted to bail, in a personal recognizance of 2000*l*, and with two sureties in the amount of 1000*l* each.

At the following assizes for the county of Lancaster, indictments were preferred against Mr E. G. Wakefield and Mr W. Wakefield, for 'having at Liverpool feloniously carried away one Ellen Turner, spinster, then a maid and heir-apparent unto her father, William Turner, Esq, for the sake of the lucre of her substance; and for having afterwards unlawfully and against her will married the said EllenTurner.' An indictment was also preferred against the same parties, together with Edward Thévenot, their servant, and Frances Wakefield, their stepmother, who was alleged to be concerned in the transaction, for a conspiracy. The grand jury returned true bills in both cases, in the former, however, reducing the offence to a misdemeanour only. All the parties, with the exception of Thévenot who was in France, appeared and pleaded Not Guilty to the indictments, and Mr Justice Park, upon an application by the defendants, refused to postpone the trial. Mr E. G. Wakefield then claimed a right to traverse, and after some argument it was allowed him. Upon the 21st of August, public curiosity was excited to the highest degree, in consequence of its being anticipated that the trial of Mr William Wakefield would then come on. The court was crowded to excess, and the ladies formed, as usual on such occasions, the principal part of the audience; but on Mr Wakefield being called, it was found that he was not in attendance. Great disappointment was felt by the public in consequence, and an order was made by the learned judge that the recognizances of the bail and of the defendant should be estreated. The interest which the public took in this case from its commencement was now doomed to be suspended for a considerable time, for it was not until Friday, March the 23rd, 1827, that the general curiosity which was entertained with regard to the termination of the case was satisfied. The three defendants were then put upon their trial at Lancaster, Mr Brougham appearing with others for the prosecution, and Mr Scarlett for the defence. After a trial which occupied the whole day, and in the course of which the circumstances which we have already detailed were proved in evidence, the jury returned a verdict of Guilty against all three defendants.

The most remarkable part of the case was the examination of David Laing, the blacksmith at Gretna. His evidence simply amounted to proof that the Messrs Wakefield and Miss Turner had come to Gretna, being apparently agreeable to the match, and that he joined their hands and heard their acknowledgment in the usual form. The young lady, he said, presented him with a twenty-shilling note, and afterwards 'embraced her husband very agreeably.' The fellow, in his examination, declared that he had formerly been a merchant (that is, a Scotch pedlar), and that he had been forty-five years employed in joining hands at Gretna Green. He had 30*l* or 40*l* for this job. In appearance the old man had been made to assume an air of respectability. Someone had dressed him in a black coat, and a velvet waistcoat and breeches of the same colour, the shape of his hat being that commonly known as the 'clerical cock'. He seemed a vulgar fellow, though not without shrewdness and that air of familiarity which he might be supposed to have acquired by the freedom necessarily permitted by persons of a superior rank, to one who had the power of performing for them clandestinely a most important ceremony. On his entering the witness-box, he leaned forward towards the counsel with a ludicrous expression of gravity on his face, accompanying every answer with a knitting of his wrinkled brow, and a significant nodding of his head, which gave peculiar force to the quaintness of phraseology which he assumed, and occasionally convulsed the court with laughter.

On the following day, Messrs E. G. and W. Wakefield submitted to a verdict of Guilty on the second indictment, and upon the two findings the male defendants were committed to Lancaster Castle, there to remain until the ensuing term, when they were to be brought up for judgement in the Court of King's Bench.

On Monday the 14th of May, Messrs E. G. and W. Wakefield were carried to the Court of King's Bench at Westminster to receive judgement, when affidavits were put in on their behalf, declaring that the latter had acted entirely under the guidance and direction of his elder brother. Mr E. G. Wakefield also swore, that the expenses of his trial to him had exceeded 3000*l*. The counsel on behalf of the prosecution having addressed the court in aggravation, pressing for the severest penalty allowed by the law, Mr Justice Bayley addressed the prisoners. He dwelt in impressive terms upon the falsehood and art used by them to entrap the young lady into the marriage, and the gross delusions resorted to for the purpose of lulling her suspicions and inducing her to yield to the design in carrying her off. Having then referred separately to the conduct of the defendants, the learned Judge passed sentence that Edward Gibbon Wakefield should be imprisoned in Newgate for the space of three years, and that W. Wakefield should be imprisoned in Lancaster Castle for the like term of three years. Mrs Frances Wakefield, against whom a verdict of Guilty had also been returned, was not brought up for judgement, the generous feelings of Mr Turner, much injured as his family had been, preventing him proceeding with harshness against a female.

On the next day, a motion was made in the House of Lords by Lord Redesdale, for leave to bring in a bill to annul the marriage between Miss Turner and Mr Wakefield, when, after some discussion, the bill was granted in the usual way. Mr Wakefield, upon his petition, was subsequently brought from Newgate to oppose the second reading of the bill; but the opposition was fruitless, and it eventually passed both houses of parliament. Messrs Wakefield afterwards completed the term of their imprisonment, at the conclusion of which they were liberated from the jails in which they were respectively confined.

We are unable to present the reader with any distinct or positive history of the Messrs Wakefield. At the time of the commission of the offence for the participation in which they suffered so severe a punishment, Mr E. G. Wakefield was a barrister, and although he was not known as possessing any practice in the profession of the law, he was understood to be in the receipt of an income of about 1000*l* a year. He was at this time a widower with two children, having eloped with his first wife from a school. His children were in Paris, but upon his committal to Lancaster Castle, they followed him to that place with their governess. Mr Wakefield was at that time about thirty years of age, and in a letter which was addressed by a person named Collier on his behalf to the newspapers, he denied the allegation that he was unacquainted with Miss Turner before the elopement, declaring that he had previously met her at a public ball. In the course of the time occupied by the public in the discussion of the case, he put forth a statement of facts, denying that any force or fraud had been used towards Miss Turner; and subsequently, while in Newgate, he published a pamphlet, the object of which was to show that Miss Turner was really his wife, that she was a consenting party to the marriage, and that no ground therefore existed for the divorce. Mr Wakefield has since become well known in the mercantile world from his connexion with several public companies.

Mr W. Wakefield at the time of this offence was much younger than his brother, and appears to have acted almost entirely under the directions of the latter. He was married only a few days before his apprehension to a lady entitled to move in the most respectable ranks of society. He has since, we believe, served with honour and credit to himself in the army of one of our European allies, in which he obtained the rank of colonel, and at this time he holds an important trust in a colony newly formed at New Zealand.

It is only necessary for us further to state, that Miss Turner was subsequently married to Mr Legh, a gentleman of wealth and consideration in the north of England, but that she unfortunately died in giving birth to her first child.

WILLIAM CORDER, Executed for the Murder of MARIA MARTEN

THE murder for which this most diabolical criminal merited and justly underwent condign punishment, was as foul and dark a crime as ever stained the annals of public justice. The wretched victim of his offence was born in July 1801, and was brought up by her father, who was a mole-catcher at Polstead in Suffolk, where she received an education far superior to her situation in life. Possessed of more than ordinary personal advantages—a pretty face, and a fine form and figure—it is little to be wondered at that she was beset by admirers, and that, artless and inexperienced as she was, she should have imprudently fixed her affections upon an unworthy object. An unfortunate step ruined the character of the young woman, and a second mishap with a gentleman of fortune residing in the neighbourhood of her father's house, left her a child, which at the time of her death was three years and a half old. About the year 1826 she formed a third *liaison* with the man who became her deliberate murderer.

William Corder was the son of an opulent farmer at Polstead, and having become acquainted with the unfortunate girl Marten, the consequence of an illicit intercourse which took place between them, was a child. From that time he became much attached to her, and was a frequent visitor at her father's house. The child died within a short period of its birth, and from the circumstances of its having died suddenly, and of Corder having taken it away at night, and disposed of its body in a manner which he would never explain, an idea was entertained that it had come unfairly by its death. However strongly this notion may have taken possession of the public mind, after the apprehension of Corder, it does not appear that any real evidence was ever produced publicly to support the impression which had got abroad; but certain it is, that the unhappy girl made use of the circumstance as a means of endeavouring to procure the father of the child to fulfil a promise which he had made, that he would make her his wife. On the 18th of May 1827, Corder called at the house of old Marten, and then expressed his willingness that the ceremony should be performed. He said that, in order that no time should be lost and that the marriage might be as private as possible, he had made up his mind to have it celebrated by licence instead of by banns.

The next day was appointed for the wedding, and he persuaded the unhappy girl to dress herself in a suit of his clothes, so as to secure the greatest secrecy, and to accompany him to a part of his premises called the Red Barn, where she could exchange them for her own, and from whence he would convey her in a gig, which he had in readiness, to a church at Ipswich. The girl having consented to this singular proposition, Corder immediately quitted the house, and he was soon after followed by his unhappy victim, who carried with her such part of her own clothes as would be necessary to appear with in church. In the course of a conversation which took place between Corder and the mother of the girl, before their going away, the former repeatedly declared his intention to make the girl his lawful wife, and he urged as a reason why she should go with him immediately, that he knew that a warrant had been issued against her, for her bastard children. Within a few minutes after Corder had quitted the house, he was seen by the brother of the girl walking towards the Red Barn, with a pick-axe over his shoulder. From this time nothing was ever heard of the unfortunate girl, except through the fictitious communications received from Corder, who still remained at his mother's house at Polstead.

The return of Maria Marten had been expected to take place within one or two days after the time of her quitting her father's house, but as she had occasionally before exhibited considerable irregularity in the duration of her visits to Corder, and as, besides, there was an understanding that the latter should procure her a temporary lodging, little anxiety or alarm was at first felt at her prolonged absence. A fortnight having elapsed, however, her mother proceeded to question Corder upon the subject, when he declared that she was quite safe and well, and that he had placed her at some distance, lest his friends might discover the fact of his marriage, and exhibit displeasure at the circumstance. Having thus from time to time put off the inquiries which were made of him, in the month of September, declaring that he was in ill health, he quitted Suffolk with the avowed object of proceeding to the Continent. It is not a little remarkable, that before he left Polstead, he expressed great anxiety that the Red Barn should be well filled with stock, a desire which he personally saw fulfilled. He took with him about 400*l* in money; and several letters were subsequently received by his mother, who was a widow, as well as by the Martens, in which he stated that he was living at the Isle of Wight with Maria. It was remarked that although he represented his residence to be in the Isle of Wight, his letters always bore the London postmark, and at length strange surmises and suspicions began to be entertained, in consequence of no personal communication having yet been received from his supposed wife. The parents of the unhappy girl became more and more disturbed and dissatisfied; and the circumstances, which eventually led to the discovery of this most atrocious crime, are of so extraordinary and romantic a nature, as almost to manifest an especial interposition of Providence in marking out the offender.

In the course of the month of March 1828, Mrs Marten dreamed on three successive nights that her daughter had been murdered and buried in the Red Barn. Terrified at the repetition of the vision, an undefined suspicion, which she had always entertained that her daughter had been unfairly dealt with, appeared fully confirmed in her own mind. So lively were her feelings, and so convinced was she of the truth of the augury, that on Saturday, the 19th of April, she persuaded her husband to apply for permission to examine the Red Barn, with the professed object of looking for their daughter's clothes. The grain which had been deposited in the barn had by this time been removed, and the permission having been obtained, the wretched father proceeded to the accomplishment of the object he had in view. He applied himself to the spot pointed out to his wife in her dream as the place in which her daughter's remains were deposited, and there, upon digging, he turned up a piece of the shawl which he knew his daughter had worn at the time of her quitting her home. Alarmed at the discovery, he prosecuted his search still farther, and having dug to the depth of eighteen inches, with his rake he dragged out a part of a human body. Horror-struck, he staggered from the spot; but subsequent examination proved that his suspicions were well founded, and that it was indeed his murdered daughter, the place of deposit of whose remains had been so remarkably pointed out. The body, as may be supposed, was in an advanced state of decomposition, but the dress, which was perfect, and certain marks in the teeth of the deceased, afforded sufficient proofs of her identity.

As may be imagined, the whole neighbourhood was in an uproar of confusion at this most extraordinary circumstance, and information was immediately conveyed to the coroner, in order that an inquest might be held. By the time a coroner's jury had assembled, a surgical examination of the body had taken place, and Mr John Lawden, a surgeon, proved that there were appearances yet remaining sufficient to indicate that the deceased had come to her death by violent means. He said that there was a visible appearance of blood on the face and on the clothes of the deceased, and also on a handkerchief which was round the neck; that the handkerchief appeared to have been tied extremely tight, and beneath the folds, a wound was visible in the throat, which had evidently been inflicted by some sharp instrument. There was also a wound in the orbit of the right eye; and it seemed as if something had been thrust in which had fractured the small bones, and penetrated the brain. On the finding of the body, it was partly enveloped in a sack, and it was clothed only in a shift, flannel petticoat, stays, stockings, and shoes.

No sooner had the body been discovered than all eyes turned to Corder as the murderer, and information having been dispatched to London, Lea, an officer of Lambeth Street, was forthwith sent in pursuit of the supposed offender. With a loose clue only, he traced him from place to place, until at length he found him residing at Grove House, Ealing Lane, near Brentford, where, in conjunction with his wife, whom he had married only about five months before, and to whom, it was said, he had introduced himself through the medium of a matrimonial advertisement, he was carrying on a school for young ladies. It was necessary to employ a degree of stratagem to obtain admission to the house, but at length, Lea, having represented that he had a daughter, whom he wished to put to school, was introduced to a parlour, where he found the object of his search sitting at breakfast with four ladies. He was in his dressing-gown, and he had his watch before him, with which he was minuting the boiling of some eggs. The officer having called him on one side, informed him that he had a serious charge against him, and inquired whether he was not acquainted with a person named Maria Marten at Polstead; but he denied that he had any knowledge of such a person even by name. He was then secured, and upon his house being searched, a brace of pistols, a powder-flask, and some balls, were found in a velvet bag, which on its being subsequently seen by Mrs Marten, was immediately identified by her as having been in the possession of her daughter at the time of her quitting her house for the last time. A sharp-pointed dagger was also found, and this was identified by a person named Offord, a cutler, as being one which he had ground for the prisoner within a few days before the murder was committed. The prisoner immediately on his apprehension was conducted to Polstead, in order that he might undergo an examination before the coroner, and the most lively interest was exhibited by the vast crowds of people who had assembled, to catch a glimpse of him on his being brought into the town. On his appearance before the coroner, he was dreadfully agitated, and the circumstances which we have described having been deposed to by various witnesses, a verdict of 'Wilful Murder' was returned against him.

The unhappy prisoner was immediately conveyed to the county jail to await his trial; but he had hardly been lodged within its walls, before a new charge, namely, that of forgery upon the Manningtree Bank, was laid against him. It appears, however, that through the intervention of his friends, this case was eventually compromised. The wife of the prisoner, upon his first apprehension, was under an impression that the offence imputed to her husband was that of bigamy, but she was soon informed of the real nature of the allegations made against him. During his detention in jail, she visited him nearly every day; and she continued to declare her belief that the statements which appeared in the papers with regard to his guilt were untrue, and that he would eventually be relieved by a jury of his country from the foul calumnies which were published against him.

Thursday 7th of August in the same year was appointed for the trial of this malefactor, and the anxiety to witness the proceedings in court, or to obtain early information in reference to the case, was strongly manifested by the assembling of hundreds of well-dressed persons of both sexes, round the front and back entrances to the Shire Hall, Bury St Edmunds, as early as five o'clock in the morning of that day. The rain fell in torrents, but many persons braving the weather remained without shelter until nine o'clock, when the Lord Chief Baron (Alexander) arrived to try the prisoner. At the moment his lordship gained admission to the court, the scene which presented itself beggars description. The barristers who attended the circuit, amongst whom were to be observed the counsel for the prosecution and the defence, in vain struggled against the pressure of the opposing crowd, and many of them, at the moment they had almost attained their object, were carried back in an exhausted state to the extremest verge of the assembled multitude. When his lordship had taken his seat on the bench, the names of the jury who had been summoned to try the prisoner were called over; but the crowd was so great, and the sheriff's force so ineffective, that it was almost impossible to make way for them into the court. After the lapse of nearly an hour they were brought over the heads of the crowd to the passage leading into the hall, some with their coats torn, their shoes off and nearly fainting.

Nor was the curiosity of the public confined to the court-house. Hundreds had early assembled at the door of the jail, and along the road leading thence to the Shire Hall, anxious to catch a glimpse of the accused. He left the jail at a quarter before nine o'clock, having previously attired himself with much care in a new suit of black, and combed his hair over his forehead, which he had previously worn brushed up in front. Upon his being called from his cell, he made some inquiries with regard to the number of witnesses who were to be called for the prosecution, and also with regard to the judges by whom he was to be tried, and his queries having been answered, he exclaimed, 'Well, whatever may be my fate, I shall meet it with fortitude.' He was then removed in a chaise cart from the jail to the Hall, and although he hung down his head all the way, he seemed little affected by the shouts and groans with which he was assailed. On his being taken to the felon's room, beneath the building, he remarked to Mr Orridge, the governor of the prison, 'What a great number of persons! I scarcely ever saw such a crowd.'

At a quarter past ten o'clock, the prisoner was brought into court and placed in the front of the dock. For a few moments he conversed with his solicitor, but then he looked up to the bench and bowed respectfully. On account of the number of challenges made by the prisoner, it was some time before a jury was empanelled. At length, however, the prisoner was arraigned upon the indictment preferred against him. It contained ten counts. In the first, the murder was alleged to have been committed by the prisoner on the 18th of May 1827, by discharging a pistol, loaded with powder and shot, upon Maria Marten, and thereby giving her a mortal wound on the left side of the face; and that by those means, wilfully, feloniously, and of his malice aforethought, he caused the death of the said Maria Marten. The second count laid the offence as having been committed by striking the deceased with a sword upon the left side of the body, between the fifth and sixth ribs, and thereby giving her a mortal wound, of which she instantly died; the third count stated that the murder was committed by striking the deceased with a sword on the left side of the face; the fourth, that it was done by sticking and stabbing her with a sword on the right side of the neck; the fifth, that the prisoner fastened a handkerchief around her neck, and thereby choked her; the sixth, that he killed her by discharging a gun loaded with powder and shot on the left side of her face; the seventh, that he pushed and thrust her into a hole made in the floor of a barn, and, by covering her with large quantities of earth and gravel, suffocated and choked her; the eighth was only technically different from the preceding one; the ninth laid the offence to have been committed by the joint means of sticking the deceased with a sword on the left side, and fastening a handkerchief round her neck; the tenth described it as being done by the joint force of all the felonious acts laid in the whole of the preceding counts—recapitulating the wounds, stabbing, shooting, strangulation, and smothering, as the cause of the death of the deceased.

The prisoner having pleaded Not Guilty, in a firm and distinct voice, the trial commenced. The evidence which was now adduced differed but slightly in effect from the circumstances which we have detailed. Proof was, however, given in support of the first and sixth counts of the indictment that, at the time of the discovery of the body of the deceased, marks were distinctly visible, which showed that she had received a pistol-shot or a gun-shot wound; and it was also proved, by the brother of the deceased girl, that the prisoner, at the time of his quitting the house of old Marten on the day of the murder, carried a loaded gun. A number of letters were likewise put in, which had been written by the prisoner to the father of the deceased in reference to his intended marriage with his daughter.

The prisoner, on being called upon for his defence, read a manuscript paper in a low and tremulous tone of voice. He declared that he deeply deplored the death of the unfortunate female in question, and he urged the jury to dismiss from their minds all that prejudice which must necessarily have been excited against him, by the foul imputations which had been cast upon him by the public press. He admitted that the evidence which had been adduced, was sufficient to create some suspicion against him, but he trusted that the explanation which he should give of the circumstances, would at once explain, to their satisfaction, the real bearings of the case. He then proceeded to say, 'No man regrets more sincerely than I do the death of the unfortunate Maria, the circumstances attending which I am now about to state; and much have I to regret, that I for a moment concealed them, but I did so because I was stupefied and horror-struck at the time, and knew not how to act. You have heard of the nature of my connexion with the unfortunate Maria: that connexion was contrary to the will of my mother, and to conceal her situation, I took lodgings for her at Sudbury, where she was confined. In the usual time she returned to her father's house, in a fortnight after which the infant died—not, as has been intimated, by violence, but a natural death. Being anxious to conceal the circumstance from my friends and neighbours, it was agreed between her father and mother and myself, that Maria and I should bury the child in the fields, and we took it away for that purpose.

'After this Maria returned to my house at Polstead, and by means of a private staircase I took her to my own room, where she remained concealed for two days. The pistols which have been spoken of were hanging up in the room loaded. I had before that shown her the use of them, and on returning to her father's, she, by some means unknown to me, contrived to get the pistols into her possession. It is well known that at that period Maria was much depressed in spirits, and was anxious that I should marry her, although I had reason to suspect that she was at the time in correspondence with a gentleman in London by whom she had a child. My friends objected to the match, and I declined it at the time. But although poor Maria's conduct was not altogether free from blame, I was much attached to her and at length agreed to her wishes; and it was arranged that we should go to Ipswich and obtain a licence for that purpose. Whether I did or did not say anything about a warrant having been issued by the parish officers for her apprehension, I cannot now pretend to say, but if I did, it must have been because such a report was abroad at the time. It was agreed that Maria should go in male attire to the Red Barn so often mentioned in the course of the trial. You have heard from the mother of the unfortunate Maria, that she and I had had words. As we proceeded to the Barn she was in tears. To that Barn we had often repaired before, and frequently passed the night there. When we reached the Barn, words arose and Maria flew into a passion. I told her that if we were to be married, and to live together, she must not go on so. Much conversation ensued, and on changing her dress, she at length told me, that if we were married we should never be happy together—that I was too proud to marry her and take her to my mother's, and that she did not regard me. I was highly irritated, and asked her, if she was to go on this way before marriage, what was I to expect after? She again upbraided me and, being in a passion, I told her I would not marry her and turned from the Barn, but I had scarcely reached the gate when a report of a pistol reached my ear. I returned to the Barn, and with horror beheld the unfortunate girl extended on the floor, apparently dead: I was for a short time stupefied with horror, and knew not what to do. It struck me to run for a surgeon, and well would it have been for me had I done so. I raised the unfortunate girl, in order, if possible, to afford her some assistance; but I found her altogether lifeless, and, to my horror, I discovered that the dreadful act had been committed by one of my own pistols, and that I was the only person in existence who could tell how the fatal act took place. The sudden alarm which seized me suspended my faculties, and it was some time before I could perceive the awful situation in which I was placed, and the suspicions which must naturally arise from my having delayed to make the circumstance instantly known. I, at length, found that concealment was the only means by which I could rescue myself from the horrid imputation, and I resolved to bury the body as well as I was able. Having done so, I subsequently accounted for her absence in the manner described by the witnesses, saying sometimes one thing to one person, and at other times other things to another. I may be asked why, if innocent of the crime imputed to me, I felt it necessary to give those answers? To which I answer, that some persons are driven to do acts from fear which others do from guilt, which is precisely the case with me in this instance. It may be asked, too, why I have not called evidence to prove the facts I have stated. But, gentlemen, I put it to you whether things do not sometimes take place which are only known to the parties between whom they happen; and what direct proof can I give when the only person who knew of these facts is no more? I can for the same reason give no direct proof of the unhappy woman's having got possession of my pistols. I say pistols, because I found the other loaded pistol in the unfortunate Maria's reticule. As to the stabs and other wounds described by the witnesses, I can only say that no stab or cut was given by Maria or myself, and I firmly believe that the surgeons would never have sworn to them, were it not for the circumstance of a sword having been found in the room in which I was arrested. If any stab did appear upon the body, it must have been done with the instrument used in disinterring it.'

Having concluded his address by a strong appeal to the jury upon the probabilities of the case, a number of witnesses were called, who spoke to the prisoner's good character. The Lord Chief Baron summed up, and a verdict of 'Guilty' was returned. At this point the prisoner was first observed to raise his handkerchief to his eyes, and during the subsequent passing of the sentence of death, he seemed to be dreadfully affected. On his return to the jail, he seemed to recover his spirits, but the only desire which he expressed was, that he should be permitted to see his wife. To this request an immediate assent was given, and at two o'clock on the Saturday afternoon, she was admitted to the prisoner. The meeting between her and her wretched husband was of a most affecting character, and it did not terminate until near an hour had elapsed. During that evening, the prisoner was constantly attended by the reverend chaplain of the jail, but notwithstanding the religious exhortations which he received, he exhibited no inclination to make any confession of his crime.

On the following day the prisoner attended chapel in the customary manner, and during the performance of the service he appeared deeply affected. On his return to his cell, he threw himself upon his bed and wept bitterly for a considerable time. In the course of the afternoon, it was hinted to him that his defence could scarcely be believed; but in answer he said that, 'Confession to God was all that was necessary, and that confession to man was what he called popedom or popery, and he never would do it.' It was subsequently suggested to him that he must have had great nerve to dig the grave while the body lay in his sight, when his reply was, 'Nobody knows that the body lay in the barn and in sight, whilst I dug the hole.' Then, suddenly checking himself, he exclaimed, 'O God! nobody will dig my grave.' In the course of the afternoon, he had a second and last interview with his wife, and the scene was truly heart-rending. He expressed the most anxious fears with regard to the manner in which she would be in future treated by the world, and implored her, should she ever marry again, to be cautious how she accepted a proposition reaching her through the equivocal medium of a public advertisement. The parting scene was most dreadful, and the wretched woman was carried away from the cell in a state of stupor.

After Mrs Corder had retired, Mr Orridge, the worthy governor of the jail, made the strongest efforts to induce the unhappy prisoner to confess, pointing out to him how greatly he would add to his crime, should he quit the world still denying his guilt. Corder then exclaimed, 'O, sir, I wish I had made a confidant of you before. I often wished to have done it, but you know, sir, it was of no use to employ a legal adviser and then not to follow his advice.' Mr Orridge said that there was no doubt that was very proper, up to the time at which he was convicted, but that now all earthly considerations must cease.

The wretched prisoner then exclaimed, 'I am a guilty man', and immediately afterwards made the following confession:

'Bury Jail, August 10, 1828—Condemned Cell,
'Sunday Evening, Half-past Eleven.

'I acknowledge being guilty of the death of poor Maria Marten, by shooting her with a pistol. The particulars are as follows. When we left her father's house we began quarrelling about the burial of the child, she apprehending that the place wherein it was deposited would be found out. The quarrel continued for about three quarters of an hour upon this and about other subjects. A scuffle ensued, and during the scuffle, and at the time I think that she had hold of me, I took the pistol from the side-pocket of my velveteen jacket and fired. She fell, and died in an instant. I never saw even a struggle. I was overwhelmed with agitation and dismay—the body fell near the front doors on the floor of the barn. A vast quantity of blood issued from the wound and ran on to the floor and through the crevices. Having determined to bury the body in the barn (about two hours after she was dead), I went and borrowed the spade of Mrs Stowe; but before I went there, I dragged the body from the barn into the chaff-house, and locked up the barn. I returned again to the barn, and began to dig the hole, but the spade being a bad one, and the earth firm and hard, I was obliged to go home for a pick-axe and a better spade, with which I dug the hole, and then buried the body. I think I dragged the body by the handkerchief that was tied round her neck. It was dark when I finished covering up the body. I went the next day and washed the blood from off the barn floor. I declare to Almighty God I had no sharp instrument about me, and that no other wound but the one made by the pistol was inflicted by me. I have been guilty of great idleness, and at times led a dissolute life, but I hope through the mercy of God to be forgiven.

'W. CORDER.'

'Witness to the signing by the said William Corder,

'JOHN ORRIDGE.'

On the next morning the confession was read over to the prisoner, and he declared that it was quite true; and he further said, in answer to a question put to him by the under-sheriff, that he thought the ball entered the right eye.

He subsequently appeared much easier in his mind, and attended service in the chapel immediately before his being carried out for execution. He still wore the clothes in which he was dressed at the time of his trial. As allusions were made to his unhappy situation in the prayers which were read, he appeared convulsed with agony; and when the service was over, although he appeared calm, his limbs gave up their office, and he was obliged to be carried to his cell.

At a few minutes before twelve o'clock he was removed from the dungeon in which he had been confined, and conveyed to the press-room, where he was pinioned by the hangman, who had been carried down from London for the purpose of superintending the execution. He was resigned, but was so weak as to be unable to stand without support. On his cravat being removed he groaned heavily, and appeared to be labouring under great mental agony. When his wrists and arms were made fast, he was led round towards the scaffold, and as he passed the different yards in which the prisoners were confined, he shook hands with them, and speaking to two of them by name, he said, 'Goodbye, God bless you!' They were considerably affected at the wretched appearance which he made; and 'God bless you!' 'May God receive your soul!' were frequently uttered as he passed along. The chaplain preceded the prisoner, reading the usual Burial Service, and the governor and officers walked immediately after him. The prisoner was supported up the steps which led to the scaffold: he looked somewhat wildly around, and a constable was obliged to support him while the hangman was adjusting the fatal cord. A few moments before the drop fell he groaned heavily, and would have fallen, had not a second constable caught hold of him. Everything having been made ready, the signal was given, the fatal drop fell, and the unfortunate man was launched into eternity. He did not struggle, but he raised his hands once or twice, as if in prayer: the hangman pulled his legs, and he was in a moment motionless. In about nine minutes, however, his shoulders appeared to rise in a convulsive movement; but life, it seemed, had left him without any great pain. Just before he was turned off, he said, in a feeble tone, 'I am justly sentenced, and may God forgive me.' Mr Orridge then informed the crowd that the prisoner acknowledged the justice of his sentence, and died in peace with all men. Thus did this unhappy man terminate, by an ignominious death, a life which, judging from his age and healthy appearance, might have been prolonged to an advanced period in comfort and independence.

The mob collected on this occasion was computed to amount to upwards of seven thousand persons, and occupied every spot of ground from which a glimpse of the final scene of the wretched man's life could be obtained. A considerable portion of the persons collected were women, and as soon as the execution was over, they dispersed from before the drop, and proceeded to the Shire Hall, where a large number of persons had assembled in order to obtain a view of the body.

At about two o'clock the body was exposed on the table in the centre of the Shire Hall; it was naked from the navel upwards. The crucial operation had been performed, and the skin of the breast and stomach turned back on each side. The body measured, as it lay, five feet five inches in length, and presented a very muscular appearance. The face and throat were somewhat swollen and discoloured, the right eye was open, and the left partially so; the mouth was also open sufficiently to show the teeth. The body was taken to the hospital the next day to be dissected, in pursuance of the sentence.

After the execution a spirited bidding took place for the rope which was used by the hangman; and as much as a guinea an inch was obtained for it. Large sums were offered for the pistols and dagger which were used in the murder, but they became the property of the sheriff of the county, who very properly refused to put them up to public competition. A piece of the skin of the wretched malefactor, which had been tanned, was exhibited for a long time afterwards at the shop of a leather-seller in Oxford Street.

It will be noticed that a spirited bidding took place after Corder's execution, particularly for the rope, and it is said that as much as a guinea an inch was given for it. In the days of public executions both at Tyburn and Newgate, the crowds would rush to touch the body of the hanged man and many curious superstitions came into vogue. The rope the hangman used was one of the objects about which superstitious beliefs were held. It is hard to believe, but it is a well attested fact that the hangman made a special trade in selling the rope by the inch, but the price was usually a modest sixpence, and not the guinea mentioned in the report. So great was the public interest in the hanging of Corder, however, that the crowds rioted to get possession of a piece of the rope, and not unnaturally the price went up as the demand increased!

WILLIAM BURKE, Executed for Murder

THE unparalleled atrocities of which this diabolical murderer was guilty, with his associates, can scarcely ever be obliterated from the recollection of man. Devoid of all sense of humanity—a butcher of the human race—he was guilty of almost innumerable murders, for which his only reward was the miserable amount to be paid him for the bodies of his victims, in order that they might be submitted to the knife of the anatomist.

The scene of these horrible occurrences was Edinburgh; but notwithstanding the publication of the details of the circumstances attending them which appeared at the investigations which took place before the sheriff, few could be found who had formed such an idea of the baseness of human nature, as to believe the possibility of the truth of the dreadful disclosures which were made.

The metropolis of Scotland had been long and frequently excited by statements being made of the disappearance of persons in the lower orders of life, who were suddenly missed, and of whom no subsequent traces could be discovered. Tramps entering the city with their friends were suddenly lost; Irish haymakers, on their road to the agricultural districts of the Lowlands, in the same manner seemed to vanish from among their companions; and in one instance an idiot, who in Scotland is always looked upon as a harmless playmate for the children, as a welcome guest at every table and as an object of universal pity, was on a sudden lost from the favourite haunts of his imbecile wanderings.

The occurrence which immediately led to the disclosure of these diabolical crimes was the unaccountable disappearance of a mendicant named Mary Campbell, an Irishwoman, who, after having been seen frequenting the same vicinity for a considerable time, towards the end of October 1829, was suddenly missed. The poor woman happened to have friends, who were not disposed to treat her loss lightly, and a rigid inquiry by the police was the result. An idea was suggested that her body might be found at some of the medical schools in Edinburgh, so justly celebrated for the excellence of the anatomical instruction which they afforded to the pupils, and one day's search testified the truth of the fears which had been excited of her death. Her remains were discovered at the dissecting-room of Dr Knox, a distinguished anatomist, bearing marks perfectly conclusive of their identity. The poor woman had received a wound upon her ankle from the kick of a drunken man, the aspect of which was sufficiently well known to enable her former companions to speak with certainty as to the body. The cause of death was now the subject of investigation, and here the deficiency of caution in the purchase of subjects, the necessity of a change in the law with regard to the provision of bodies for dissection, and finally, the certainty of the murder of the deceased, were exemplified. The medical men, by whom the body was examined, gave their firm and decided opinion that suffocation had been the means by which the deceased had been deprived of life—a means which it was exceedingly unlikely any natural circumstances would have produced. It was evident, therefore, that murder had been resorted to, it was believed, with a view to secure the body of the wretched woman, in order that it might be sold for dissection.

The next inquiry which followed, was that as to the individual from whom the subject had been purchased. The law at that time contained no enactment with regard to the mode by which surgeons were to be provided with those subjects which the study of anatomy, so important to the human race, positively required that they should possess. The occasional execution of a criminal, whose remains were ordered by the terms of his sentence to be given over to the surgeons for dissection, afforded no sufficient supply to meet the constant demand which existed; and the stealing of dead bodies was a practice openly encouraged by the professors of anatomy.

So long as the war continued, the period of time required for the completion of the education of medical students, so as to fit them in some measure for the Army or Navy, was very short, and the study of anatomy was consequently much neglected. At that time the dissecting-rooms were generally supplied by 'resurrection-men' who exhumed the bodies, and, as the suspicion of the public was not excited, this was attended with no great difficulty. The highest price ever obtained by these men was four guineas for each subject; but as the number of medical men increased, and many gentlemen, who had been engaged in the Army and Navy, returned to complete their education, the demand became greater, and consequently the risk of procuring subjects by the usual means was proportionately augmented. The men were frequently detected in their attempts, and punished severely: they therefore demanded an advance in their remuneration, and in consequence of no legal provision being made for supplying the schools, it was found necessary to accede to their demands. The price then became eight guineas, and it subsequently varied from that to sixteen guineas, according to circumstances.

On account of the greatly increased amount obtained for subjects, numbers of persons now engaged in the traffic, and the consequence was more frequent detection. Every means which ingenuity could suggest was used to obtain bodies which had not been buried, and for this purpose, the men, when they heard of the body of a person being found (drowned for instance) and which was lying to be owned, trumped up a story of an unfortunate brother or sister, humbugged a coroner's jury (who, by the way, were more than once so well imposed on as to make a subscription, to enable the supposed brother to bury his relative) and thus obtained possession of the body. In this sort of trickery the wives of the men were often employed, as their application was attended with less suspicion, and it was never difficult to impose on the parochial officers, who were always anxious to avoid the expense of burying the deceased. Subjects were thus occasionally procured, but they were much more frequently obtained by pretending relationship to persons dying without friends in hospitals and workhouses. As the bodies thus obtained were much fresher than those which had been buried, they produced generally (independent of the teeth) as much as twelve guineas each.

But the poor and friendless were not the only sufferers from this system; persons moving in a higher sphere of society have often suffered the loss of their friends, when they were confident in security. What will the wealthy not feel, when they are told that the very men employed to solder down the leaden coffin of a child have abstracted the body, and carried it off, without exciting the slightest suspicion, in the baskets with their tools?

The surgeons from their anxiety to obtain subjects, and from the acknowledged illegality of the proceedings, were frequently not over-nice or minute in their inquiries as to the cause of death, or the means by which the body offered to them was obtained. The impossibility of obtaining any answer the truth of which could be relied on, and the independence of the 'resurrection-men', who were always sure of a market, may be reckoned as almost sufficient excuses for this lax mode of proceeding. It is just to believe, however, that no suspicion can ever have entered the imagination of the anatomists that unfair means had been resorted to, to take away the life of the subjects offered to them, merely with a view to their bodies being submitted to dissection. To such causes may be ascribed the non-discovery of the suspicious cause of death of the numerous miserable victims whom investigation proves to have been murdered.

In this case, happily, the frequency of the visits of the supposed *resurrectionist* or body-stealer to the same dissecting-room enabled the police to discover his haunts, together with the circumstances attending the disappearance of the deceased, which were sufficient to afford convincing proof of her murder at his hands. Paterson, the porter to Dr Knox, was well acquainted with the persons of Burke and a man named Hare, by whom this subject had been sold, and he related the circumstances attending its purchase to the police serjeant by whom the investigation was carried on, in such a manner as at once secured their apprehension. He said that on the 31st of October, Burke and Hare called at the dissecting-rooms, and said that they had got something for the doctor, at the house occupied by the former. Paterson had before visited this place on similar occasions and was well acquainted with its position, and on the next morning he went to the house in Tanner's Close, where he was told the body lay. He found there Mrs M'Dougal, who passed as the wife of Burke, and Mrs Margaret Laird, who stood in the same relation with regard to Hare. Upon his entrance, Burke pointed to a heap of straw under the table, signifying that the body was there, and the witness gave them *5l* to be divided between the two men, *3l* more being agreed to be paid, if the subject should turn out to be such as was desired. The men divided the money, and promised to carry the body on the same night to the dissecting-room. It arrived, packed in a tea-chest, and at the time of the visit of the police, which was on the following day (the 2nd of November), it had not yet been looked at. Upon the chest being opened, appearances presented themselves which induced Paterson to believe that the body had never been buried; the face was livid, and blood was running from the nostrils and mouth. As we have already said, subsequent examination proved that death had been caused by suffocation.

Coincident with the discovery of this evidence, the voluntary testimony of two other witnesses was obtained, which afforded conclusive proof of the violent means resorted to by Burke and Hare, to procure the death of the deceased. Mr and Mrs Gray, poor persons who were travelling through Edinburgh, informed the police, on the same day, of occurrences which they had witnessed on the night of the 31st October, which induced the most dreadful suspicions in their minds. They stated that they had taken up their lodgings in the house occupied by Burke in the course of that day, and towards the evening they had seen Mrs Campbell go in with that person. They retired to rest without holding any communication with her, as she appeared to be intoxicated, but in the morning, they were surprised to find that she was gone. They inquired of Mrs Burke what had become of her, and she said that they had turned her out because she was impudent. But an undefinable apprehension lurked in their minds of some wrong having been done, and seizing an opportunity they peered into Burke's room, and there, under the table, they saw marks of blood, and upon further investigation, the body of the murdered woman concealed beneath some straw. Terror-struck with the discovery, they immediately gathered up their bundles and proceeded to quit the house, but were dissuaded from their intention by Mrs Burke, who had ascertained the fact of their having made so important a discovery, and urged them to stop, 'as it might be 10*l* a week to them'. They, however, rushed from the place as soon as they could escape, and on the following day conveyed intelligence to the police of what they had seen.

Upon the arrival of the authorities at the Tanner's Close, they found it to be a scene well fitted for the performance of such tragedies as had been recently enacted within its limits.

The close itself was narrow and dark, and contained only one house, which was situated at the bottom. Here, almost shut out from the light of heaven, lived this detestable murderer, letting out lodgings either by the night or otherwise, to such poor wretches as would put up with the accommodation which he could offer. The house consisted of two rooms only, one of which was occupied by Burke and his wife, while the other was devoted to his lodgers. The former contained nothing but a miserable bed, a table, and some straw, still reeking with the blood of the murdered woman, while the latter was totally devoid of furniture. Fortunately for their purpose, the whole party, four in number, was assembled; and they were all immediately secured and conveyed to prison. Burke, it appeared, had carried on a pretended trade of shoemaking, and in one corner of his room was found a pile of old boots and shoes, consisting of nearly forty pairs; but the discovery also of a great number of suits of clothes, of various sizes, and bearing distinct marks of blood, afforded sufficient proof, that the murder of Mrs Campbell was not the only one which had been perpetrated within the apartment.

The examinations of the prisoners before the magistrates of Edinburgh served only to bring to light fresh atrocities and to excite fresh horror; and eventually the whole of the prisoners were committed for trial, the evidence being clear and conclusive as to the implication of the men, although that which affected the women left great doubts as to the possibility of their conviction being secured.

During the period which elapsed subsequently to their committal, and preparatory to their trial, Hare, with a degree of villainy excelling that of his fellow in guilt, offered to make disclosures upon the subject of the system which had been carried on, upon condition of his own indemnification from punishment, and that of his wife. Mrs Laird, it had been discovered, was the least guilty of the whole party, and so far as her discharge was concerned little difficulty was experienced, but upon the question of the other terms desired by Hare considerable doubt was entertained. Long and frequent consultations were held by the magistrates upon the subject, in which the probabilities of the conviction of these associates in villainy were most anxiously weighed, and it was at length determined that, for the sake of that justice which imperatively demanded the most satisfactory and complete evidence of the guilt of one at least of the gang, the offer should be accepted. The prisoner then made a statement to the officers of the jail, which was reduced to writing.

On the 23rd December in the same year, the two prisoners, William Burke and Helen M'Dougal, were put upon their trial before the High Court of Justiciary at Edinburgh. The indictment charged against them several murders, founded upon the communications made by Hare, but after much discussion on the part of the counsel for the Crown and on behalf of the prisoners, it was determined that that part only of the indictment which alleged them to have murdered Mary Campbell should be proceeded with, inasmuch as that the disclosure of any of the particulars of one murder in the course of a trial for another would materially prejudice the minds of the jury against the persons charged. The murder of Mrs Campbell was alleged to have been committed by suffocation.

The preliminary witnesses produced a plan of the house of the prisoners in Tanner's Close, and proved the identity of the remains found at the house of Dr Knox.

William Noble, the shopman to Mr Rayner a grocer at Portsburgh, near Tanner's Close, was then examined, and proved that on the night of the 31st October Burke, who had been in the habit of dealing at his employer's house, called there in order to purchase some trifling articles of grocery. While he was standing at the counter, Mrs Campbell entered the shop, and begged for charity. She said that she had come to Edinburgh to search for her son, a boy of eleven years old, but that she had been unable to find him and that she was now quite destitute. Burke inquired her name, and on her mentioning the name of Campbell he at once claimed acquaintance and relationship with her, and finally took her away with him, saying that he would provide her with lodging for the night. The woman at this time was sober. The witness added that on the following day, Burke called again and purchased an old tea-chest, and Mrs Hare, whom he knew, as well as her husband and Mrs M'Dougal, carried it away about half-an-hour afterwards.

Mrs Ann Black and Hugh Alison gave evidence tracing Mrs

Campbell to Burke's house, and as to the occurrences of the dreadful night of her death. The former said that she was a lodger of Burke's and upon going home on the night of the 31st of October, she saw Mrs Campbell sitting in Burke's room by the fire. She was ill-clad, and was eating porridge, and in answer to a question which the witness put, Mrs M'Dougal said that she was a Highland woman, a friend of her husband's, and that she had been assisting them in washing. The witness then quitted the room, but subsequently in passing through it after dark, she saw that Mrs Campbell was much intoxicated. Hare and his wife were then there, and had brought in some spirits with them, and they were all merry, and laughing and singing together. The witness afterwards heard dancing, and on looking into the room, she saw that it was Mrs M'Dougal, Hare, and Mrs Campbell. Between ten and eleven o'clock she heard a disturbance, as if Burke and Hare were fighting, and a woman screaming, but she took no notice of it, as such occurrences were frequent with her landlord's friends. In the morning she inquired of Mrs M'Dougal where Mrs Campbell was, and was told that she and her husband (Burke) had got too friendly, and that she had kicked her out of the house. Alison, the witness, corroborated the evidence of Mrs Black, as to the disturbance which occurred in the house of Burke at about the hour mentioned, and which he had heard in his residence at one of the upper flats of a house nearly adjoining, but he had distinguished screams of agony and cries for help, succeeded by a noise as if some person had been strangling or suffocating. He afterwards heard the voices of two men in conversation in the close, whom he had taken to be Burke and Hare.

Mr and Mrs Gray, whose names we have already mentioned, were also examined upon the same point, and having proved the presence of Mrs Campbell in Burke's house at the time of their arrival, they stated that Mrs M'Dougal had told them in the morning, that she had turned out the deceased because she was impudent. They, however, watched their opportunity, and slipping into the room unseen, discovered her body concealed among the straw under the table.

Other confirmatory evidence was also given upon the same subject, and David Paterson, the porter at Dr Knox's, detailed his account of the transaction of the purchase of the body in the

The mob pursuing Mrs M'Dougal (page 162)

manner which we have already described, and of its arrival in a tea-chest. Other witnesses having proved that they saw the prisoner (Burke) and Hare carrying a tea-chest in the direction of Dr Knox's, but in such a line of street as clearly showed their object to be to escape observation, William Hare, the approver, was called.

Lord Meadowbank, a learned and very distinguished judge, presided upon this occasion, and with the most humane feelings earnestly cautioned this witness to give his evidence with truth. The fellow, whose appearance in the witness-box excited great interest and indignation, sullenly answered, that he intended to do so, but that he only came there as a witness in the case of the 'old woman', as he emphatically described the deceased Mrs Campbell, as distinguished, doubtless, from other miserable victims; his examination then proceeded. Having been sworn in the common form, he said he was a native of Ireland, and had resided in Scotland ten years. He had been acquainted with Burke about twelve months. M'Dougal lived with Burke as his wife; witness lived in the West Port, not far from Burke. He was in a public-house in the West Port on the forenoon of the 31st of October, when Burke came in, and they had a gill; he asked witness to go down to his house, to see the shot he had got to take to the doctor's; he said he had taken an old woman off the street, and wished witness to go down and see her, and see what they were doing. He understood by the word 'shot', that he was going to murder the woman. He went to Burke's house, and found there was a strange man and woman (their name was Gray), the old woman, and Helen M'Dougal; the old woman was washing her short-gown; it was white and red striped. [Identified the bedgown.] Witness remained in the house about five minutes, and then went home. Between eight and nine on the same night he was at the house of a man named Connaway with his wife, and Burke, Mrs M'Dougal, the old woman Campbell, and a lad named Broggan, Mrs M'Dougal's nephew, came in. Liquor was introduced, and after a while Burke and Broggan went away. Witness remained some time longer, but then he also quitted the house, and went to Tanner's Close. There had been some dancing at Connaway's, and at this time he had no idea that any harm was to be done to the old woman on that night. Soon after he arrived at Tanner's Close, Burke, M'Dougal and Mrs Campbell also came in, the latter being so much the worse for liquor as scarcely to be able to keep her feet. A quarrel arose between him and Burke (which was evidently got up for the purpose of murdering the old woman in the confusion which would be the result of it), upon the subject of his being in the house, Burke declaring that he had no business there, while he asserted that he had been invited by Mrs M'Dougal. They began to fight, and Mrs Campbell appeared alarmed, and called police and murder. She ran into the passage twice, but was brought back each time by Mrs M'Dougal, and upon her re-entering the room the second time, witness intentionally pushed her over a stool upon the floor. She got up so as to rest upon her elbow, but was so drunk as not to be able to regain her feet; she called on Burke to quit fighting, and he did so, but then having stood for some minutes on the floor, Burke stood stride-legs over her, and laid himself down above her—his breast being on her head. She gave a cry, and then moaned a little; he put one hand on her nose and mouth, and the other under her chin, and stopped her breathing; this was continued for ten or fifteen minutes; he never spoke while this was going on; after he had risen from above her he put his arm upon her mouth for some minutes; she appeared quite dead; witness was sitting all the while on a chair. When he saw the woman was dead, he stripped the body of the clothes, put it into a corner, doubling it up and covering it with straw. Witness's wife and M'Dougal, when they heard the first screech of the old woman, ran into the passage, and did not come in again until the body was covered with straw; before this they were lying in the bed, and witness sat at the head of the bed; did not observe blood on the floor, or on the woman's face at the time; did not observe the woman in the passage cry—but nobody came to the door during the time. Burke had not been above the woman more than a minute or two, when the women started out of bed and ran to the door; he saw none of them attempting to save or assist the old woman, and such could not have happened without his seeing it. When it was all over the women came in again, and then Burke went out; the women asked no questions, nor did they make any remark, but they went to bed again without a word being exchanged. When Burke returned, he brought with him the man from Dr Knox's (Paterson), and he looked at the body; he said it would do well enough, and they were to get a box and put it in, in order to carry it to his master's house. At this time the women were in bed, but he could not tell whether they were awake or not, and he soon afterwards fell asleep himself. He was rather the worse of liquor, but he knew well enough what he was about.

He awoke about seven o'clock in the morning; he found himself on a chair, with his head on the bed; the women were in the bed, and John Broggan was lying beyond his aunt; Burke was at the fireside. He and his wife got up and went home. In the course of the day, Burke called on him, and asked him to assist in procuring a box. They went first to Surgeon's Square, where Dr Knox's school was situated, but failed in obtaining one there, and then Burke went and purchased a tea-chest at the grocer's. M'Culloch, a porter, took the box home, and witness arrived there with him before Burke came in. They were standing at the door when he came, and he asked whether they had put up the body. He answered that they had not, and Burke then remarked that they were worth little if they had not done that. They, however, directly went in, and witness and M'Culloch assisted in placing the body in the chest, the latter forcing it down in its place. M'Culloch also, on seeing some of the woman's hair hanging out, pushed it into the box, remarking that it would be 'a fine thing to have that seen!' The chest was corded, and M'Culloch was instructed to carry it to Surgeon's Square, witness and Burke accompanying him. On their way they met Mrs M'Dougal and his (witness's) wife, in the High School Yard, and they all went together. Having delivered the chest to Paterson, it was placed in a cellar, and the latter then went with them to Dr Knox at Newington, where he and Burke were paid *2l 7s 6d* each, *5s* being given to the porter.

The witness was cross-examined by Mr Cockburn on behalf of the prisoners, when he admitted that he had followed many businesses, both in Ireland and in Scotland. He had been frequently concerned in supplying medical schools with subjects, but had never assisted in raising any bodies from churchyards. He had often seen bodies carried to the houses of medical lecturers, but declined to say how often; he also declined to say whether he had been concerned in the murder of any other person but the old woman, or whether he had been present at any other murder in the course of the same month of October.

Mrs Laird, the wife of this witness, gave evidence very similar to that of her husband, corroborating his statements to as many of the transactions as had fallen within her knowledge and observation.

This completed the case for the prosecution, and a most humane and able address having been delivered to the jury by Lord Meadowbank, at half-past eight o'clock in the evening, they retired to consider their verdict. During the period of their absence, which extended to fifty minutes, the most breathless anxiety was exhibited as to the result of the trial, and upon their re-entering the court, an eager silence prevailed amongst the persons assembled. The verdict consigned Burke to an ignominious fate by a declaration of his guilt; but the jury, contrary to all expectation, declared, that as to Mrs M'Dougal, the offence alleged was 'not proven', a finding which relieved her from all immediate consequences upon the indictment.

Lord Meadowbank immediately passed the sentence of death upon Burke, and ordered him to be hanged on the 28th January, 1830, and his body to be delivered over to the surgeons for dissection.

He and his fellow prisoner, M'Dougal, were then immediately conveyed to the lock-up house attached to the court, where they met Hare and his wife, who, although they had been examined as witnesses, were detained to answer any charge which might be preferred against them.

On the succeeding Friday, Mrs M'Dougal, who had been allowed to remain so long in custody from motives of humanity only, fears being entertained that if she were to go at large, her life would be sacrificed to the vengeance of the mob, was discharged, and forthwith proceeded to her old abode, the scene of so many horrible transactions. On the next day she ventured out to a neighbouring liquor-shop to purchase whisky, but she was instantly recognized, the spirit was refused her, and the mob gaining intelligence as to who she was, she was compelled to fly for her life. Fortunately for her, the police interfered, and conducted her again to the prison, thereby saving her from violence; but there can be little doubt that, but for this fortunate intervention in her behalf, she would have fallen a victim to the vengeance of the justly indignant populace.

In the meantime Burke had become scarcely less communicative than Hare had previously been. He made no denial of the truth of the statements which had been made by that wretch, declaring that he had sold as many as thirty or forty subjects to the surgeons, although he subsequently admitted, like his companion, that he had never once been concerned as a resurrectionist, so that it could only be inferred that he had been a party to as many murders as he had sold dead bodies.

The following conversation, which took place between him and one of the officers of the jail, sufficiently indicates the state of his mind at this time, and the respective degrees of guilt attributable to him and to Hare:

He was first asked how long he had been engaged in this murderous traffic? To which he answered, 'From Christmas 1827, till the murder of the woman Campbell, in October last.' 'How many persons have you murdered, or been concerned in murdering, during that time? Were they thirty in all?'—'Not so many; not so many, I assure you.' 'How many?' He answered the question; but the answer was, for a reason perfectly satisfactory, reserved.

'Had you any accomplices?'—'None but Hare. We always took care, when we were going to commit murder, that no one else should be present—that no one could swear he saw the deed done. The women might suspect what we were about, but we always put them out of the way when we were going to do it. They never saw us commit any of the murders. One of the murders was done in Broggan's house, while he was out; but before he returned, the thing was finished and the body put into a box. Broggan evidently suspected something, for he appeared much agitated and entreated us "to take away that box", which we accordingly did; but he was not in any way concerned in it.'

'You have already told me that you were engaged in these atrocities from Christmas 1827 till the end of October 1828: were you associated with Hare during all that time?'—'Yes: we began with selling to Dr —— the body of a woman who had died a natural death in Hare's house. We got 10*l* for it. After this we began the murders, and all the rest of the bodies we sold to him were murdered.'

'In what place were these murders generally committed?'—'They were mostly committed in Hare's house, which was very convenient for the purpose, as it consisted of a room and a kitchen.'

'By what means were these fearful atrocities perpetrated?'—'By suffocation. We made the persons drunk, and then suffocated them by holding the nostrils and mouth, and getting on the body. Sometimes I held the mouth and nose, while Hare knelt upon the body, and sometimes Hare held the mouth and nose, while I placed myself upon the body. Hare has perjured himself by what he said at the trial about the murder of Campbell; he did not sit by while I did it, as he says; he was on the body assisting me with all his might, while I held the nostrils and mouth with one hand, and choked her under the throat with the other. We sometimes used a pillow, but did not in this case.'

'Now, Burke, answer me this question: were you tutored or instructed, or did you receive hints from any one, as to the mode of committing murder?'—'No, except from Hare. We often spoke about it, and we agreed that suffocation was the best way. Hare said so, and I agreed with him. We generally did it by suffocation.'

'Did you receive any encouragement to commit or persevere in committing these atrocities?'—'Yes; we were frequently told by Paterson that he would take as many bodies as we could get for him. When we got one, he always told us to get more. There was commonly another person with him of the name of Falconer. They generally pressed us to get more bodies.'

'To whom were the bodies so murdered sold?'—'To Dr ——. We took the bodies to his rooms in ——, and then went to his house to receive the money for them. Sometimes he paid us himself; sometimes we were paid by his assistants. No questions were ever asked as to the mode in which we had come by the bodies. We had nothing to do but to leave a body at the rooms, and to go and get the money.'

'Did you ever, upon any occasion, sell a body or bodies to any other lecturer in this place?' 'Never. We knew no other.'

'You have been a resurrectionist (as it is called), I understand?' 'No, neither Hare nor myself ever got a body from a churchyard. All we sold were murdered, save the first one, which was that of the woman who died a natural death in Hare's house. We began with that: our crimes then commenced. The victims we selected were generally elderly persons. They could be more easily disposed of than persons in the vigour of youth.'

Such were the horrible disclosures made by this man—disclosures of the truth of which there cannot be the smallest doubt. The general impression raised by Burke's declaration was, that he had been originally the dupe of Hare, and that the latter having been before engaged in a similar traffic had driven him on, after having once enlisted him in the service, to commit atrocities of which he would not otherwise have been guilty.

On Wednesday the 28th of January, pursuant to his sentence, Burke underwent the last penalty of the law. During the latter portion of his confinement, he declared that his confession had tended materially to relieve his mind; and he professed great contrition for his crimes. On the day of his execution he was removed from the jail to the lock-up, at the Court-house, where the scaffold had been erected, under a strong escort of police. The crowd which had assembled to witness his final exit from the scene of life was tremendous, and seats commanding a view of the gallows were let at a large price. Upon his coming forth on to the platform, he was assailed by the hideous yells of public execration. The concluding moments of his existence must have caused him the most acute suffering, for, stung to madness by the horrible shrieks with which he was greeted, he appeared anxious to hurry the executioner in the performance of his duty, as if desirous to escape from that life which he had spent so ill. Very soon after eight o'clock, he was tied up to the gallows in the usual way; and he immediately gave the signal for the falling of the drop, by throwing down his handkerchief. A short, but apparently a severe struggle succeeded; and in less than two minutes he ceased to move. His body hung suspended for half an hour, when it was cut down and placed in a shell, which had been brought to the scaffold for its reception. A struggle took place among the officials present for scraps of the rope with which he had been hanged, shavings of his coffin, and other relics of a similar character, but by nine o'clock, the crowd had dispersed.

The case of Hare was argued before the Scotch judges on the 5th of February, and by a majority of four to two, they determined that the public faith had been pledged to him, when his evidence was received against Burke, and he was ordered to be discharged. It was found, however, that by an ancient form of law he might be detained for the costs of the suit, and his final deliberation was therefore delayed until Thursday, the 12th of the same month, when he and his wife were set at liberty. They appear upon their discharge to have parted company, for Mrs Hare was nearly sacrificed to the fury of the mob at Glasgow, to which place she wended her way, while her husband proceeded by mail to Dumfries, where he was near meeting a similar fate. The mail, it appears, landed him at about seven o'clock in the morning, and although there was no intimation of his arrival, he was recognized by the mob, who immediately assailed him with the bitterest execrations, and with stones and other missiles. He succeeded in effecting his escape from them into the King's Arms Inn, where he obtained a refuge, but a crowd of persons surrounded the house, and demanded that he should be given up to their fury. For a considerable time consequences of a dangerous nature were apprehended, but night having arrived, the people dispersed; and when all was quiet, Hare quitted the house, and made a precipitate retreat from the town —whither, it was not known. The subsequent history of this atrocious ruffian, and of his wife and Mrs M'Dougal, must, we believe, for ever remain a mystery.

On the trial of Burke, his accomplice in crime, Hare, turned Queen's evidence, that is to say, he offered to give evidence against Burke on condition that he and his wife went free. That is why he is called an Approver in the text, for that was the name by which an accomplice went who had undertaken to give the evidence to prove the guilt of his companion in crime. The circumstances under which an accomplice should be admitted as an Approver are discussed in many criminal cases, and Macaulay makes use of the word in his history when he speaks of the 'testimony of a crowd of approvers swearing for their necks'. Once the evidence of Hare had been obtained on the conditions agreed, it would have been a great injury to the prestige of the law if the conditions had been broken, and it is also doubtful whether any proper evidence could have been brought against him to secure his conviction. It was undoubtedly this consideration which convinced the authorities that without the evidence of Hare it might well be that Burke would escape conviction. Mrs Hare was believed to be, and might well have been, Hare's wife, and if so, she could not have given evidence against him. The persons put on trial were therefore Burke and his paramour M'Dougal.

There is no property in a corpse and it cannot therefore be the subject of larceny, but there can be larceny of coffins, shrouds or property buried with corpses. It is a misdemeanour at common law to remove, without lawful authority, a corpse from a grave, whether in a churchyard or elsewhere, and it is no defence that the motives were pious and laudable for so doing. At common law the coroner can direct the exhumation of a body for the purposes of an inquest, but in practice this is usually done on the authority of the Secretary of State for the Home Department. A person who without authority disposes of a dead body for the purpose of dissection is indictable at common law and it matters not whether it was or was not done for gain. The Anatomy Act of 1832 now governs the situation, but those who are interested further in this rather gruesome matter would find much instruction in the account of the trial of Burke in the series of Famous Trials *recorded by the first Earl of Birkenhead.*

WILLIAM BANKS, Executed for Burglary

WE do not recollect that we have ever met with an instance of a burglary having been committed attended with greater violence or atrocity, than that for which this man underwent the punishment of death.

The Reverend William Warrington, it appears, was a gentleman of large property, residing at Grove Cottage, West Moulsey, in the vicinity of that well-known spot, Moulsey Hurst, Surrey. On the night of Wednesday, 19th of November 1828, his house was entered by four burglars, and a great quantity of valuable property carried off. Mr Warrington's house adjoined that of Mr Jeffs, a magistrate of the county, and a ladder, which had been accidentally left in the garden of the latter gentleman, was employed by the thieves in effecting an entrance to the house which they had determined to rob. The circumstances attending the burglary are as follows:

Between one and two o'clock on Wednesday morning, Mrs Warrington was in her bed-chamber engaged in writing and Mr Warrington was in the same room in bed, asleep, when the former was terrified by hearing some persons at the back part of the house attempting to force a window on the first floor, which opened to a staircase and to a passage leading to the bedroom. Before she had time to alarm her husband, the fastenings of the window were wrenched off, without breaking the glass, and as she opened her bedroom door, she beheld four men, who had entered at the window by means of the ladder beforementioned, in the act of ascending the stairs and approaching her chamber. Her fears were so excessive, that she was struck speechless for a few seconds. When she recovered, she shrieked, and exclaimed, 'Good God, we shall be murdered; there are thieves in the house.' Her husband was awoke instantly by her cries, and he had just time to leap from his bed and proceed in his shirt to the mantelpiece, on which he constantly kept a loaded pistol, before the four villains entered the chamber. He seized the pistol, levelled it at one of the thieves and fired, but without effect. The first man who entered the room, a dark, ferocious-looking fellow, in turn drew from under his coat a pistol and presented it at Mr

Warrington. The villain pulled the trigger, but the powder did not ignite. He recocked it and pulled it a second time, but it flashed in the pan. Mrs Warrington fell upon her knees, and in the most earnest and affecting manner implored the villains not to murder her husband, but to take all the property without interruption.

The thieves then produced some cords (which they had stolen from Mr Jeffs' garden) and tied Mr and Mrs Warrington's hands and feet. Their hands they tied fast behind their backs, and cautioned them to be silent as they valued their lives. They then left Mr and Mrs Warrington in their bedroom for a few minutes, and proceeded upstairs to the servants' sleeping apartments. There they bound two female servants (the only persons in the house beside Mr and Mrs W.) with cords, in the same manner in which they had previously bound the others. After they had bound them, the four robbers carried them downstairs to a vault which was under the house, and fastened them in that cold place with scarcely any covering. The villains then returned to Mr Warrington's bedroom, searched his clothes, broke open his desks and drawers, and, in truth, ransacked the house completely. They took cash to the amount of about 30*l*, and jewels and plate of considerable value, with which they decamped.

The servants had been confined for several hours in the vault, when one of them, after much exertion, released one of her hands from the cord and forced her way through the door of the vault. After ascending the steps, she found another door fastened, and she had to break through that before she could assist her master and mistress, who were in the most deplorable state of agitation. She unloosed the cords which secured them, and having released her fellow-servant also, they alarmed Mr Jeffs' family and the other neighbours. Mr Warrington found that not only all his portable property of value was carried off, but that the villains had actually stolen a horse, value 80 guineas, from the stable, had taken his phaeton from his chaise-house, and by these means had carried off their booty. Mr Warrington sent information of the robbery to Mr Cooke, constable of Kingston, who set off in pursuit of the robbers. He was able to trace the phaeton and two of the robbers from the house of Mr Warrington, by a very circuitous route, to Walton Bridge, and from thence through several by-roads to Knightsbridge.

On the same day Mr Warrington also gave information of the robbery at Bow Street, and Ellis, Ruthven and Bishop were directed to institute an investigation with a view to the apprehension of the thieves.

Upon the arrival of the officers at the house of Mr Warrington, various minute circumstances transpired which induced a strong belief in their minds that the robbery had not been committed by experienced thieves, and that it had been 'put up' or sanctioned by some person in the house. The clumsy manner in which the boxes and drawers had been opened seemed to point to the first impression, and the undoubted circumstance of six buck-shot having been withdrawn from Mr Warrington's pistol which had been lying on the mantelpiece during several days, led to the latter conclusion. Suspicion seemed to attach to one of the female servants, who had been familiarly accosted by her name, 'Fanny', by one of the robbers, and who had been the first to secure her escape from the cords by which she had been confined. She was therefore taken into custody, but after a few days' imprisonment, the officers declared themselves unable to produce any positive evidence against her and she was discharged.

From this time the most anxious exertions were made by the police-officers to secure the robbers. Every means in their power was tried; but although they succeeded in tracing them by witnesses to London, where Mr Warrington's carriage and horse were found, they were unable to discover who were the persons by whom the burglary had been perpetrated.

In the month of July 1829, however, the long-pending mystery was solved. A man named Barnett, a Jew, had been convicted of a burglary in the house of Mr Colebatch, in Thames Street, for which he had been sentenced to transportation for life. Anxious to save himself from the infliction of this punishment, he tendered information as to the parties who had composed 'The Moulsey Gang', as they were now called, upon condition of his liberty being restored to him. The proposition was at once accepted, and he immediately impeached Banks and four other men named John Smith, William Johnson, James Taylor and William Potts, *alias* Emery. The officers instantly set about endeavouring to procure the apprehension of these persons, and Cragg, a resolute officer of Bow Street, was directed to proceed in search of Banks. This fellow was a notorious thief, suspected to have been concerned in many robberies which had recently been committed, and Cragg heard that he had frequently declared his resolution not to be taken alive. The officer, however, was determined in his object, and attiring himself in the garb of a butcher, he proceeded in search of him. Many days elapsed before he could find him, but at length meeting with him, he rushed at him, and presenting a pistol at his head, called upon him to surrender himself a prisoner. Banks appeared astounded at this salutation and made no resistance, but exclaimed, 'I am a dead man.' On his person being searched, a loaded pistol was found in his pocket: on his back was a coat, part of the produce of a robbery in the house of Mr Campion at Waltham Cross, in which he had been recently concerned.

The other prisoners were apprehended nearly at the same time, and Potts was proved to have pawned a pair of shoes which had also been stolen from Mr Campion's. Upon their examination before the magistrates at Bow Street, Banks' participation in both burglaries was clearly proved, and he was committed for trial. Both Mr and Mrs Warrington identified him as one of the persons who had entered their house, but pointed him out as having acted with some degree of humanity, strongly protesting against the exercise of any cruelty by his companions.

Banks alone was committed for trial upon the charge of burglary at Mr Warrington's, the evidence against the other prisoners not being sufficiently conclusive to warrant their being indicted. He was found guilty, and sentenced to death at the succeeding Surrey assizes.

After his conviction, he professed himself to be perfectly willing to meet his fate, as he knew nothing of a state hereafter, declaring that all he cared about being hanged was for the pain it would cause him. He refused to receive any consolation from the chaplain, and was perfectly unmoved up to the time of his being pinioned.

He was hanged at Horsemonger Lane jail on the 11th of January 1830.

JOHN SMITH, *alias* WILLIAM SAPWELL
Executed for the Murder of a Policeman

THE cold-blooded and atrocious murder of which this man was convicted, showed him to merit most fully the awful punishment which befell him.

The object of the dreadful crime of which he was guilty, was a constable of the G division of the Metropolitan Police Force, then only recently established in London and its vicinity. In laying before our readers the circumstances of the case, it will not perhaps be considered out of place if we shortly recite the manner in which that most admirable body was first called into existence and operation.

The necessity of some improvement in the police of the metropolis had long been felt, and the utter inadequacy of the few Bow Street patrols hitherto employed to guard the streets of London by day, and of the watchmen, upon whom the same duty devolved by night, had for a considerable time attracted the attention of the public and of parliament. Committees of the House of Commons sat for the purpose of receiving evidence upon the subject, and a vast number of suggestions were thrown out upon the proper measures which should be taken with a view to obviate the existing difficulty. Statements were published in many of the newspapers, in which the faults of the system were pointed out and partial remedies suggested, but it was universally felt that no amendment of the plan then in operation could be sufficient to secure the object in view, and that a general and complete alteration and reorganization of the whole police of the metropolis was requisite. A plan of this description was long and ably advocated in a weekly journal of large sale (*Bell's Life in London*), the Editor of which had turned a great portion of his attention to a subject so nearly connected with the most minute interests of the community. A series of articles appeared in that newspaper, upon which there can be no doubt that the new police system, now so deservedly popular for its competency and for its admirable effects in securing our common safety, was founded. In the session of parliament of the year 1829

Mr Peel, at that time Secretary of State for the Home Department, introduced a bill to the House of Commons, founded upon principles directly in consonance with those supported in the journal in question—principles which were eventually adopted with the almost unanimous consent of the legislature. The general scheme which was put forth as being most desirable, was that of making a police throughout England, the centre and focus of which was to be fixed in London. The great towns throughout the kingdom would act as corresponding agents for the diffusion of that intelligence, the rapid and regular transmission of which was properly looked upon as so important to the success of any system of this description. In London, again, a smaller focus was to be formed under a board of commissioners, who would have daily communication with every division of the metropolis in which the police should be established, as well as with those country districts to which we have already alluded.

The minor details of the measure were to be carried out by the marking out of divisions, to be governed by superintendants, inspectors, serjeants, and privates in their various grades, constant communication being kept up throughout the metropolis, by day as well as by night, between each division. The advantages to be derived from a scheme so comprehensive in its details, and so complete in its organization, must be at once obvious to the mind of every person, and it is needless to point out to our readers the vast variety of instances in which its effects would be attended with the very best results. It was felt, however, by Mr Peel, that so large and general a measure could not be carried into operation with immediate success, and that much delay must take place before a universal scheme of rural police could effectually be established. He was yet convinced of the great utility which would be produced even from its partial adoption, and he lost no time in proposing a bill in parliament, which should have for its object the immediate appointment of a body of men capable of performing all the police duties of the metropolis. The proposition was at once assented to by both houses of the legislature, and on Tuesday the 29th September 1829, the 'new policemen' first entered upon their duties. Their dress, their supposed military character, and the extreme jealousy with which all classes of Englishmen view anything which may be supposed to derogate from their rights and privileges, long conspired to make this most useful force in the highest degree unpopular. Epithets of the most odious character were heaped upon them, attacks both abusive and violent were levelled at them from all quarters, and a few instances of irregularity amongst their numbers were eagerly seized hold of, as arguments to be employed against the general body. But at length, the increased safety obtained for the community, the quiet and orderly manner of the men themselves, as well as the improvement in the general conduct of the lower classes, obtained for them a reputation of the very highest description. The system which, first, was confined to the limits of the metropolis, has been joyfully extended to all large towns and to manufacturing neighbourhoods, and so anxious have even the most remote rural districts become for this new safeguard for their property and their lives, that almost every month sees the adoption of the plan in some new quarter. The improvement of the morals of the lower orders is no less than that which has taken place in their manners, and many of the crimes by which society was formerly so frequently disgraced, have now happily disappeared from the dreadful catalogue which the life of degraded man presents.

There can be no doubt that the offence of which we are about to enter into a description was in some degree attributable to that feeling of hatred for the police which was so peculiarly exemplified among the lower orders of the people. Long, the unfortunate object of the attack of this determined murderer, was a police-constable, No 43 of the G division, and occupied a beat in Gray's Inn Lane. On the night of Monday the 16th of August 1830, he was engaged in the performance of his duty when, at about half-past twelve o'clock, he observed three men of suspicious appearance lurking about the vicinity. Entertaining an apprehension of their intention to commit a burglary, he communicated his opinions to a brother constable on the adjoining beat, and it was determined that the men should be watched. They remained within Long's district of duty, and he followed them as far as the burial-ground of St Andrew's parish, which is situated at the back of Mecklenburgh Square. Here they stopped and remained in conversation for some time, and Long, believing this to be a favourable opportunity for convincing them of

William Sapwell stabbing Police-Constable Long
(*page 175*)

his intention to prevent the success of any marauding schemes which they might have in view, warned them to retire. The words had scarcely escaped the lips of the unfortunate man, ere he was violently seized by the arm by two of the party, while the third stabbed him to the heart. So desperate was the wound, that the murderer was unable to withdraw the weapon with which it was inflicted; but in his effort to do so, he pulled away the handle, and then all three ran off. This diabolical act was witnessed by more than one person, and several individuals instantly rushed to the spot. Long had fallen to the ground, with an exclamation that he was 'a dead man', and upon his head being raised upon the knee of one of the witnesses, he immediately expired. In the meantime, Newton, the constable to whom the unfortunate man had communicated his suspicions, had followed the assassins, and Smith was secured by him, having run a considerable distance and being in a state of the greatest agitation and alarm. Two other persons were also taken into custody, but it turned out that they were unconnected with the dreadful occurrence, and they were set at liberty. The truth of the suspicions of the constable was amply exhibited by the discovery of a number of housebreaking implements near the spot, which it was evident the thieves had intended to employ, but had thrown away in their flight. The handle of the knife was also discovered lying in the road at about one hundred yards from the spot where the murder was committed.

Several examinations of the prisoner subsequently took place before the magistrates at Hatton Garden, and witnesses were called who swore positively that his was the hand by which the wound was given which had caused the death of the deceased. During his imprisonment, he continued firm in his denial of participation in the murder, and maintained a sullen silence as to his occupation in life as well as his connexions. He appeared to associate with none of his fellow-prisoners.

His trial took place at the Old Bailey sessions, on Friday the 17th of September, when it turned out that his name was Sapwell and that he was a baker by trade. He still protested his innocence, but the evidence of the witnesses being of the most conclusive description, a verdict of guilty was returned, and he was sentenced to be executed on the following Monday.

On the day after his conviction he was visited by his wife and his six children, to whom, as well as to the officers of the jail, he continued loud in his declarations of his having been wrongfully convicted. He asserted that he had been to the Bedford Tea Gardens at Camden Town on the night of the murder, and that on his way home he heard a cry of 'Stop thief', and had joined in the pursuit of four men whom he saw running away, when he was himself taken into custody. He was exhorted by the Rev Mr Cotton, the ordinary of the prison, to whose humane advice he paid some attention; but he declined to receive the sacrament. In the course of the following day (Sunday) he also received a visit from the Sheriff (Ward), to whom he made no secret of his having intended to commit suicide if an opportunity had occurred, and with whom he argued against the sinfulness of such a mode of terminating his life. He instanced the cases of Sir Samuel Romilly, Mr Whitbread, and other distinguished individuals, who he said were perfectly justified in depriving themselves of existence when it became irksome to them.

On the morning of his execution (the 20th of September 1830), he entered freely into conversation with Sheriff Ward, and with new asseverations that he was not guilty of the crime for which he was about to suffer, declared, in an imaginary dialogue with the Almighty, that on his arrival at the gates of heaven, he should be unable to account for his standing there, and that the Almighty would give him admission; protesting, however, that he ought not to have been sent there so soon. He appeared sensible of his situation, and requested that the proceedings on the scaffold might occupy as little time as possible. He was turned off at the usual hour, and his remains were given to the directors of St George's Hospital for dissection.

The wretched man occupied the greater part of Saturday and Sunday, previous to his death, in drawing up statements of the manner in which he was by mistake drawn into the situation in which he stood, which amounted simply to a repetition of the story he had related to his family. He appears to have been very illiterate, his letters being both ill-spelt and ill-written, and he expressed none of those fears usually exhibited by persons in his situation.

Long, the constable, appears to have been a man of excellent character, having for a considerable time occupied a situation as watchman before he entered the police. He left a wife and several children, for whom a liberal public subscription was afterwards raised.

This case is noteworthy for the history of the police force in this country.

During the second half of the eighteenth century the state of crime in England was an intolerable evil. Horace Walpole has set on record the fact that coaches were held up by highwaymen in broad daylight and Fielding's Inquiry into the Causes of the Late Increase in Robberies *bears witness to the existence of many organized gangs of criminals. In the sixty years before 1828 Parliament had appointed six different committees to inquire into the state of the police forces of the country, but nothing was done until the provincial police were established by the Metropolitan Police Act of 1829, which is referred to in the text of this case.*

There is a deep-seated reason why reform was so long delayed when conditions obviously cried out for drastic action to be taken. Englishmen knew that in some countries the police were used as instruments of oppression and the establishment of Sir Robert Peel's disciplined professional force was regarded in many quarters as a direct threat to liberty. Anonymous posters even appeared which read: 'Liberty or Death! *Englishmen! Britons! and Honest Men!!! The time has at length arrived. All London meets on Tuesday. Come armed. We assure you from ocular demonstration that 6,000 cutlasses have been removed from the Tower for the use of Peel's bloody gang. These damned police are now to be armed. Englishmen, will you put up with this?*'

Generally speaking public anxiety did not, of course, reach this extreme pitch, but it was—and very properly still is—none the less real, and the judges of the land have been very wise and tactful in dealing with the problem from time to time. The police have been given very few privileges, and in most respects are subject to the same rules of law as the ordinary private citizen. If, for example, the police should arrest a man without lawful authority that man has the same rights against the police as he would have against a private citizen. Lord Denning, a Lord of Appeal, put it strongly and emphatically in his Hamlyn lectures when he said: 'He is entitled to resist the unlawful arrest, if need be, by force. If a ticket collector or a policeman tried to arrest a man for travelling without paying his fare, when he was willing to give his name and address, he would be entitled to knock them down, rather than go with them. If he submitted to the arrest and went, he would be entitled to obtain his immediate release by means of a writ of Habeas Corpus; *and after obtaining his release, he would be entitled to bring an action for damages against them for false imprisonment. Social security requires that the police should have power to make a lawful arrest, but individual freedom requires that a man should have power to resist an unlawful arrest, and, if need be, by force'.*

At the present time the police are regarded as the friends of the people and when a policeman is murdered when doing his duty the anger of the public is very great. It will be noticed that the report of this case concludes with a reference to the 'liberal public subscription' raised for the widow and children of the policeman, and in a recent case in our day public *funds were immediately called on for the same purpose.*

In the Homicide Act of 1957 it is still a capital murder punishable by death to murder a policeman acting in the execution of his duty or of a person assisting a police officer so acting.

It will be noticed that Smith was 'turned off', i.e. hanged, and his remains were given to the Directors of St George's Hospital for dissection. It will come as a surprise to many that at one time the bodies and clothes of persons who were hanged became the property of the hangman. The relatives could buy the bodies if they wanted, and if there were no purchasers, the bodies were sold to surgeons for dissection. These dissections were done in public at Barber Surgeons' Hall and were attended by great mobs of people. It seems an extraordinary thing that the most terrible and hardened murderers were very much afraid of being dissected after execution, but there are many remarkable examples of this fear recorded in the books. The Act of 1752 'for better preventing the horrid crime of murder' was passed to add some 'further terror and peculiar mark of infamy' to the punishment of death; and amongst the provisions of the Act it was provided that the body of the murderer should be delivered to the surgeons for dissection. In 1786 William Wilberforce brought in a Bill to extend this last provision to the offences of Rape, Arson, Burglary and Robbery. The Bill passed the Commons but was thrown out in the

Lords. Lord Loughborough who was then Lord Chancellor said of the clause extending the punishment of dissection—'The Act of 1752 had a strong deterrent value. Was it wise therefore to destroy this salutary effect by making the deprivation of the rights of burial a common and ordinary consequence of every conviction of almost every capital offence?' Ten years later a motion to bring another Bill into the Commons for 'Anatomizing the bodies of felons executed for Burglary or Highway Robbery' was defeated and leave to bring in the Bill refused.

Incidentally, the Bill of 1786 brought in by Wilberforce sought to discontinue the burning to death of women found guilty of petty or high treason. Lord Loughborough opposed this on the ground that the spectacle was likely to make a stronger impression as a deterrent on those who saw it than mere hanging, and there was no more personal pain in the burning than in hanging because the women were always strangled before the fire got near them.

John St John Long, Convicted of Manslaughter

THE extraordinary investigation touching the offence of which Mr Long was guilty attracted to him more than ordinary public attention. It appears that about the month of August 1830, a lady named Cashin, of great respectability and considerable fortune, came to London from Dublin with her two daughters for the purpose of procuring medical assistance for one of the young ladies, who was labouring under consumption. The ladies took up their abode in the house of a Mrs Roddis in Mornington Place, Hampstead Road, and Mrs Cashin having heard much of the wonderful cures effected by Mr St John Long, determined to seek his advice and aid for her daughter. Mr Long, it seems, had not been regularly educated as a surgeon, but had acquired considerable celebrity for a line of practice which he had adopted, and occupied a house in Harley Street, Cavendish Square. Thither Mrs Cashin repaired, and a short attendance upon the young lady, who was only sixteen years of age, was sufficient to confirm the melancholy fears of her mother that all human exertions in her behalf would be of no avail. The insidious nature of the disease by which she was affected was known and acknowledged by Mrs Cashin, and a desponding apprehension seized upon her mind, that her eldest daughter might also be attacked with this dreadful disorder. A new application on her behalf was therefore decided upon to Mr St John Long, who was requested to devise some means by which the impending mischief might be prevented. Mr Long participated in the fears of the young lady's mother and acknowledged the prudence of the course which she had adopted. Bidding them at once give up their fears, he assured them of his perfect ability to attain the object which they so anxiously had in view.

Miss Cashin at this time was twenty-four years of age, and in the full enjoyment of health, but, notwithstanding the absence of any necessity to take any active steps in her case, Mr Long determined upon employing his line of treatment towards her. The general nature of this treatment may be simply stated to be this: in case of internal disease, it was proposed by creating an external wound and a discharge, to carry off the malady. In a few days the external wound was produced in the case of Miss Cashin, by what means did not appear, as the general mode of treatment was kept secret by the quack, and the effect was of the most dreadful description. The wound daily increased, and appearances soon presented themselves which so alarmed Mrs Roddis, the landlady, that she felt herself called upon to adopt measures on behalf of the young lady.

She wrote to Mr Long, and in a day or two he called. Mrs Roddis humanely urged that danger might arise from symptoms which appeared so violent; but the doctor laughed at her apprehensions, declared that the wound was going on remarkably well, and that he would give a hundred guineas if he could produce similar favourable signs in some other of his patients. It was represented to him that the wound had wrought a disease upon the young lady of another description—she was unable to retain anything upon her stomach. For this, he said, he had a remedy with him if he chose to apply it. He was an enemy, however, to physic, the sickness was a favourable symptom, and the young lady would find relief from its disagreeable effects by taking mulled port wine. This, however, like everything else, was ejected from the stomach. Mr Long called again: in vain were certain angry appearances about the wound pointed out to him. He remained positive in his declared opinion, and refused to take any new measures for the young lady's immediate relief.

Every day brought new symptoms, which were looked upon by Mrs Cashin as unfavourable and dangerous, and at length Mr Brodie, of Saville Row, was called in. This eminent surgeon took every step possible for Miss Cashin, but all his efforts were useless, and the very morning after his assistance had been obtained, the young lady expired. Mr Long was acquainted with the circumstance of new aid having been procured, but he assured Mrs Cashin that this was quite unnecessary, and he never afterwards called.

Circumstances of so remarkable a character were not likely to pass unnoticed or unquestioned, and on Saturday the 21st of August 1830, a coroner's jury was summoned to inquire into the cause of the death of the deceased young lady. The investigation created much interest, and professional gentlemen attended on behalf of Mr Long, as well as of Mrs Cashin, to watch the proceedings.

Mrs Roddis was the first witness examined, and she deposed to the circumstances which are above detailed. Upon her cross-examination by Mr Long's solicitor, it was attempted to elicit from her that the deceased had eaten a great quantity of plums. But this was distinctly denied, and Mrs Roddis asserted that, ten days before her death, the young lady was in perfect health.

Mr Brodie's evidence was conclusive as to the cause of the death of the deceased. He said that he had been called in to attend the deceased young lady, and found a wound on her back, with considerable sloughing. He saw but slight hopes of her recovery but applied such remedies as he deemed fit. On the next morning he found that she was dead. Mr Brodie added that he had no knowledge of the manner in which the wound had been produced, but there was no doubt that it was that which had caused the sickness complained of, and which had also been the cause of death. He was at a loss to imagine how the production of such a wound could be supposed to have any effect in curing a patient of consumption, or in preventing such a disease.

At this point of the inquiry it was determined that the body of the deceased lady should undergo a post-mortem examination, and the further investigation of the case was, therefore, postponed until the following Monday.

On that day the inquest was resumed, new advocates appearing for the respective parties.

Sir Francis Burdett then came forward to speak to the mode of treatment adopted by Mr Long with some of his patients, which he did not think dangerous. By his recommendation two persons had put themselves under Mr Long's care. He did not know the nature of the application used by Mr Long: he had used it on his hand for the gout, but it did neither good nor harm. He had waited on him, understanding he could cure the tic douloureux, and he wished to have some information on the subject, with a view of apprising his friend, the Marquess of Anglesea, who was affected occasionally with that disease.

Dr Alexander Thompson, who had examined the body of the

deceased, was called, but he could form no positive opinion of the cause of death, as he was not permitted by the family to inspect the spine and head. In this state of things, it was resolved that Dr Thompson should pursue the examination of the body, and for that purpose was requested to have it exhumed from the burial-ground in Moorfields, where it had been interred.

On Wednesday the coroner and jury again assembled, when Dr Alexander Thompson, Mr Thomas King, surgeon, Mr Wildgoose, surgeon, Dr John Hogg, Dr Thomas Goodeve, Dr James Johnson, Mr John Maclean and Mr Thomas Evans, who had all been present at the last opening of the body, and examination of the spine and head, were examined. They all concurred that it was a perfectly healthful subject—beautiful in form, and free from all disease, save that occasioned by the wound in the back. Few people could recover after such a local injury, which appeared to them perfectly unjustifiable. A notion was entertained by some that it was advisable to produce an external illness, for the purpose of drawing off an internal disease. Here was no internal disease, and the concurrent opinion of all was that death had been occasioned by the wound in the back. The wound possessed much of the character of a burn, not produced by fire but by some application that would cause the same result. The mode of inflicting the wound was kept secret.

Mr Patrick Sweetman was then called: The deceased left Dublin about two months before, in perfect health. He saw her two days before she died, and had an interview with Mr Long, who described her situation as most favourable and said that there was no danger whatever. The deceased was twenty-four years of age: her younger sister was sixteen. The latter was in a consumption, and left Dublin to be put under Mr Long's care. He believed she had also a wound in her back. From the first Mr Long said he could not undertake her cure. Mr Long stated to him the causes of the deceased putting herself under his care. He told him that a young lady, one of his patients, had asked him what he thought of the health of Miss Catherine Cashin, who was in the habit of going to his house with her sister Ellen. Mr Long told the young lady that Miss Cashin would be seized with consumption in less than two months, unless she allowed herself to be rubbed by him with his mixture. She informed the mother of what Mr Long had said, and she consented to her undergoing this treatment, lest she might have to accuse herself of any neglect in the care of her children. Mr Long said he required everyone to sign a book. He required those who signed it not to divulge anything regarding the mixture and the inhaling which he prescribed. 'The inhaling was going on in the house while I was there. I signed the book, as a mere matter of form, at his request. He charged a guinea each visit for each young lady. I did not inhale: I should be very sorry to do so. He demanded no fee from me.' Miss Ellen Cashin was pronounced by the most eminent medical men in Dublin to be consumptive. Mrs Cashin heard of Mr Long in consequence of a book which he had published. The faculty in Dublin endeavoured to dissuade her from bringing her daughter here, but she would. At the conclusion of this witness's evidence, the inquiry was adjourned until Friday.

On Friday the jury once more assembled, and the evidence, touching the death of Miss Cashin, having been closed, Mr Adolphus addressed the jury on the part of Mr Long. He said that even supposing for a moment that the death of Miss Cashin had been caused by Mr Long's application, there was no evidence of malice prepense to constitute murder. As to 'manslaughter', it had been recently decided by two learned judges that if a man, whether ignorant or skilful, acted honestly and with intention to do good, he was not accountable for the result. Different practitioners adopted different modes of treatment: it often happened that that which was deemed advisable by one was considered quite the contrary by others and yet the practice objected to was the more successful.

Miss Matilda Christian of North Bank, Regent's Park, said she had been a patient of Mr Long's for some time. Her complaint was a consumption. Mr Long treated her as he did his other patients: he made wounds on the chest, on the left side, on the back, and on the temples. She recovered entirely under his care. The wounds left some marks, which might be seen when she was cold. Her former medical attendant expressed great astonishment at her cure. In cross-examination by the jury, she said the sores did not affect her inside, nor did they confine her to her bed. Mr Long had employed rubbing, as he did to the deceased, but what the ingredients were she did not know. For the rubbing he used a sponge. There was considerable discharge from the sores. She expectorated some stuff, which was put in water and sunk to the bottom. She had lost her father, brother and sister, by consumption of the same kind she had when she went to Mr Long.

Other witnesses, who had been patients to Mr Long for different diseases and to whom the same mode of treatment had been applied, spoke in the same terms of the advantageous effects which had accrued.

This evidence, however, was declared by the jury to have nothing to do with Miss Cashin's case, for Mr Long might have committed many harmless acts, which, nevertheless, would not relieve him from the consequences of one which was not harmless. The inquest was again adjourned until the following Monday.

On that day the inquiry terminated.

Among the witnesses examined were the Countess of Buckinghamshire, Mr Prendergast, M.P., and Mr Higgs, the brewer, all of whom spoke in high terms of Mr Long's treatment, and of the virtues of his lotion for curing various complaints. All the witnesses said that, in consequence of the benefit they derived from Mr Long's treatment, they had recommended many persons to him and would employ him again themselves in case of necessity.

The coroner, in summing up the case, observed that if Mr Long appeared to have possessed the necessary skill and knowledge for carrying on medical practice, and had used due diligence and care in the case of Miss Cashin, they must arrive at the conclusion that in this matter he was no wise to blame. It would be a lamentable thing if every medical man who committed an error of judgement was to be held responsible, as if he committed a criminal act. At five o'clock, the jury retired to consider their decision upon the case, and at eight o'clock returned into the room and announced their verdict of Manslaughter against Mr St John Long. A buzz of approbation was heard in the room when the verdict was pronounced, and one or two persons cried out 'Bravo!' Others exclaimed, 'Shame, shame!' The coroner then asked if Mr Long were present, and having been informed he was not, issued a warrant for his apprehension, and bound the witnesses over to attend at the sessions and prosecute the offender. The jury-room was crowded to the last moment.

Mr Long subsequently surrendered to the warrant, and was admitted to bail to answer the charge, but on the case being called on for trial at the ensuing Old Bailey sessions on the 18th of September, it was postponed, owing to the absence of some material witnesses for the prosecution.

On the 30th of October, Mr Long was placed upon his trial, when the same facts which we have detailed were stated in evidence. After an ample investigation, a verdict of manslaughter was again returned. Mr Long was then committed to Newgate to await his sentence, but on the following Monday he was again placed at the bar. The Court then passed upon him a sentence, condemning him to pay a fine of 250*l* to the king. The money was immediately paid and the defendant was discharged out of custody.

The case had already created a great degree of interest in society from the vast number of persons whom Mr Long had attended, and many honourable and right honourable persons were present at his trial, but the public excitement was still further aroused upon a subsequent charge of a similar nature being brought against him. The result of this charge was different from that of the indictment preferred in the case of Miss Cashin, but the affair was regarded with no less astonishment by the larger proportion of the community, who wondered at the folly of any one submitting to the absurd mal-treatment of this person for the cure of any real or supposed disease.

On Wednesday morning, November 10th 1830, at eleven o'clock, J. H. Gell, Esq and a highly respectable jury assembled at the Wilton Arms, Kinnerton Street, Knightsbridge, to inquire into the death of Mrs Colin Campbell Lloyd, aged 48, the wife of Captain Edward Lloyd of the Royal Navy, whose death was alleged to have been occasioned by the treatment she had experienced under the hands of Mr St John Long.

The inquiry excited the most intense interest, and the jury-room was crowded to excess, principally by gentlemen of the medical profession anxious to hear the result of the proceedings.

Mr Wheatley, a barrister, attended on behalf of the family of

Mrs Lloyd, and Mr Wooler appeared to watch the proceedings for Mr St John Long.

After the jury were impanelled, they proceeded to view the body of the unfortunate lady at her lodgings, No 33 Wilton Place, and on their return the following evidence was adduced:

Mr George Vance of No 27 Sackville Street, Piccadilly, surgeon: I visited Mrs Lloyd on the 21st October last which, as I was informed by her medical attendant, Mr Campbell, was about ten days from the commencement of her illness. Mrs Lloyd informed me that she had inhaled from a tube a few times at Mr St John Long's in Harley Street, and had been rubbed on the chest with a liniment twice: she did not say who rubbed her. The first rubbing, she said, produced no inconvenience, but the second a sense of burning heat. She stated that she was quite well at the time, and had not suffered any important indisposition for three years, which was the time I had attended her. From the inhalation, it appeared to me that her tongue, mouth and fauces had eroded. On examining her chest I found a sloughing sore of great extent (where she had, by her own account, been rubbed with a liniment) which extended from the arm-pits across the chest in one direction, and from the collar bones above, under the nipples, in the other direction. The stomach was much disturbed, and she was in a state of great exhaustion and despondency, frequently expressing a desire to die. In a day or two after my attendance some of the constitutional distress (by which I mean fever and irritation, as well as the sickness of the stomach) subsided in a degree, and her spirits revived. The dead parts began to separate more freely, and in a correspondence with her friends I gave encouraging hopes of her amendment. No granulations, however, appearing in the clean parts of the sore, and the surface having become dry and flabby, exhibiting the appearance of the dissected parts of a dead body, I imparted to her friends the certainty of her death. The deceased gradually grew weaker, and died on Monday morning the 8th of November. In my opinion, the application of some corrosive matter, applied to the parts which I found in a state of mortification, was the cause of her death. Mr Vance added that about three years before, he had attended Mrs Lloyd for an affection in the throat, which he considered to be Globus Hystericus. It was a nervous complaint, but soon disappeared. This was the only disease which he observed in Mrs Lloyd: she was, in all other respects, a stout woman, very richly covered with fat. He had never known any disease of that nature terminate fatally. Mrs Lloyd said that she had been persuaded to apply to Mr Long.

Mr Brodie of No 16 Saville Row, surgeon, and Mr Campbell, surgeon of No 23 Wilton Place, confirmed the testimony.

Captain Lloyd was then examined: He said he came to London with his wife and family on the 15th July. Mrs Lloyd was in good health but subject to a nervous affection of the throat when she took ill from the rubbing of Mr Long. On the 5th I accompanied her to Mr Long's house: she merely had a conversation. She went on the following day, when she inhaled. On the 7th she inhaled again, also on the 8th, when she paid him 1*l*. She went to him on the 9th, when she was rubbed for the first time across the bosom, as she described to me. On the 10th October she told me that she had inhaled as before, and afterwards was rubbed—as they termed it, 'rubbed out'. She told me that there was but a small portion of liquid in the saucer, but more was added when that was expended. She became so unwell while the rubbing was going on, that the rubber became alarmed and went for Mr Long, who did not come for some time. When he did, he said it was nothing and would soon go off, which it did after some time; but an odd sensation remained, which continued during the evening. She came home in her sister's carriage, and continued uneasy the rest of the day. She complained of a cold and chillings all the evening: a cold shivering fit came on when she retired to bed, and she took some hot wine and water. She had a restless night, and on the 11th October was unwell all day. There was a vivid redness across the breast where the rubbing had taken place, and a dark place in the centre of the breast, from which a discharge was taking place. She expressed great surprise that Mr Long did not call. She was inclined to be sick during the day, could not take any nourishment, and complained of a dreadful burning heat in the breast. She passed a restless night, and on the morning of the 12th of October, on looking at her breast, it appeared to me that wherever the matter discharged from the wound rested it caused fresh blisters, some of which I cut to relieve her pain, as she complained all over. A wicker cradle was forced to be made to place over her to prevent the bed-clothes touching her. On this day I called upon Mr Long, who expressed his surprise at not having seen Mrs Lloyd to go on with her inhaling. On explaining her inability and great sufferings, he said that he would come in the evening, which he did, and found that she had applied some common blister dressing to alleviate the heat and burning feeling. Mr Long said that was wrong and contrary to his practice, but he would rub it out, which Mrs Lloyd exclaimed against, saying that she had suffered so much that she could not endure these parts being rubbed at all—the very idea of touching them, even by herself, was excruciating. Mr Long said that the only thing necessary to be applied to the wound was old dry linen, to absorb. He then asked for a towel, and began rubbing it dry on the large black spot, as I suppose to absorb the discharge. Mrs Lloyd said she had always healed any little blister by a simple blister-dressing, and Mr Long said he saw no objection to her using it, and then departed. During the time Captain Lloyd was giving his evidence he appeared deeply affected, and frequently burst into tears.

The inquiry was then adjourned until the next day.

The jury resumed the inquiry on Thursday morning, when a post-mortem examination of the body took place.

Further evidence was given in corroboration of that heard on the preceding day, when the gentlemen who had examined the body of the deceased read a report, from which it appeared that the body was perfectly healthy. The lungs were sound and free from all disease. The heart was healthy, and the windpipe equally so. In fact, the medical gentlemen added, in their professional researches they had seldom seen a body that had lived forty years with internal structures so generally healthy and so fine in their proportions.

Several of Dr Long's dupes were called to swear to the general excellence of his treatment.

The coroner addressed the jury, stating that the question for their determination was, whether the deceased came by her death from gross ignorance or inattention from her medical attendant, or whether she died a natural death.

The jury retired for about half an hour, and then returned the following verdict:

'The jury, having attentively and deliberately considered their verdict, can come to no other than Manslaughter, against John St John Long.'

The coroner inquired on what grounds they found their verdict?

Foreman: On the ground of gross ignorance, and on other considerations.

Upon this second charge Mr Long was tried at the Old Bailey on the 19th of February 1831.

Mr Long appeared somewhat confused on his entering the dock, but he soon recovered his self-possession and bowed to many persons who entered the court. The case was tried before Mr Baron Bayley.

The evidence of Captain Lloyd, and of the other witnesses examined before the coroner, was now again gone into, and the additional testimony of Mr Campbell, who had first seen Mrs Lloyd after she had quitted Mr Long, was also given. His statement was as follows:

I am a surgeon. I visited Mrs Lloyd some time before her death. She appeared to me a healthy person. She told me a few days before her death that she was suffering great pain in her breast, which, from its appearance she must have done—there were very extensive wounds, no doubt produced by strong corrosive liquid. I applied a simple dressing. I saw the deceased afterwards, every day until her death. I considered the wound dangerous to life from the first moment that I saw it. When Mr Vance was called in, he applied the same dressing, and I described to him the treatment I had pursued. I gave the deceased some internal medicines; it was not until mortification had commenced that bark and mineral acids were administered. According to the best of my judgement, I should say that the deceased died of the wound in her chest. It certainly was not necessary to produce such a wound to cure a difficulty in swallowing. I know of no disease where it would be necessary to produce such a wound.

Cross-examined by Mr C. Phillips: I have practised as a surgeon for seven years. From the time that I was called in Mr Long had no opportunity of prescribing for Mrs Lloyd. Generally speaking, the remedy applied by the surgeon must be regulated by the description the patient gives him of his disease. I was not present when the deceased first described her symptoms to Mr Long. I do not recollect whether I proposed to Mrs Lloyd to call in some eminent surgeon. I did not consider that I was authorized in calling in another surgeon without the party wished it: the general practice in dangerous cases certainly is to mention it to the friends, and leave them to act as they please.

Mr Phillips: Seeing, as you express it, that it was a wound dangerous to life, did you not wish for further assistance? Witness: I had no objection to take the chance. Mortification came on about seven or eight days after Mrs Lloyd was under my care; I was from the beginning apprehensive of gangrene, but I cannot say how soon afterwards it commenced. I applied nothing but simple dressing until Mr Vance was called in. I stated at first to the friends of the deceased the danger that I anticipated from the wound. I attended her nearly a month before she died, during which time Mr Long had no opportunity of seeing or prescribing for her.

Re-examined: I fully believed that I understood how to treat the wound. I saw the body examined after death, but from nothing I then saw do I think there is any reason to suppose that I mistook the cause of death. I never saw a wound like the one on Mrs Lloyd's breast produced by a blister, and in such cases, where fatal results have followed, there have generally been appearances to account for them.

By the court: I think simple dressing best calculated to have reduced the inflammation.

When the whole of the evidence had been given, Mr Alley and Mr Adolphus addressed the court and urged that there was nothing in the proofs, which had been adduced, which fairly brought the prisoner within the jurisdiction of the court.

Mr Baron Bayley, however, held that any man presuming to meddle with what he did not understand—unacquainted with the principles of medicine, venturing to prescribe for the sick, and thereby causing their death—incurred a heavy responsibility, and indisputably, in some cases, was guilty of manslaughter. It would be for the jury to decide whether the present case assumed such a complexion.

The prisoner was then called on for his defence.

He addressed the court and jury at some length, urging that the death of the deceased was occasioned, not by any improper treatment of his—for that, if he had been permitted to attend her for a few days longer, he would have restored her to perfect health—but to the inexperience of Mr Campbell, into whose hands she was thrown, to his utter exclusion. He complained of the prejudices which had been excited towards him by practitioners who were jealous of his success, for while he was earning ten or twelve thousand a year, they were not obtaining more than one-third of that sum. It was true that he was not a member of either the College of Surgeons or Physicians, but he had spent a fortune in the attainment of his professional knowledge, and in pursuit of his practice had given the most universal satisfaction—so much so, that were he acquitted that day, he was persuaded he should be again honoured with the confidence of those distinguished and respectable individuals who had already from experience placed implicit confidence in his skill and judgement. Of those, he was proud to say, he had many in attendance, to whose testimony in his behalf he should refer. He complained that he had not himself been examined as a witness before the coroner's inquest, and repeated, that if guilt attached anywhere, it did so to Mr Campbell more than to himself; for that there was nothing in his treatment which could have occasioned the melancholy result, which no man deplored more than himself. The prisoner spoke in rather a low tone of voice, and, having a slight impediment in his speech, his address did not seem to make a very forcible impression.

The counsel of the prisoner then proceeded to call evidence in his behalf.

Mr Abingdon was examined: He said he had several times been under the care of the prisoner: he had an asthma, and subsequently a determination of blood to the head.

The Attorney-General here interfered, and submitted that the course of the present examination ought to be confined to the general character of the prisoner, in which the court, after hearing arguments from Mr Alley and Mr Phillips, acquiesced.

Mr Phillips endeavoured to shake this decision, contending that as the indictment raised the question whether Mr Long was grossly ignorant, or had been grossly careless, it was impossible to establish his innocence otherwise than by showing, as he verily believed they could, that he was both learned and skilful, and most attentive and humane in his practice of the healing art.

Mr Baron Bayley: We cannot go into specific cases; we must confine ourselves to general evidence.

Mr Phillips resumed the argument at length, but

The Attorney-General, in reply, said that if his learned friends found themselves at liberty to go into all the successful cases of the prisoner, he should go into the several failures in his practice.

The court having repeated its former decision, the examination of Mr Abingdon was resumed, and he stated that the prisoner had attended him for several disorders, and he had the fullest reason to be satisfied with his skill, care and attention.

Mrs Ashworth, the wife of General Ashworth, Miss Rook, her sister, Mrs Prendergast, Mrs M'Donnell, Mrs M'Dougall, and a vast number of other ladies and gentlemen were then examined, and every one of them bore testimony, in the strongest manner, to the skill, assiduity, and humanity of the prisoner, and to the extraordinary success which had uniformly attended his practice.

Mr Baron Bayley then proceeded to sum up, observing, that the question for the jury to decide was, whether the prisoner had been guilty of gross rashness, or had manifested culpable ignorance. The point at issue was, not whether, after the medicine had been administered, the prisoner had been inattentive, for his services were prevented, but whether, before it had been administered, he was ignorant of its nature and probable effect upon the constitution of the unhappy person to whom it was applied. His lordship then proceeded to read over the evidence, and to comment upon it as he proceeded. If the jury were of opinion that the death took place from the wound given on the morning of the 10th, they would give their verdict against the prisoner; but they must be fully satisfied that the death arose from that alone. If they entertained any doubt, the prisoner would be entitled to the benefit of that doubt: they must be satisfied that the crime imputed to him had been committed feloniously.

The jury retired at half-past eight o'clock, and returned in an hour with a verdict of 'Not Guilty'.

Several ladies, elegantly dressed, remained with the prisoner in the dock throughout the day, to whom this verdict appeared to give great satisfaction.

Mr Long, upon his discharge, resumed his 'rubbing in' practice, as before, and, we believe, still with much success. Many reports were circulated as to his habits and history, and many calumnious statements were made, both as to his mode of life and the system which he had adopted to carry on his business. For one of these libellous publications he brought an action in the Court of Common Pleas, which was tried on Tuesday, 14th June 1831, and he obtained a verdict with 100*l* damages.

Mr Long, we believe, was a native of Mallow, in Ireland, where his father carried on the useful but humble trade of basket-making, in which he was assisted by his son. At an early period of the life of our hero, he became acquainted with some members of the family of a gentleman named Hill. The young Hills were at the time engaged in perfecting themselves in a knowledge of drawing, and young Long being observed by them to possess some taste and considerable aptitude as a draughtsman, his patrons generously provided him with means of obtaining a knowledge of the art for which he had taken such a fancy. A short time served to render him a tolerable proficient, and he repaired to London, where for a considerable time he supported himself by the productions of his pencil. We have no means of learning the manner in which he discovered his system of medical treatment, but it is true that he numbered amongst his patients persons of the highest eminence in this country, and that he obtained an extent of practice which enabled him to live in excellent style.

He died in the year 1834, and his body was consigned to the tomb in the Harrow Road cemetery, where a monument has been erected to his memory at the cost of his former patients, who, in an inscription, pay a handsome tribute to his talents.

This case is of no legal importance but it possesses a good deal of human interest. It shows in a very striking way the gullibility of human nature and the rich field that is always open to the quack.

Manslaughter may be committed in many forms, and it would

seem that if a medical man or a layman performs an operation on another in good faith, even by a dangerous instrument, then if the person dies he is not guilty of manslaughter; but if the medical man or the layman is guilty of criminal misconduct due to ignorance or neglect he will be guilty of manslaughter. In Bateman's case (which I argued many years ago in the Court of Criminal Appeal) the law as to manslaughter by negligence is authoritatively laid down and the distinction drawn between civil and criminal negligence.

Lord Lyndhurst in an early case laid down the law as follows:

> *In these cases there is no difference between a licensed physician or surgeon and a person acting as physician or surgeon without licence. In either case, if a party having a competent degree of skill and knowledge makes an accidental mistake in his treatment of a patient, through which mistake death ensues, he is not thereby guilty of manslaughter; but if where proper medical assistance can be had, a person totally ignorant of the science of medicine takes upon himself to administer a violent and dangerous remedy to one labouring under disease, and death ensues in consequence of that dangerous remedy having been so administered, then he is guilty of manslaughter.*

Those words would seem to fit the case of Long, for more blatant quackery it is difficult to conceive, but in the one case he was fined, and in the other the jury returned a verdict of Not Guilty. It certainly seems in the highest degree surprising that quite eminent people should be willing to testify on his behalf, and that a jury's verdict in his favour should be greeted with public approval.

Riots at Merthyr Tydfil

THESE riots, as alarming in their nature as they were distressing and mischievous in their consequences, occurred at Merthyr Tydfil in South Wales, on the 3rd of June 1831. The district surrounding Merthyr Tydfil was at that time, as it is now, densely populated by persons engaged in the iron manufactories with which that district abounds, and the alleged insufficiency of the wages was the immediate cause of the desperate riot which took place.

The preliminary to this distressing occurrence, it appears, was a turnout, or strike among the workmen; and the alarming manner in which these men assembled, and the threats which they held out, produced a well-grounded apprehension that violence might be done both to the persons and the property of the iron-masters. In order to meet any attack which might be made, the magistrates assembled at the Castle Inn, Merthyr Tydfil, for the purpose of devising means to meet and repel the rioters, and the result was that an application for military assistance was determined on.

In consequence a detachment of the Ninety-third Regiment, under the command of Major Folkes, proceeded into the town, and on the 3rd of June took up their quarters at the Castle Inn, the chief inn in the town, where the magistrates still remained assembled in consultation.

By this time, the mob had already exhibited its riotous and unlawful determination by an attack upon the Court of Requests. This court, it would appear, had become hateful to them, from its being also the place where offences affecting the relations of master and servant were usually adjudicated upon, and they demanded that the books should be given up to them. This was, of course, refused, as indeed they had been already removed to a secure place, upon which the mob commenced a most violent and determined assault upon the building. The residence of Mr Coffin, the officer of the court, was also an object of their angry demonstrations, and the two places having been stripped of their books and furniture, a fire was immediately made of them in the street and they were burned.

This done, the rioters proceeded at once to the Castle Inn, there to give fresh proofs of their power and determination. At this time they exceeded a thousand in number, and they were loud in their demands that justice should be done them. A deputation was called in to explain their wants, who respectfully but firmly demanded an increase of wages, but the magistrates, having earnestly desired them to return to their work, pointing out to them that it was impossible that they could suffer themselves to be dictated to by a lawless mob, desired them to retire. Upon their return to their partisans they communicated what had taken place, and symptoms were soon observable in the countenances of all, which denoted their determination to proceed to measures even more violent than any they had hitherto adopted.

They were addressed by several of the iron-masters present at the inn, both in English and Welsh, but without effect, for they persisted in their demands for further wages, and declared their intention to persevere until their desires were acceded to.

At this time there was a guard of soldiers stationed at the door of the inn, the smallness of whose numbers was remarkably contrasted with the vast assemblage of the workmen. The weakness of the position of the military, in case of an attack, was at once seen, and steps were immediately taken to secure the safety of the post at which they had fixed themselves. For this purpose three men were ordered to each window in front of the building, to be ready with their muskets in case of necessity. Renewed efforts to procure the dispersion of the crowd were then made by Mr Crawshay and Mr Guest, and a long parley took place. No amicable decision was, however, arrived at, and at length, when it was least expected, a spontaneous rush was made by the people upon the soldiery occupying the doorway and its vicinity, whose arms appeared to be the object of the attack. The force in the street was absolutely as nothing against the numbers by whom they were assailed, and orders were given to the soldiers above to fire.

At this period a scene of dreadful conflict was witnessed. The men in the windows advanced one by one to the front to fire, and each man, before he discharged his piece, took deliberate aim at one of the most violent of the mob, whom he seldom failed to bring down. As each man fired, he fell back and re-loaded, so that there was a constant succession of discharges upon the heads of the misguided people in the street. The personal conflict below was no less dreadful. The first person whom the mob had attempted to seize, was a soldier whose back was turned to them, and his assailant was a brawny fellow of upwards of six feet in height. The musket was seized from behind, but the soldier, no less active than his antagonist, immediately turned round, still maintaining his hold of his piece. By a dexterous twist he pushed his opponent from him, and received him, on his return, on the point of his bayonet, so that he fell dead at his feet. The soldier was at once felled to the ground by a blow from a bludgeon, and his gun was secured by another of the rioters. At the same moment a scene almost precisely similar occurred within two yards of the same spot. A fellow seized hold of a drummer's sword, but immediately had a bayonet run though his body. The muskets, meanwhile, were cracking from every window, and the street was raked from one end to the other. Many of the rioters penetrated to the interior of the house, where they committed acts of violence upon the officers of the regiment and upon the magistrates, many of whom, in their efforts to secure these assailants, received severe contusions. The rioters exhibited a degree of determination which was truly surprising, and the position of those who were in the inn was at one time highly critical. The superior discipline of the soldiery, however, prevailed against their numbers, and at length the neighbourhood was cleared.

Upon a search being now made, it was found that thirteen of the rioters lay dead upon the ground, and the mob were seen carrying off many others, who were believed to be dead or severely wounded. The soldiers themselves did not escape injury: nearly twenty of them were wounded, exclusive of Major Folkes, who had received a serious contusion on the back of the head from a bludgeon. One of the men had had his bayonet taken from him and was stabbed in his side, while others were bleeding profusely from places where they had received blows or wounds from the people. The bodies which had been found in the street were conveyed to the stables of the inn—many of them only now parting with the last quivering remains of existence—there to wait a coroner's inquest, while those persons who had been secured and who were wounded, received immediate surgical assistance.

The danger to the town, however, had not yet altogether ceased. The rioters having succeeded in escaping from its precincts, ascended the neighbouring heights, from whence they continued to fire upon the immediate vicinity of the Castle Inn with much precision. Many of them had procured fowling-pieces, while others employed the muskets which they had taken from the soldiery.

It may readily be supposed that an occurrence like this produced a very great degree of alarm in the vicinity of Merthyr Tydfil; and the assertion that men were hourly swelling the ranks of the insurgents, tended to increase the apprehensions which already existed. The magistrates, with great promptitude, summoned additional military force to their aid, and by night a body of cavalry, infantry and militia, amounting in number to near five hundred men, was at their disposal. During the whole of the day exaggerated and alarming accounts of the proceedings of the rioters were brought into the town, and the number of rioters assembled in the evening was stated to be nearly eight thousand men, all of whom appeared to be endeavouring to station themselves at Coedycymer. A large body of troops, both cavalry and infantry, was in consequence dispatched to Penydarran House, to keep them in awe and prevent any further acts of mischief in that quarter.

This state of things continued during the whole of that night, but on the ensuing day a circumstance occurred which is worthy of notice, as exhibiting the ferocious intentions of these misguided men. Their headquarters at this time were at Hirwain, and there two red flags were hoisted, as typical of their bloody determinations. This, however, was not significant enough in their opinion, and they actually procured a basin of calf's blood, in which the flags were soaked, and with which the standard-bearer's hands and arms were smeared on his appearing at their head. They were approaching Merthyr Tydfil with this emblem, when, however, they perceived the increased strength of the military, and prudently retired until they should procure fresh numbers.

On Sunday the rioters remained perfectly inactive; but on

Monday it had been determined that a general meeting of the working classes should be held on the Wain Hill, near Dowlais, which was to include all the men engaged, not only in the local districts, but in the counties of Brecon and Monmouth, and nearly twenty thousand persons were expected to assemble.

At an early hour men were seen drawing towards that spot in every direction, and at ten o'clock it was announced that there were thousands in the road coming down to Penydarran, armed with bludgeons. The troops, now consisting of one hundred and ten Highlanders, fifty of the Glamorganshire Militia, and three hundred Yeomanry Cavalry under the command of Colonel Morgan, accompanied by the magistrates, proceeded to meet them, and at Dowlais the road was found filled with the dense masses. Mr Guest ably addressed them, but to no purpose, and the Riot Act was read. Still no disposition to disperse was manifested, but a determined resistance was shown and maintained. The Highlanders were at length ordered to level their muskets; but the coolness and forbearance of all parties allowed the words of command to be given so slowly, that the consideration of the consequences intervened between them, and the last word 'Fire!' became unnecessary, to the great satisfaction of all the gentlemen present. The rioters now gave way, and many returned home. Some parted on one side, others on another, but the greater part crossed the hill to the ravine in the Brecon road, where, by regular concert, all the arms were collected under the most determined and hardened of the villains; and they were observed from the tower of Cyfarthfa Castle exercising in line with the sabres and pistols taken from the cavalry, and with the muskets of the Highlanders and their own fowling-pieces. This exercising was observed to continue during the whole morning, and repeated shots were heard fired. About twelve o'clock a scout who had been sent out brought intelligence that two black flags were flying in the Brecon road—a symbol of the determination of the men who fought under the banner to conquer or die. Soon after this, a movement was observed among the rioters, as if they would assume an offensive position, and every preparation was made to give them such a reception as would effectually disperse them. Their march was observed, however, to be hesitating and wavering, numbers flung away their arms and returned home, and at length the main body became so disheartened that they fairly took to their heels and disappeared.

During the whole of the remainder of that evening and the next morning, the magistrates and military were exceedingly active in apprehending such men as were suspected or were known to have taken part in these disgraceful proceedings, and fourteen of the worst among them were taken in their beds. On Wednesday night, Richard Lewis, who had led the attack upon the Castle Inn, was secured. He was found skulking in a wood by two men, who secured him in a low public-house until they had obtained the aid of the military, and the prisoner was escorted into the town by a body of cavalry. His appearance and demeanour were ferocious in the extreme—in which he differed materially from the other prisoners, of whom there were now near forty, all of whom admitted their fault, and ascribed the lamentable bloodshed which had taken place to their own unjustifiable attack on the military. This expression of feeling on their part was also sufficiently accorded to by the conduct of their fellows at liberty, who, without saying one word against the course which had been taken, buried their dead companions as quickly and as quietly as possible—a sure proof that their own consciences convicted them of lawless violence. Those who had been wounded, exhibited an equal consciousness of guilt, by abstaining from seeking medical aid, until pain or inflammation rendered such a step absolutely necessary to save their lives.

In the course of the week, the greater proportion of these misguided men who were still at liberty returned to their work, while the cases of those who were in custody were disposed of by the magistrates. Several who appeared to have acted as ringleaders in this dreadful affair were committed for trial, but the larger number were dealt with summarily, by the infliction of the penalties of fine or imprisonment, or by their being held to bail, to be of good behaviour. Many of the muskets and sabres which had been carried off were restored, and all exhibited the greatest terror at the guilt in which they had involved themselves, and apprehension lest they should be placed in the same position of difficulty in which their less fortunate companions were thrown.

At inquests held on the bodies of the rioters who had been

killed by the soldiery, the juries returned the invariable verdict of 'Justifiable Homicide'—a sufficient assurance to the country that the steps taken by the magistracy had been neither uncalled for nor too violent.

The trials of the prisoners who had been committed for various offences of which they were alleged to have been guilty during these disturbances came on at the Cardiff summer assizes, held in the month of July.

The following sentences were passed upon those who were convicted:

Lewis Lewis and Richard Lewis—Death, without a gleam of hope of mercy.

David Hughes, Thomas Vaughan and David Thomas—Death recorded: the judge intimating that the sentence would be commuted to transportation for life.

Eight were sentenced to imprisonment for different periods and hard labour.

Several other persons, committed to Cardiff jail for having participated in the riots, were acquitted.

The charge upon which Richard Lewis was convicted, was that of having, during the scuffle with the military before the Castle Inn, wounded Donald Black, a private in the Ninety-third Regiment of Highlanders, with a bayonet: the wound in this case was never considered dangerous.

The soldier gave his evidence upon the trial in a very manly and creditable manner, but could not identify the prisoner as the party who had used the bayonet. The only evidence of identity was that of a person who, till the riots, was unacquainted with the prisoner.

The prisoner persisted in a denial of his guilt, and declared that he would do so with his dying breath.

Lewis Lewis (called Lewis the Huntsman, from his having been a huntsman to a gentleman of the name of Llewellen, about eleven years before) was indicted jointly with Hughes, Vaughan and Thomas, together with three other persons. He was charged with having, on the 2nd of June (the day preceding the affray near the Castle Inn), stood upon a chest in the street, opposite the house of a man named Thomas Lewis, and addressed the mob to the following effect: 'I understand that the mob has taken a chest of drawers from a widow woman, who had purchased it for two guineas from the bailiffs of the Court of Requests, and restored it to another poor widow, from whom it had been taken in execution. Now I don't think that is fair, unless she has her two guineas back, and if you are of my mind, we will go to Thomas Lewis and get it back. All you that are of my mind, raise up your hands.' Upon this, the mob all raised their hands, and several of them went into Thomas Lewis's house, and compelled him to deliver up the two guineas which he had received (being the plaintiff in the execution) to one David Williams, the widow's son. They also compelled Thomas Lewis to give up several other articles. During the whole of this time Lewis Lewis remained in the street. Upon this evidence the jury found Lewis Lewis, Hughes, Vaughan and Thomas Guilty, and acquitted the other prisoners.

It appears that the two guineas thus extorted were restored to the prosecutor, Thomas Lewis, about a month before the assizes.

Looking at this offence with all its bearings, there seems a much less degree of moral turpitude in the crime, than that of an ordinary robbery, committed for the sake of plunder. Here the offender sought no plunder, but, from a mistaken sense of right and wrong, did that which he thought justice, by restoring to the widow the money she had paid for the chest of drawers.

At the conclusion of the trials, John Thomas of Merthyr Tydfil, who was employed during the riots as a peace-officer, and who apprehended the prisoner when he was committed to jail, was called by the prisoner's counsel, and was ready to prove, upon oath, that whilst the mob were assembled before the house of Mr Coffin at Merthyr Tydfil, some of them attacked him (J. Thomas) and violently beat him. And but for the timely aid of the prisoner, who actually fought in his defence, and in which he was himself severely beaten, he would, in all probability, have been killed.

This evidence, however, was declared inadmissible at the trial, although it was subsequently made the ground of an application for mercy on behalf of the prisoner.

The circumstances attending the conviction of these unhappy men procured for them almost universal commiseration, and petitions, signed by many thousands of persons unconnected with them in any way, were presented to the Crown, with a view to obtain for them a mitigation of punishment.

In the cases of Hughes, Vaughan and Thomas, in obedience to the suggestion of the learned judge, an immediate reprieve was granted, together with a commutation of punishment. In that of Lewis Lewis, the huntsman, a respite for a week was at the same time allowed. The same favour was almost immediately afterwards accorded to Richard Lewis, but the most painful doubts were entertained as to his ultimate fate.

On Friday, the 5th of August, Lewis Lewis received a reprieve, together with a notification that his punishment was commuted to transportation for fourteen years (an arrangement which was also at the same time made in the cases of Hughes, Vaughan and Thomas) and on the same day a respite for Richard Lewis for a fortnight was transmitted to the sheriff.

This postponement of the fatal day was looked upon by most persons as preparatory only to a commutation of punishment, but this favourable anticipation was contradicted by its being eventually determined that the case of the prisoner did not entitle him to any further consideration.

On the night before the execution, the unhappy convict was urged to make a confession of his guilt, but he positively denied that he had been in any way connected with the transaction in which he was alleged to have been an actor. He continued firm in this declaration up to the time of his death, and Lewis Lewis, who so narrowly escaped the same fate and who was his brother, subsequently confirmed the assertion which he had made, and stated that he could have given satisfactory evidence of his brother having been altogether absent from the affray.

The execution took place at Cardiff, on Saturday the 20th of August 1831.

Dennis Collins, Convicted of High Treason, in throwing a stone at King William IV

THIS extraordinary attack on the person of His Majesty took place at Ascot Heath races, for many years the resort of the royal family, on Thursday, the 19th of June 1832.

His Majesty, accompanied by his consort, had just reached the grand stand on the race-course, and had advanced to the front window to acknowledge the respectful greetings of his people, when two stones, thrown in quick succession after each other, were seen to fly in the direction of the window at which the royal party was stationed. The first stone rebounded from the building to the ground below, but the second entered the open window and struck His Majesty a somewhat severe blow on the front of the head. An instant alarm was raised, and a thousand arms were extended to seize the individual by whom the attack was made, and whose act was attributed to an intention far more dangerous than it eventually appeared the unfortunate man had had. His Majesty was much agitated, and retired to the inner part of the room, apparently in alarm lest any further violence should be attempted. He was observed to express considerable fear lest Her Majesty, or any of the females of the suite, might receive injury, but in a few moments he regained his self-possession and presented himself at the window to assure the public of his safety. His Majesty had received a slight injury only, owing to the stone having fallen upon his hat, and the royal party appeared perfectly reassured long before the alarm created in the minds of those present had subsided, and they had become convinced that the attack was not the subject of some deep laid and villainous plot.

The wretched author of the mischief had been immediately secured, and he was now carried before Sir F. A. Roe, the chief magistrate of Westminster, who was always in attendance upon His Majesty upon such occasions and who held a species of court in a room under the Grand Stand. Gardiner, the Bow Street officer, had the prisoner in charge and conducted him to the presence of the magistrate. In a few moments the room where the examination was held was crowded with persons in attendance on His Majesty or attached to the royal suite, who were anxious to learn the particulars of this extraordinary act, as well as to ascertain the station and occupations of the assailant of the king.

The prisoner was found to be old and decrepit, with a wooden leg and wearing the tattered garb of a sailor. He gave his name Dennis Collins, and surveyed the assembled throng with a calm composure. There appeared, however, to be considerable incoherence in the expressions which he occasionally let fall, produced apparently by the confusion in which he was involved, consequent upon the somewhat rough treatment which he had received from the mob before he had reached the custody of the police-officers. The circumstances which have been already detailed were now proved in evidence; and witnesses were examined who had seen the prisoner on the race-course during the morning and had remarked his demeanour. He appeared to be occupied in begging, but an angry resentment seemed to be exciting his mind. This had evidently reached its height at the moment of his attack upon His Majesty, but his premeditation appeared to be exhibited beyond a doubt by his possession of the missiles, which must have been brought from a somewhat distant part of the ground.

The miserable old man was considerably below the middle height, and the general aspect which he presented was the reverse of pleasing on account of the want of cleanliness of his person. His countenance was by no means ill-favoured, and a bright sparkling eye appeared to lend to it an expression of considerable intelligence. He made no statement before the magistrates, and was eventually committed to Reading jail for re-examination on the following Wednesday.

On that day the necessary witnesses to his crime were called, and their depositions formally taken. The prisoner was then called upon for his defence. His address to the magistrates was highly characteristic of the old sailor, a station to which it appears the prisoner was entitled. He said, 'I own myself in a great fault for throwing these stones at His Majesty. I was in Greenwich Hospital on the 16th of December last as an in-pensioner.

Riots at Merthyr Tydfil (*page* 199)

I had been there eighteen months. The ward-keeper was sweeping the place, and I told him he had no business to sweep it more than once a day. The boatswain's mate abused me, and I returned it. A complaint was then made to Sir Richard Keats (the governor), and I was expelled for life. I petitioned to the Lords of the Admiralty to have the pension which I had before I went into the hospital restored to me. I am entitled to that pension by an act passed in the reign of George IV, which entitles a pensioner to have the same pension which he had before he became an in-pensioner, unless he struck an officer, or committed felony, or did anything of the kind, which I did no such thing. On the 19th of last April I petitioned the king to have my pension restored. He answered by sending the petition to the Lords of the Admiralty, and Mr Barrow, the secretary, sent a letter to me at the public-house, the Admiral Duncan, with the same answer the king gave. The answer was that "His Majesty could do nothing for me". This was part in writing and part in print. I had neither workhouse nor overseer to apply to, and had not broke my fast for three days; merely distress drove me to it. His Majesty never did me an injury, and I am exceedingly sorry I threw a stone or anything else at His Majesty. On the 17th of the present month I went to Admiral Rowley's. He swore at me and kicked me. I can only say I am very sorry for what I have done, and must suffer the law. They had no right to take my pension from me, to which I was entitled by Act of Parliament.'

This was all the wretched man said, and he was then fully committed for trial in the customary form, upon the charge of high treason.

His trial took place at Abingdon on Wednesday the 22nd August, when he was arraigned upon an indictment, charging him with assaulting His Majesty, with intent to kill and murder him; with intent to maim and disable him; and with intent to do him some grievous bodily harm.

The prisoner pleaded Not Guilty, and the case was immediately commenced. The evidence was conclusive as to the facts which we have stated, and a verdict of 'Guilty' upon the last count was returned.

The sentence awarded by the law to the offence of high treason was immediately passed, the prisoner being ordered to be drawn and quartered, in obedience to the ancient and long existing practice.

It was directly known that a sentence so severe would not be carried into full effect upon a man whose only crime appeared to have been insanity, and on the following Friday a respite was received at Abingdon jail, by which the punishment of death was removed in the case of the wretched old convict.

Collins, at the time of his trial, was upwards of seventy years of age and, as his defence before the magistrates imported, he had served in the Navy for many years. His gallant conduct in an action was the cause of his losing his leg and he was compelled to quit the service. He subsequently exerted himself to procure his admission to Greenwich Hospital, and eventually he succeeded, but he was expelled for the misconduct which he pointed out. From this time he appears to have supported himself by begging, and he was well known at the various fairs and race-courses.

His sentence was eventually commuted to transportation for life, and he was sent from this country to Van Dieman's Land. A short residence in that colony ended his days. He died at Port Philip in the spring of the year 1834.

Job Cox, Transported for Letter-Stealing

THE offence of which this young man was convicted, at the time of its commission subjected its perpetrator to capital punishment. The particular case is not remarkable for any peculiarity, but it is fit that it should be mentioned in connexion with the observations made about the conduct of the learned recorder of the city of London, and his neglect of the highly important duties entrusted to him.

Cox, a postman in the service of the General Post Office, was charged with abstracting a letter from those entrusted to him for delivery, and appropriating its contents to his own use. It appeared that on the 18th of March 1833, a Mr Foreman of No 101 Grafton Street, Dublin, had sent a letter containing a 10*l* bank note addressed to his brother, Mr H. Foreman in Queen Street, Clerkenwell, which never reached its destination. Inquiry being made at the post-office, Cox was found to have signed a book in the ordinary way as having received the letter, and it was subsequently ascertained that he had paid the same note to Mr Lott, a publican in Lambeth, who had given him change for it. There were reasons to believe that Cox had been guilty of other offences of a similar character, and he was taken into custody.

At the ensuing sessions at the Old Bailey, held in the month of May 1833, the prisoner was tried and convicted of the offence imputed to him, and on the 20th of the month he received sentence of death, in obedience to the requisites of the act of parliament.

At this time it was the practice of the recorder of London to report to His Majesty in council the cases of the various prisoners in custody upon whom sentence of death had been passed. The case of Cox was reported, with others, as usual, and upon the return of the learned recorder to London, he caused it to be made known to the prisoner that his execution was directed to take place. The unhappy wretch had looked forward with confidence to the result of the exertions of his friends in his favour, and received this intelligence with deep dismay. He was told to prepare for death, and the reverend ordinary of the jail proceeded to pay to him those attentions usually expected at his hands.

A blunder of a most extraordinary nature, however, was soon discovered to have been made. This discovery is thus described in a newspaper of Sunday, the 23rd of June:

'On Thursday morning, Sir Thomas Denman, Lord Chief Justice of the King's Bench, on casting his eyes on a newspaper, saw the paragraph representing the fact that Job Cox was ordered for execution on Tuesday. His lordship thought the statement had been published from false information, and he adverted to the circumstance in the presence of one of the under-sheriffs, as of a very mischievous nature. The under-sheriff, in some surprise, observed to his lordship that the paragraph was correct—that the recorder's warrant had been received on Wednesday evening, at half-past six o'clock, at Newgate, that the intelligence had been communicated to the unfortunate culprit, and that notices had been sent to the sheriffs and the other officials. "What (said Sir Thomas Denman) Cox ordered for execution! Impossible! I was myself one of the privy council present when the report was made, and I know that no warrant for the execution of any one was ordered. Cox was ordered to be placed in solitary confinement, and to be kept to hard labour previously to his being transported for life, to which penalty the judgement to die was commuted."

'The under-sheriff repeated the extraordinary information to his lordship, who instantly requested that he would forthwith apply at the Secretary of State's office, when he would be reassured of the fact, and receive an order in contradiction of the learned recorder's warrant. It is needless to say, that the under-sheriff, who was very glad to be the bearer of such good tidings to a poor unhappy fellow-creature, very speedily executed his mission. He found that the correction of Sir Thomas Denman was accurate, according to Mr Capper's books, in which the allotted punishment was regularly entered; and Lord Melbourne, immediately upon being informed of the mistake under which they laboured at Newgate, sent thither an authority to countermand the warrant with the black seal. Cox had just twenty-two hours previously been told in the usual solemn way to prepare for death, and as he had calculated largely and correctly upon the merciful character of the administration, he received the awful news as if he had been struck to the earth with lightning. The mistake, upon being mentioned to him, it is unnecessary to state, gave full relief to his heart.'

Mr Knowlys, who at this time filled the office of recorder, was immediately called upon to explain to the Common Hall of the City of London the circumstances attending the very remarkable error into which he had fallen, but having heard from him whatever excuse he had to urge, on Monday 24th of June, they came to the following resolutions:

'Resolved unanimously, That this Common Hall has learnt with feelings of the deepest horror and regret, that the life of John Cox, a convict under sentence of death, in Newgate, had well-nigh been sacrificed by the act of the recorder of London, in sending down a warrant for his execution, notwithstanding His Majesty in privy council had, in the gracious exercise of his royal prerogative of mercy, been pleased to commute his sentence for an inferior punishment.

'Resolved unanimously, That the mildest and most charitable construction which this Common Hall can put upon this conduct of the recorder is, that it was the result of some mental infirmity incident to his advanced age; but contemplating with alarm the dreadful consequences which, though happily averted in the present instance, may possibly ensue from such an infirmity in that important public functionary, this Common Hall feels it an imperative duty to record the solemn expression of its opinion, that the recorder ought forthwith to retire from an office, the vitally important duties of which he is, from whatever cause, incompetent to discharge.'

The recorder, who was present, was received with deep groans. The resolutions of the Common Hall were followed by a Resolution of the Court of Aldermen, announcing the receipt of a communication from the recorder, that from his advanced age, ill-health and debility consequent upon a late very severe fit of illness, he had felt himself bound, after serving the city for more than forty-seven years, upwards of thirty as common-serjeant and recorder, to resign the office of recorder.

The useless form of reporting the cases of felons sentenced to death has since been removed, and the capital penalty in cases of letter-stealing has also been taken away, and the less severe punishment of transportation substituted for it.

The Calthorpe Street Riot

THIS affair, which produced much bitterness of feeling between the people and the Metropolitan Police, occurred on Monday, the 13th of May 1833. For some time before, the streets of London had been placarded with bills announcing the intention of certain parties to hold a meeting in a place called the Calthorpe Estate, at the back of the Cold Bath Fields Prison, its professed object being to adopt measures preparatory to a National Convention being held. In consequence, a government proclamation was issued, declaring a meeting for that purpose to be illegal, and warning all persons to abstain from attending it or taking any part in its proceedings.

This proclamation, there is little doubt, tended in a very material degree to produce the very evil which it was intended to repress. The intention to hold the meeting was little known, for the party by which it was called was an obscure though violent political sect, but the effect of the government notification was to excite the curiosity of many who were driven to the spot, to which otherwise they would have had no attraction, for the purpose of witnessing whatever might take place. Precautions were taken by the Government to secure the public peace, which, had they been adopted in a proper spirit, would have been most praiseworthy. The very consequence, however, of the extensive preparations which were made, was to attract fresh curiosity, and to draw new observers to the scene of the proposed meeting.

The assemblage was appointed to take place at two o'clock, but long before that hour several hundreds of persons had collected upon the spot indicated as the place of convocation. Groups of idlers were to be observed dispersed in different directions, among which women and children were intermingled to a very considerable extent; and there were not wanting among them the partisans of the disaffected, to amuse them with declamations on the sufferings of the people and the necessity of their taking strong measures to obtain redress.

In the meantime, the police force of the metropolis were to be seen marching from all quarters of town towards the scene of action. Between two and three thousand men were placed on duty, all of whom were distributed at certain appointed places of rendezvous, under the orders of their superintendants and inspectors, while Viscount Melbourne, the Home Secretary, and Messrs Rowan and Mayne, the commissioners of police, with a considerable number of police magistrates, sat as a species of council to direct their future movements, at the White Hart tavern in Gray's Inn Lane. The formidable appearance of the police on their march created new food for curiosity, and they were followed by hundreds of persons anxious to ascertain the inducement for such an assemblage. The numbers of the mob collected were thus every moment increased.

At one o'clock, between six and seven hundred persons had assembled, and this crowd, comparatively insignificant considering the parade which had been made, kept gradually swelling until three, when a van was driven up at the end of Calthorpe Street, which a young man named Lee, who was afterwards taken into custody, mounted, together with three or four other shabby-looking persons. At almost the very moment of the van taking its station, however, the driver appeared to become alarmed and, notwithstanding the entreaties of Lee and his companions, drove off. Mr Lee and the others were in consequence compelled to quit their intended rostrum and to adopt one somewhat less convenient, namely, a paling which stood on the spot. Lee was soon raised upon this new pulpit and, after a few prefatory remarks, he proposed that Mr Mee should take the chair. It had been stated that 'The National Union of the Working Classes', a society of men bound together for the purpose of procuring the achievement of certain political objects, would attend the meeting, and their committee was known to be assembled at a neighbouring public-house, called 'The Union', engaged in arranging the programme of the proceedings of the day. Mr Mee was recognized as an active member of the Union, and he was immediately elected chairman by acclamation.

Mr Mee then got upon the paling, and after thanking the meeting for the honour which they had conferred upon him, proceeded to address them upon the objects with which they had been called together. He declared that he was thankful to the ministry for having given the meeting an air of importance which, but for their proceedings, it would have wanted, but the question which they had to consider was whether, as they had met under such disadvantages as surrounded them, they should go on, or whether they should adjourn to a more favourable opportunity? (Cries of 'No, no! Go on!') He was, he said, but a working man with a family, and if they were not prepared to give his family one-tenth of their earnings they should not cry 'go on'. He might fall a martyr in the cause, and in that case, he should expect his family to be supported. (Cries of 'Yes! Yes!')

The 'Union', which had been expected every moment, and for which an anxious look-out was maintained, at this time appeared in sight. The procession, into which it was formed, consisted of about one hundred and fifty persons, and they carried among them eight banners. The most conspicuous of these was one which bore the motto 'Liberty or Death', with a skull and cross-bones on a black ground and a red border: others bore mottoes of 'Holy Alliance of the Working Classes', and 'Equal Rights and Equal Justice'. There were also to be seen a tri-coloured flag, the flag of the American republic, and a pole bearing at its head the Cap of Liberty. The procession with these ensigns walked in good order to the spot at which the speakers had assembled, but they had scarcely taken up their position, when a body of police marched into Calthorpe Street with the greatest order and precision. Their formidable appearance seemed to make a momentary impression on the mob, but a person pointing to the flag bearing the motto 'Liberty or Death', cried out, 'Men, be firm!' and shouts of 'Go on! go on!' instantly resounded from all sides. The police had now reached the middle of the street, the crowd clearing the way for them to advance, and staves in hand they pressed forward to a man who was still addressing the mob. As they advanced near what may be termed the platform, however, they met with much resistance. A conflict ensued, and under circumstances respecting which the evidence was of the most contradictory nature, one policeman named Robert Cully, No 95 of the C division, received a mortal wound from a dagger and died instantly. Two others, Serjeant Brooks of the C division, and constable Redwood of the C division, were wounded with the same or a similar instrument.

In the course of the afternoon a great number of persons who had been observed to be active in the proceedings of the day, were taken into custody, and all the flags were captured. By six o'clock the whole of the mob had been dispersed and quiet was restored.

Pursuant to the instructions of Viscount Melbourne, the prisoners who had been secured were taken to Bow Street on the same evening to be examined before Sir F. A. Roe, the chief magistrate. The whole street was filled with persons interested in the fate of the prisoners, and the proceedings excited a vast degree of interest. The result of the examinations taken on that night was the remand of a person named Robert Tilly, on suspicion of having been concerned in the murder of Cully (a charge which subsequently proved unfounded), and of a man named Fursey, on the charge of stabbing Redwood and Brooks. A great number of others were held to bail, or fined for the various offences of assault, or rioting, preferred against them.

On Thursday, Fursey was fully committed on the capital charge of stabbing Redwood and Brooks, and on the next day, a true bill was returned against him by the Grand Jury.

On Wednesday, May the 15th, an inquest was held before Mr Stirling, the coroner for Middlesex, on the body of Cully. The investigation lasted for several days, and the inquest-room and the neighbourhood of the house where the jury sat, were crowded by persons interested in the proceedings. A great number of witnesses were examined, many of whom declared that the police had acted towards the people with unwarrantable harshness, striking and beating them with their truncheons, making no distinction between active parties in the meeting and defenceless women, but conducting themselves with equal and undue severity towards all, and that they had been guilty of this misconduct without any provocation being offered. On the other hand, it was sworn, that the mob were violent, and that many of them were armed with formidable weapons. Truncheons loaded with lead were used by them in striking the police, and the pikes upon which their banners were mounted were headed with iron, in obedience to instructions published by Colonel Maceroni, which were contained in a book called *Defensive Instructions for the People*. It was admitted, however, that there was no disposition to riot among the people until the arrival of the police, that neither the Riot Act nor the Government Proclamation was read, and it was further proved, that the deceased had struck the man who wounded him before the wound was given. In reference to this part of the case there was considerable contradiction in the evidence, for one witness distinctly swore that the deceased was speaking to her, and desiring her to go home, when a man suddenly rushed from the mob and stabbed him, and grave and important doubts appeared to exist as to the proper result to be arrived at. At the conclusion of the inquest on Monday, May the 20th, the jury returned the following verdict: 'We find a verdict of JUSTIFIABLE HOMICIDE on these grounds: that no Riot Act was read, nor any proclamation advising the people to disperse; that the Government did not take the proper precautions to prevent the meeting from assembling, and that the conduct of the police was ferocious, brutal, and unprovoked by the people. We moreover express our anxious hope that the Government will in future take better precautions to prevent the recurrence of such disgraceful transactions in the metropolis.'

The announcement of this finding was received with immense cheering among the people assembled, but not without remonstrance on the part of the coroner. He urged the jury to reconsider their decision, but with obstinate pertinacity they refused to alter the determination to which they had arrived.

The verdict was, however, declared by the law officers of the Crown to be at variance with law and with the evidence on which it was founded, and on Thursday, May the 30th, upon the motion of the attorney-general in the Court of King's Bench, the inquisition was quashed.

On Thursday, July the 4th, the trial of George Fursey took place at the Old Bailey. He was indicted for having riotously and tumultuously assembled at Cold Bath Fields, on the 13th of May, with five hundred others, and with having assaulted and wounded Sergeant Brooks, and Redwood, the constable, with intent to murder them.

The evidence by which it was sought to bring home the charge to the prisoner was first the positive declarations of Brooks and Redwood, that the prisoner was the man who had stabbed them, and secondly, the allegation by a man named Hayles, a constable, that after the prisoner had been apprehended, he was conveyed to a stable, where he and Tilley were confined together. They lay down on some straw, and when they had been removed to a lock-up house, the witness found on the spot where they had lain, a loaded pistol and a powder-flask, which Tilley had acknowledged belonged to him, and also a short dagger apparently made out of a foil blade, which was alleged by Redwood and Brooks to be exactly similar to that with which they had been stabbed and which besides was found to correspond in shape with the wounds which they had received. Here, as well as before the coroner's jury, there was much contradictory evidence as to the conduct of the police. Many witnesses were called for the defence, who described their demeanour as having been extremely violent, and who said that they saw them strike many persons whose proceedings had not rendered such a course justifiable. The trial lasted until two o'clock in the morning, the defence being conducted by Messrs C. Phillips and Clarkson, and Mr Justice Gazelee having summed up, the jury pronounced the prisoner 'Not Guilty'. This determination was received with loud demonstrations of applause by the people assembled within and outside the court, which the judges and officers in vain attempted to repress.

Much ill-feeling was produced by this unfortunate affair towards the police and the Government. The police at their establishment had been exceedingly unpopular, from the military constitution of the force, but their usefulness had now begun to counterbalance the feeling which had so unfavourably prevailed. Their conduct at the Calthorpe Street riot did much to make them hateful to the lower orders, who were unable to draw the distinction between the intemperance of a few and the usefulness of the main body. The conduct of the mob can be justified only by the attack which it is clear was made upon them, but the act of murder and the attempt made to kill or disable Brooks and Redwood, are offences which appear to have been quite unwarranted by the circumstances which preceded them.

Fursey, after his trial, recovered 40*l* damages against the proprietor of *The Morning Chronicle* newspaper, for publishing a libel, imputing to him the murder of Cully. Tilley, whose name has been mentioned, was liberated on bail, on Fursey's acquittal taking place, the charge against him, as has been already said, being found to be without foundation.

JAMES LOVELACE and others, transported for administering Unlawful Oaths

IN the instance of the riot in Calthorpe Street, reference has been made to a combination or union of the working classes, confederated for the purpose of securing certain political objects. The system of 'Unions', which was commenced in the metropolis and the larger towns of the kingdom, was not, however, confined exclusively to those thickly populated districts, nor were the objects of these societies limited to those which were merely of a political nature. In various parts of the country associations were formed with a view of maintaining the prices of labour, and with other objects more especially connected with the social welfare of the community.

The case of the Dorchester labourers is one which has attracted a vast degree of general observation and attention. The evil effects of the system may be collected from the following statement of the charges preferred against them, at the Dorchester assizes, on the 17th of March 1834, and of the facts which were proved in evidence upon their trial.

The names of the prisoners were James Lovelace, George Lovelace, Thomas Stanfield, John Stanfield, James Hammet and James Brine, and they were indicted for 'administering and causing to be administered, and aiding and assisting, and being present at, and consenting to administer, a certain unlawful oath and engagement, purporting to bind the person taking the same not to inform or give evidence against any associate or other person charged with any unlawful combination, and not to reveal or discover any such unlawful combination, or any illegal act done or to be done, and not to discover any illegal oath which might be taken.' Mr Gambier stated that the charge against the prisoners was that on a certain day in December, they, all together, or one of them, administered an unlawful oath to a person of the name of Legg, for the purpose of binding the party to whom it was administered not to disclose any illegal combination which had been formed, and not to inform or give evidence against any person associated with them, and not to reveal any unlawful oath which might be taken. The first part of the charge was that the purport of the oath was to bind the party to obey the orders of a body of men not lawfully constituted. The indictment was framed on an Act of the 37th George III, cap. 123, and his lordship would be aware that the preamble of that act related to seditious meetings, but the enacting part was of a more general nature, including confederacies not formed merely for seditious purposes, but for any illegal purpose whatever. There was an authority which had decided that the enacting part of the statute was not restrained by the preamble, but extended to all societies the object of which was unlawful. One clause of the act related to oaths administered for the purpose of binding a party not to reveal an unlawful combination. The allegation in the indictment was that the prisoners administered an illegal oath to certain persons, binding them not to disclose an illegal confederacy. It would be for them to see whether the facts bore out the conclusion to which he had come, that a combination formed under the circumstances that would be stated, was a combination which the law had pronounced to be illegal, and would depend on this—whether any member was required to take any oath of this description, or any oath which the law did not require or authorize. He would, therefore, show that the combination was illegal—that it was the practice of the association to administer oaths, and that they were administered, and that the members were bound to obey the commands of men not legally constituted, and that they were bound to secrecy. With regard to the form of the oath and the mode of administering it, it was proper he should call his lordship's attention to the 5th section of the 37th George III, cap. 123, which provided that any engagement in the nature of an oath should be deemed an oath within the meaning of the act in whatever form or manner the same should be administered.

The learned counsel then proceeded to state the facts of the case to the jury, and to call his witnesses. From the evidence it appeared that the prisoners were agricultural labourers, and that on the day stated in the indictment Legg and others were conducted to the house of Thomas Stanfield at Tolpuddle and, after waiting a short time, were blindfolded and taken into a room, when certain papers were read over to them while on their knees: on the bandage being taken from their eyes, they saw the figure of a skeleton with the words 'Remember your end' written over it. They were then sworn to obey the rules and regulations of the society, and not to divulge its secrets or proceedings. They were to pay a shilling on entrance, and a penny a week afterwards, to support the men who were out of work (those who had struck) till their masters raised their wages. The defendants were all present, and Lovelace wore a dress like a surplice. The general laws of the society were produced and read to the jury, from which it was collected that the society was to be called 'The Friendly Society of Agricultural Labourers'. Regular officers and periods of meeting were appointed, and the mode of making collections pointed out. The twentieth and twenty-first rules were as follows: 'That if any master attempts to reduce the wages of his workmen, if they are members of this order they shall instantly communicate the same to the corresponding secretary, in order that they may receive the support of the grand lodge; and in the meantime they shall use their utmost endeavours to finish the work they may have in hand, if any, and shall assist each other so that they may all leave the place together and with as much promptitude as possible.' 'That if any member of this society renders himself obnoxious to his employer solely on account of taking an active part in the affairs of this order, and if guilty of no violation or insult to his master, and shall be discharged from his employment solely on consequence thereof, either before or after the turn-out, then the whole body of men at that place shall instantly leave the place, and no member of this society shall be allowed to take work at that place until such member be reinstated in his situation.'

After the counsel for the defendants had addressed the court, contending that no offence had been proved, the judge summed up, enforcing on the jury that they must satisfy themselves as to the illegality of the oath which Legg had taken, and which had been administered to other members of the society. The precise formality of the oath, his lordship observed, was not under inquiry; but the Act of Parliament referred to an oath fixing an obligation on a party to whom it is administered. To sustain and prove this charge, the jury must be satisfied that the oath administered to Legg was to bind him not to divulge the secrets of the society: if so, it came within the meaning of the act. It was also a question whether the dress of James Lovelace, which resembled a clergyman's surplice, was not intended to give a degree of solemnity and additional force to the proceedings. The representation of a skeleton seemed also to have been intended to strike awe on the minds of the persons to whom the oath was administered. In taking the oath, if they were satisfied that it was intended as an obligation on the conscience of the person taking it, it clearly came within the meaning of the act. His lordship proceeded to remark on the rules of the society, which spoke of the violation of an obligation, evidently referring to the oath which was administered by the prisoners, and that such violation would be deemed by the society a crime. His lordship also read from a book belonging to the society the names of several persons (the prisoners among others), who had contributed to its funds, leaving the jury to draw their conclusions from these facts, and the whole chain of evidence which had been repeated to them. The jury, after about five minutes' consultation, found all the prisoners 'Guilty', and they were sentenced to be transported for seven years.

In pursuance of this sentence the prisoners were subsequently conveyed to New South Wales by the Surrey transport ship, the offence of which they had been convicted being deemed to be of a nature so heinous as not to be expiated by an imprisonment in this country. This proceeding was looked upon by the political supporters of the system of unions as one which was exceedingly harsh and unjustifiable under the circumstances of the case, and loud and repeated remonstrances were made, both within and without the walls of parliament, against it. For a considerable time the Government declared its unwillingness to interfere to direct any amelioration in the punishment directed to be inflicted upon the offenders, but at length they yielded to the constant exertions of the friends of the prisoners and granted a free pardon to them all.

At the commencement of the year 1838, those who had chosen to return to England were landed at Plymouth—several of them, however, having preferred to remain in the colony to which they had been transported. An attempt was made to excite great sympathy in their behalf, and a species of public entry was made by them into London, but the whole affair turned out a failure, and the good sense of the general order of people was found to have induced a feeling not altogether in accordance with a supposition that these men had been martyrs.

This case takes a most important place in the history of trade unions. It is better known as the case of the 'Tolpuddle Martyrs', because it was in a house at Tolpuddle that the offence of administering unlawful oaths was committed. The details are fully set out in the text and the relevant passage from the indictment is cited. The offence was to administer an oath to a man named Legg and other persons binding them not to inform or give evidence against any persons charged with an unlawful combination. By the common law of England combinations of workpeople were generally regarded as illegal. They were held to be contrary to public policy and were described as conspiracies in restraint of trade. To be a member of such a body was to commit an offence punishable by fine and imprisonment, and although the common law applied equally to combinations of masters, it was only against the men that the common law was enforced. On the statute book of England from the time of Edward I to the early nineteenth century there were no less than forty statutes embodying the common law against unlawful combinations in one form or another. The great objective was to prohibit labourers joining together to improve their conditions.

A Select Committee of the House of Commons which reported in 1824 had condemned the combination laws as useless and dangerous and recommended the repeal of the statutes and the alteration of the common law. This was in fact done, but in 1825 another Select Committee was appointed to reconsider the situation and in consequence of their recommendations the legislation of 1824 was repealed and the common law restored to its former state. The Act of 1825 provided however that no persons were liable to punishment for meeting together for the sole purpose of consulting upon and determining the rate of wages or prices . . . or the hours for which they would work. . . . But all persons were subject to a maximum punishment of three months' imprisonment with hard labour who should by violence, threats or intimidation or obstruction . . . do certain things defined in the statute inconsistent with freedom of contract. This partial protection naturally led to a great advance in the growth of trade

Courtenay shooting Lieutenant Bennett during the Canterbury riots (pages 229–30)

unions and the Grand National Consolidated Trades Union came into being in 1834 but was not destined to have a long life because of the attitude of the Government as displayed in the prosecution of the Dorchester agricultural labourers described in this case. A sentence of seven years' transportation was a very heavy sentence and it is interesting to see that public opinion was not ready unanimously to support it. When, however, a free pardon was eventually granted to all the defendants only a lukewarm welcome was given to them on their return to England.

In the nineteenth and twentieth centuries the legislation concerning trade unions placed the unions in a position of security and they now form part of the industrial life of Britain recognized by governments as essential to the life of the community.

At the present time it is still an offence to administer an unlawful oath but the oath must bind the party taking it to engage in a seditious or mutinous purpose, or to disturb the public peace, or to be of some confederacy formed for any such purpose or some matter of the like kind.

Riots at Canterbury

THESE singular but mischievous riots occurred on Thursday, the 31st of May 1838, at a place called Bossenden Wood, situated about five miles from the ancient city of Canterbury, and were the result of the pranks of a madman who had assumed the title of Sir William Percy Honeywood Courtenay, Knight of Malta, and whose insane spirit communicated itself to the rustics, and produced severely calamitous consequences. The infatuation with which this insane impostor was followed, and even worshipped, by the peasantry of the district into which he intruded himself, affords a striking and melancholy proof of the magic powers of fanaticism. But while one is not surprised that among the lower orders he should find persons incapable of resisting his wily and specious arguments and the impudent falsehood of his assertions, it cannot but be the subject of the greatest astonishment that he should have procured the countenance, during a very considerable period, of individuals of superior rank and education in the county.

The best mode of introducing this extraordinary event will be by detailing succinctly the circumstances of the early life of the supposed Sir William Courtenay. The real name of this pretender was John Nichols Thom, and he was the son of a small farmer and maltster at St Columb in Cornwall. While yet a lad, he procured employment in the establishment of Messrs Plumer and Turner, wine-merchants of Truro, as cellarman, but after five years' service, the firm was broken up and the business ceased. Thom now commenced trading on his own account, as a wine-merchant, maltster and hop-dealer, and for three or four years he carried on his trade with great apparent respectability. At the end of that time his premises and stock were consumed by an accidental fire, and he recovered from an Insurance office, for the losses which he alleged he had sustained by this event, the sum of 3000*l*, being a much larger amount than many judged him to be entitled to. Subsequently he rebuilt his house and continued his trade, and, after about two years more, he made a considerable sum of money by a successful venture in malt which he disposed of in Liverpool. For two years after this event he was lost sight of by his friends and it was presumed that he was out of England, and the first intimation which was received of his return was his declaring himself a candidate to represent the city of Canterbury in Parliament, under the name of Sir William Courtenay, in the month of December 1832. He was found to have taken up his residence at the Rose Hotel, Canterbury, and the splendour of his dress, and the eccentricity of his manners, soon gained for him many admirers, even among the respectable inhabitants of the town. During his canvass he increased the number of his friends, and his success in procuring supporters was most extraordinary. His effort, however, was not fortunate. His opponent candidates were the Hon R. Watson and Lord Fordwich, the former of whom obtained 832 votes and the latter 802, while Courtenay polled 375. This attempt gained him many friends, and great popularity among the lower orders. His persuasive language was exceedingly useful to him, but the peculiarity of his dress, combined with the absurdity of many of his protestations, induced a belief among some of those to whom he procured introduction that he was insane.

After his defeat, he did not confine his proceedings to Canterbury alone, but passed through most of the towns in Kent, declaiming against the poor laws, the revenue laws, and other portions of the statutes of the realm which are usually considered by the poor to be obnoxious to their interests. By his speeches he obtained much éclat, but his exertions in favour of some smugglers led him into a scrape, from which he was likely to have suffered serious consequences. An action took place near the Goodwin Sands in the month of July 1833 between the revenue cruiser *Lively* and the *Admiral Hood* smuggler, and, in the course of the flight of the latter vessel and her exertions to escape from the *Lively*, her crew were observed to throw a great number of tubs overboard, which, on their being picked up, proved to contain spirit. The *Admiral Hood* was captured, but no contraband goods were found on board, and, on the men being taken into custody, Courtenay presented himself as a witness before the magistrates. He swore positively that he had seen the whole of the action, and that no tubs had been thrown from the *Admiral Hood*. He further stated, that he had observed those which had been picked up by the revenue men floating in the sea all day. This was so diametrically opposed to the truth, that a prosecution for perjury was determined on, and he was indicted at the Maidstone Assizes on the 25th of July 1833. A verdict of conviction followed, and Mr Justice Park, the presiding judge, passed a sentence of imprisonment, to be followed by seven years' transportation. The difficulty in which he was placed, however, having reached the knowledge of his friends in Cornwall, they made representations to the Home Secretary that he was insane, and, after having suffered four years' confinement in a lunatic asylum at Barming Heath, he was at length liberated, on bail being given for his future good behaviour.

He now took up his abode at the residence of Mr Francis, a gentleman of fortune, of Fairbrook near Boughton in the neighbourhood of Canterbury, and speedily resumed his wild efforts to gain popularity for himself. His dress now was similar to that which he had worn before his incarceration; and the following sketch of his personal appearance, extracted from the romance of *Rookwood* by Mr Ainsworth, well describes him. 'A magnificent coal-black beard decorated the chin of this worthy; but this was not all—his costume was in perfect keeping with his beard, and consisted of a very theatrical-looking tunic, upon the breast of which was embroidered in golden wire the Maltese Cross; while on his shoulders were thrown the ample folds of a cloak of Tyrian hue. To his side was girt a long and doughty sword, which he termed, in his knightly phrase, Excalibur; and upon his profuse hair rested a hat as broad in the brim as a Spanish sombrero. Exaggerated as this description may appear, we can assure our readers that it is not overdrawn.'

His impositions, unfortunately, proved as mischievous as they were plausible. He succeeded in persuading many of the ignorant peasantry that his origin was as high as that of the Saviour. His visits to the cottages of the labouring classes were numerous, and his striking appearance seems to have had considerable influence upon the minds both of men and women. Many of the poor people believed that he was in the habit of receiving barrels of sovereigns every week to meet his current expenses, and that he was the rightful owner of some of the largest estates in Kent, from the possession of which he was only driven by the violence and fraud of their present holders.

A misunderstanding with Mr Francis compelled his retirement from that gentleman's house, and he took up his abode at the residence of one of his most devoted followers named Wills, from whence subsequently he again removed to the farm house of a person named Culver, at Boughton. During these changes he was constant in his exertions among the poorer classes, and the influence which he obtained over them was extraordinary. The women excited their husbands and sons to join him, 'because he was Christ, and unless they followed him, fire would come from Heaven and burn them'. They asserted, as he had declared, that 'he had come to earth upon a cloud, and would go away from it on a cloud'; and instances were not infrequent in which the misguided people, the subjects of his imposture, had actually worshipped him as a God.

At length this excitement was destined to be brought to a conclusion, but not without the occurrence of events which are deeply to be lamented.

On Monday, the 28th of May, Courtenay, with about ten or fifteen followers, sallied forth from the village of Boughton, without having any very distinct or apparent object in view, and proceeded at once to the cottage of Wills. Here they formed themselves into a species of column, and a loaf having been procured, it was broken in halves and one half of it was placed on the top of a pole, which bore a flag of blue and white upon which a lion rampant was drawn. Wills having joined them, they all proceeded to Goodnestone, near Faversham, Courtenay, as they went along, haranguing them and the country people whom they met, and producing a great deal of excitement and astonishment at his proceedings. From thence they went to a farm at Herne Hill, where they received food, and then to Dargate Common. By Courtenay's desire they all went to prayers here, and after that they returned to Bossenden Farm, where they retired to rest in a barn. At three o'clock on Tuesday morning, they went to Sittingbourne, and Courtenay provided them with breakfast, for which he paid twenty-seven shillings, and then they went to Newnham where, at the George Inn, they had a similar treat. After visiting Eastling, Throwley, Seldwich, Lees and Selling, where, as at Sittingbourne and Newnham, speeches were made and new followers obtained, the party again returned to Bossenden Farm.

During these progresses, it appears that Mr Curling, a respectable farmer, lost some of his labourers who were enticed away from their work by the crowd, and disinclined to permit them to join the riotous proceedings of Courtenay and his party, he went before a magistrate of the district, by whom a warrant was issued for their apprehension. Nicholas Mears, a constable, and his brother, were entrusted with the warrant for execution, and on Thursday morning at about six o'clock they went to Culver's farm-house to secure the men. Upon their presenting themselves, Courtenay and several of his followers appeared, and almost before the unfortunate Mears could state his object, Courtenay drew a pistol from his breast and shot him dead. He returned into the house, exclaiming to the men who were there, 'Now, am I not your Saviour?' and going out again, he discharged a second pistol at the body of Mears and mutilated it with his sword.

This diabolical murder was communicated to the magistrates directly afterwards, and they proceeded to take steps for the apprehension of Courtenay. But the latter immediately called out his men and marched them to Bossenden Wood, and there he administered the sacrament to them in bread and water. This over, a man named Alexander Foad knelt down in the presence of the rest and worshipped him, and while on his knees, he demanded to know whether he should follow him in the body or whether he should go home, and follow him in the spirit? Courtenay answered, 'In the body,' upon which Foad jumped up with great exultation, exclaiming 'Oh! be joyful, be joyful; the Saviour has accepted me. Now go on; I will follow you till I drop.' Another man, named Blanchard, also worshipped him. Courtenay then, in answer to a question which was put to him, said that he had shot the constable and had eaten a good breakfast afterwards, and added, 'I was only executing the justice of heaven in consequence of the power God has given me.' At twelve o'clock Sir William and his followers had shifted their position to the Osier-bed, and here he harangued them, informing them that he was invulnerable, and that they also could not be hurt by reason of the faith they put in him. He defied the attack of the magistrates, which he declared would do neither him nor them any harm, but then he proposed that they should take up a position in ambush in the wood. This was agreed to, and on their way thither, seeing the Rev Mr Handley of Herne Hill observing their motions, Courtenay fired at him but happily missed his aim.

In the meantime, the magistrates had been taking such steps as they deemed advisable for the maintenance of the public peace, and in order to secure the person of the leader of these extraordinary proceedings with his followers. Acquainted with the desperate violence of Courtenay, by his act of the morning, they deemed it unfit that an unarmed force should be brought in opposition to him and his party, and they in consequence dispatched a messenger to Canterbury, requiring the aid of the military. A detachment of one hundred men of the 45th Foot, under the command of Major Armstrong, was at once placed at their disposal and marched to Boughton. The rioters were known to be posted in Bossenden Wood, from the information of outscouts, and in that direction the troops, accompanied by the magistrates and special constables, were marched. The position of Courtenay was ascertained to be about a mile from the road in Bossenden Wood. The wood was of very considerable extent, but was intersected by two roads; and it was found that the insurgent party were placed so that their front and rear were covered by the roads right and left. The military were in consequence divided; and while one party of fifty under the command of Captain Reed took the road nearest Canterbury, the other was conducted by Major Armstrong, assisted by Lieutenant Bennett and Lieutenant Prendergast, along the road next Boulton-under-Blea. Thus the insurgents were placed between the two bodies of troops and their only chance of escape was to take a straight line through the woods. For this, however, the madman who was their leader was in no wise disposed, and he soon presented himself to Major Armstrong's troop. He was required to surrender, but without waiting to give any answer, he called upon his followers—now only between thirty and forty in number—as if to prepare for the approaching conflict and rushed at Lieutenant Bennett, who was rather in advance of the soldiers. Lieutenant Bennett observing this movement, rushed forward also, sword in hand, but almost before he had reached his assailant, Courtenay presented a pistol, fired, and the ball entered the right side and passed completely through the body of the young officer, killing him instantaneously. At this moment Courtenay was felled to the ground by a constable named Millwood, but he jumped up again, and at the instant of his regaining his feet, he was shot by the troops. The order to 'fire', was then given by Major Armstrong, and being mounted, he dashed in among the peasantry. By the discharge eight men were killed on the spot, and several others were wounded; but the wretched peasantry fought desperately, until at length, perceiving the dreadful consequences which must result from persevering in their resistance, they dispersed and scattered themselves through the woods. In the course of the afternoon twenty-seven prisoners were made by the military and constables, and of these seven were wounded, two of them mortally. Of the party who were employed in maintaining the law, George Catt, a constable, who acted with much determination, was shot, and Lieutenant Prendergast received a contused wound on the head from the bludgeon of an insurgent.

During the remainder of the week the coroner of the county was engaged in conducting the necessary inquiries into the cause of death of the deceased persons. Verdicts of 'Wilful Murder' were returned against Courtenay and his adherents, in the cases of the constable Mears and Lieutenant Bennett, while in the case of Catt, the jury found 'That he had been killed upon an erroneous belief that he was a rioter'. In the cases of death which had occurred amongst the insurgents, the jury found a verdict of 'Justifiable Homicide'. The scene which presented itself, during the sitting of the jury, was distressing in the extreme. The Red Lion at Boughton was the place at which the coroner conducted the investigation, and there also all those prisoners who were suffering from the wounds which they had received were detained, while in the stable attached to the house, the bodies of the slain were extended. In the yard were the wives, widows and children of these deluded men, lamenting bitterly the position of danger into which the fanaticism of their relations had drawn them. During the sitting of the jury, two of the wounded men died and, upon their decease being communicated to the crowd outside, they gave vent to new expressions of grief. The body of Lieutenant Bennett lay in an upper chamber of the inn and was a melancholy spectacle. The unfortunate gentleman was about twenty-five years of age, and had just obtained leave of absence when, the news of the riots reaching the barracks, he applied for and obtained permission to join the party.

At the conclusion of the proceedings before the coroner and the magistrates, the following prisoners were committed for trial, viz: Thomas Mears *alias* Tyler (the cousin of the murdered constable), Alexander Foad, William Nutting, William Price, James Goodwin, William Wills, William Spratt, John Spratt, John Silk, Edward Curling, Samuel Edwards, Sarah Culver, Thomas Myers *alias* Edward Wraight, Charles Hills, Thomas Ovenden, William Couchworth, Thomas Griggs, William Foad and Richard Foreman.

The prisoners Mears, Alexander Foad and Couchworth were wounded. Foad was a respectable farmer, cultivating a farm of about sixty acres, and it was a matter of some surprise that he should have been implicated in so extraordinary a proceeding. The prisoner Sarah Culver was a woman about forty years of age, of respectable connexions, and possessing considerable property. She had been a devoted follower of Courtenay, but it was presumed that she, like him, was insane. The other prisoners were all persons of inferior station.

On Tuesday, the 5th of June, the greater number of those who had been killed at the riot were interred in the churchyard of Herne Hill. Amongst these was Courtenay; and the funeral attracted a vast assemblage to the place. Considerable apprehensions were entertained lest the mob should use any violence to prevent the burial of their late fanatical leader, for many had been heard to declare their firm belief that he would 'rise again', but the whole affair passed off quietly and no new outrage was committed. The bodies of the other deceased persons were buried by their friends.

At the Maidstone Assizes, on Thursday, the 9th of August 1838, the trial of the prisoners commenced before Lord Denman.

The first persons who were tried were Mears and Price, and after a long investigation they were found guilty of being parties to the murder of Mears the constable, but recommended to mercy, on the ground of their having been led astray by their infatuation in favour of Courtenay.

Sentence of death was at once passed upon the prisoners, but they were informed that their lives would be spared.

On the next day, William Wills, Thomas Myers *alias* Edward Wraight, Alex. Foad, Edward Curling, Thomas Griggs, Richard Foreman, Charles Hills and William Foad were indicted for the murder of Lieutenant Bennett, but upon their being arraigned they pleaded guilty, on the same understanding as that which existed in the former case, namely, that their lives should be spared. The prosecutions in the cases of the other prisoners were not proceeded with, and they were discharged from custody.

On Friday, the 17th of August, the extent of the commutation of the punishment of the convicts was made known to them. Mears and Wills were ordered to be transported for life; Price was ordered to be transported for ten years; and Wraight, the two Foads, Curling, Griggs, Foreman and Hills were directed to undergo one year's imprisonment and hard labour in the House of Correction, during which, each of them was to pass one month in solitary confinement. A pension of 40*l* per annum was granted to the widow of Mears the constable, in consideration of the death of her husband.

The unfortunate Courtenay appears to have been a man by no means devoid of ability, and who had turned what little education he possessed to the very best account. His speeches were energetic and well put together, and he possessed an ample flow of language. He was abundantly supplied with scriptural quotations, and appeared to be fully and intimately acquainted with the Old and New Testaments.

Shortly before the dreadful affray in which he lost his life, he left off the picturesque attire in which he had hitherto been in the habit of dressing, and assumed one of a more homely character. This was a blouse or frock of brown holland with a black belt, in which he carried a brace of pistols; and a round hat. He was usually also armed with a sword and dagger, but his miserable followers possessed no other weapons than those which the hedges or woods through which they passed afforded them. It is remarkable that none of them were of so low a station as to render it at all probable that want had induced them to listen to the insane promises of their leader. The precise object which was held in view appears to have been unknown even to the misguided men themselves; but the general impression was, that Courtenay, by his power, would take possession of all the private estates of the county, which he would bestow upon his trusty followers. The Sunday after the riot, according to the statements and promises which he made, was to have been 'a glorious but a bloody day', and some persons did not scruple to assert that it was his intention on that day to fire Canterbury. It is probable, therefore, that the distressing events of the 31st of May served to prevent the occurrence of scenes even more terrible.

The visual proof of the existence of a degree of superstition so gross as that which is shown here to have been exhibited is almost necessary to induce its belief, but there can be no doubt that the lamentable ignorance and fanaticism of the peasantry was even more striking than we have described it to be. The general happy contentedness of the inhabitants of the county of Kent, the proximity of their position to the metropolis, and the high state of cultivation to which the soil of that county has been brought, one would have thought would have tended to forbid the possibility of such occurrences among them. These remarkable details, however, only serve to afford an additional proof of the facility with which the human mind is moved, and how open it is to the operations of the allurements of fanaticism.

George Cant, Convicted of Rape

THE case of this individual presents circumstances of so remarkable a character to our notice, that we should be guilty of a neglect of our duty if we omitted their recital.

At the Central Criminal Court on Thursday, the 31st of October 1839, George Cant, a publican aged forty years, was indicted for a rape upon Jane Bolland, and in order that the course which the case took may be understood, we shall repeat the evidence which was given by the witnesses at the trial in preference to a general narrative of the proceedings.

Jane Bolland deposed that she resided with her brother in Solomon Terrace, St George's-in-the-East. On the 30th of September she went to live as barmaid at the Windsor Castle public-house, Holborn, kept by the prisoner. She slept in one of the attics and the prisoner and his wife slept in the room underneath. The prisoner called her on the morning of Thursday, the 3rd of October. When she came down to the bar, the prisoner patted her on the cheek with something; he laid his hand upon her breast and insisted upon kissing her. She threatened to inform Mrs Cant of his conduct, and he said, 'What the eye did not see the heart would not believe.' He then wished her to leave the door of her room open that he might come in when he came to call her in the morning, but she told him that she was not the sort of person he imagined her to be and left the parlour. In the course of the day her brother and a person named Balfour called upon her, and she communicated to them what the prisoner had said and done to her. Mr Balfour said that, after what had passed, he did not think the prisoner would again attempt to use indecent liberties with her, and her brother, at the suggestion of Mr Balfour, advised her not to leave her situation. Subsequently on that day she became unwell, and about eight o'clock in the evening she was conveyed upstairs to bed, but she was then so ill that she could not recollect who went up to her room with her. She was insensible when she reached her bed, but during the night she partially recovered, and then she found the prisoner at the bedside. He placed one of his hands upon her mouth to prevent her calling out, a struggle took place and she fainted. There was a candle on the table in the room. About six o'clock in the morning she recovered her senses, and found her clothes, which had not been taken off, in disorder, and the bone of her stays broken: the offence charged in the indictment had been committed when she was in a state of insensibility. She then saw the prisoner standing at the door of her room, and she cried out to him, 'You villain, you shall not come in.' He answered that she was a drunkard and should not again enter his bar. She went downstairs to inform Mrs Cant of what the prisoner had done, but when she told that person that her husband had used indecent liberties with her, Mrs Cant said, 'I will not hear you, you drunken hussy.' She immediately left the house and went to her brother's, where she told what had happened to her. On the Saturday following she was examined by a medical gentleman.

On her cross-examination by Mr C. Phillips, who appeared for the prisoner, she stated that a young man named Joseph Edwards had slept at her master's house on the night of the 3rd of October, and that he accompanied her home on the next day. He was a friend of Mr Cant's and she had observed him in attendance at the Court. She was subject to a swimming in the head, and was suffering from this complaint when she went to bed on the evening in question. She was not intoxicated and had taken nothing during the whole day, with the exception of one glass of half-and-half.

The brother of the prosecutrix and Mr Balfour, a wine-merchant's clerk, corroborated that part of the evidence of the witness, which referred to her conversation with them. Bolland further deposed, that his sister had some years previously suffered from a severe attack of erysipelas in her head, from the effects of which she had been for some time insane. She was still occasionally subject to determination of blood to the head.

The wife of Bolland, and the medical man referred to, both gave evidence which left no doubt that the offence which was complained of by the prosecutrix had been committed upon her person, and Mrs Bolland declared that her sister-in-law, when she saw her on the Friday, exhibited all the agitation which might be supposed to be incident to such an occurrence.

The prisoner was proved to have been taken into custody by

a constable named Wells, when he said that he had 'only kissed the girl'. This closed the case for the prosecution.

Mr Phillips then addressed the jury for the prisoner, and disclosed a most extraordinary defence on his behalf. He disclaimed all intention of impeaching the young woman's character and was happy that he had no reason for making even an insinuation against her in regard to her conduct previous to this occasion. That she was deeply to be commiserated he owned, and that she had come here to tell what she believed to be the truth, he had not the least doubt. He was sure, however, that both reason and a sense of justice would compel the jury (if the witnesses he intended to call for the prisoner should speak the truth) to say that they could not see their way through the case, and that such doubt was created in their minds, as would warrant them in acquitting the man at the bar.

He approached the defence of the prisoner with the greatest anxiety of mind, because, if the evidence he intended to adduce should be discredited, the consequences to the prisoner would be truly awful. The giddiness in the head had induced those who had only been acquainted with the girl for four or five days to believe that she was intoxicated; and this was most natural, for the swimming in the head would produce all the appearances of intoxication. She was taken upstairs by a servant of the prisoner, who would describe her appearance at the time, and would also state that the young man Edwards came to the door with her. That she had been violated there was not the least doubt, but that the prisoner had committed the offence was by no means clear, and it would be his duty to call the young man Edwards, who, if he (Mr Phillips) was rightly informed, would state that he was the guilty party. The young woman had given her evidence very fairly, however, and had doubtless stated only what she considered to be truth. After Mr Cant had been committed, Edwards had called at the office of Mr Williams, the solicitor for the prisoner, and made a disclosure which left no doubt of the innocence of the man at the bar. He did not mean for an instant to justify the conduct of Edwards, and it was a pity that he did not make all the amends in his power to the young woman. He was a young unmarried man and might have done so. It was unlikely the prisoner committed the offence, for, if he had been guilty, it was not probable that he would have conducted himself towards the young woman as she had stated he had done in the morning after she had recovered from her illness. He (Mr Phillips) believed he had been a foolish man in using even the liberty he himself confessed he had done with the girl, and it would be a warning to others to beware of the consequences of the smallest deviation from a virtuous line of conduct. The liberty he had used in the morning had induced the girl to suppose that he had committed the capital offence upon her during the night. Unfortunately there were many cases in which the innocent suffered for the guilty, but there was no instance in which the innocent had actually come forward to place himself in the situation of the guilty. It was very unlikely that an individual, entirely innocent of a capital charge like the present, would come forward and put a rope about his neck, in order to free the man who had actually committed the crime. He could not, therefore, see any reason to throw doubt on the testimony of Edwards.

Jane Hollier was then called, and, on being sworn, stated that she was at the Windsor Castle public-house, when this transaction was stated to have occurred. At about eight o'clock she assisted the prosecutrix to bed. Witness thought she was in a state of intoxication at the time. About twelve o'clock witness again went up to the bedroom of the prosecutrix, accompanied by Joseph Edwards. Edwards remained at the door while she went in. She asked him to come up with her, as there was only one candle. The poor girl was lying on the bed, with her clothes on, asleep; witness covered her with blankets. Witness was in the room about five minutes, and the door was closed during that time. When she came out she found Edwards at the door. She gave him the light and he went towards his bedroom. She neither saw the prosecutrix nor Edwards again that night.

Cross-examined by Mr Adolphus: The prosecutrix was not able to speak on her way upstairs. She heard the prosecutrix say to the prisoner, 'You took liberties with me, you villain.'

Mr George Williams, the attorney for the prisoner, stated that he knew Joseph Edwards: that person came to his office after Cant was committed, and made a communication to him. The communication was made after the prisoner had been admitted to bail.

Thomas Shipton, pot-boy at the Windsor Castle, stated that the prosecutrix appeared to be intoxicated on the day in question. He saw her before she went upstairs, and she then presented the appearance of a person who had taken liquor.

Mrs Sarah Goodchild, a washerwoman, stated that she was employed by Mr Cant. She went up to the bedroom of the prosecutrix about nine o'clock on the night in question, accompanied by the prisoner and his wife. The girl was then lying across the bed, and witness, assisted by Mr Cant, placed her straight upon the bed. They all left the room together. No light was left in the room.

Joseph Edwards was called and examined by Mr Phillips: He was a bootmaker, and formerly slept at the house of the prisoner. He now resided at No 2 Fenton's Buildings. He was in the habit of visiting the prisoner's family occasionally, and he slept there on the 3rd of October when the girl Bolland was there. She went upstairs, he believed, between nine and ten o'clock. She appeared then to be intoxicated. He saw her the next morning about half-past six o'clock, and went to her brother's house with her. They went down Chancery Lane, along Fleet Street and over Blackfriars Bridge. He told her that was the way to the Commercial Road, believing that she lived near the Commercial Road, Lambeth, but it appeared that it was Commercial Road East, she wished to go to. After the prisoner was committed, he called at the office of Mr Williams, and made a communication to that gentleman which was true. He made a similar communication to a friend of the name of Murphy. He went into prosecutor's room about eleven o'clock on the night of the 3rd of October. He had no light with him. She was in bed. Edwards proceeded to state that he had criminal intercourse with the girl, and he felt it his duty, when the prisoner was committed, to inform Mr Williams of what he had done.

Cross-examined by Mr Adolphus: Witness was out of employment at the time of this transaction. He knew Mr Cant, and the first time he slept at the Windsor Castle was on the 3rd of October. He had known Cant for four or five years. He had lodgings at Bartholomew Close on the 3rd of October. When he stayed at the Windsor Castle late, he was asked to sleep there. The girl did not appear at all unwilling to submit to the intercourse, but on the contrary, appeared quite willing. He had not gone to bed before. She was not covered with blankets. He heard all that had been stated that day, when the prisoner was examined before the justices, but he did not then mention a word of what he had now said. On the way home on Friday, the prosecutrix said that Mr Cant had called her a drunkard, and she would fix him for it. She then seemed happy enough.

Murphy corroborated this statement by declaring that the witness had told him of what he had done, after the time at which the communication had been made to Mr Williams.

A number of witnesses were then called, who gave the prisoner an excellent character, and

Mr Adolphus proceeded to reply. He rejoiced that Mr Phillips had not attempted to cast any aspersion upon the character of the prosecutrix, and declared his belief that no attempt could be successfully made to show that she was unworthy of belief. The case depended entirely now upon the testimony of Edwards, and the simple question was, whether the jury would credit his statement in preference to that of the girl Bolland. No attempt was made to deny the advances which Cant had made to the girl on the morning of the 3rd of October, and he asked the jury first, whether having made those advances, it was improbable that he should have followed them up, and secondly, whether they could believe a person who came forward and told such an improbable tale as Edwards. The testimony of the prosecutrix was materially sustained in many particulars—that of Edwards received no important confirmation. True, he had gone to two persons to relate his story before he told it here, but at that time the prisoner was at large on bail, and it was to be observed that he might have done so for the express purpose of propping up an improbable story. He had said nothing about it at the police office, although he had heard the prosecutrix examined there, and the whole relation bore so much of the impress of fiction, that the jury, he was sure, would attach no credit to his declaration.

The learned judge (Mr Baron Gurney) in summing up contrasted the statements of the prosecutrix and Edwards with great force, and having instructed the jury upon the law affecting the case, informing them that the offence of rape might have been committed upon the prosecutrix while she was in a state of insensibility, although no resistance had been made by her, left the whole case to them for decision.

After about two hours' consideration, a verdict of 'Guilty' was returned. The prisoner appeared somewhat astonished at this conclusion of the case, and loudly declared his innocence. Judgement of death was, however, recorded against him, and he was removed from the bar.

The very peculiar circumstances of this case attracted a large share of public attention; and a feeling was commonly entertained that the verdict was founded upon an erroneous view of the facts of the case. The persons who adopted this impression lost no time in conveying their opinion to the Secretary of State for the Home Department, but in spite of their most strenuous exertions in favour of Mr Cant, the Government declined to give a decision in opposition to that which had been arrived at by the jury, although it was resolved that the sentence of death should be changed for a punishment of transportation for life.

In obedience to this determination Mr Cant was subsequently sent out of the country.

The offence of Rape has always been regarded as one of the most serious crimes a man can commit. It is a common law offence but the punishment is statutory. Rape is the unlawful carnal knowledge of a woman without her consent by force, fear or fraud, and it is punishable by imprisonment for life or such other sentence of imprisonment the judge deems right. In the case of George Cant he was sentenced to death but his sentence was commuted to transportation for life and Cant was banished from the country. The case is only now important because it would appear that in all probability Cant was wrongly convicted. The evidence can be examined almost as the judge examined it, with this most important difference. The judge saw the witnesses, as the jury did, and judge and jury could form their own opinion about the truthfulness of the girl Jane Bolland and the witness Joseph Edwards. The suggestion would appear to be that when Cant was on bail he induced Edwards to come forward with this confession, but Edwards must have known that he was in fact saying that he was guilty of an offence punishable by death, and any reward given to him by Cant for making the confession could not have been of much benefit to him.

In the administration of the criminal law it has always been the practice of the judges to warn juries about the evidence of women who bring charges of rape or other sexual offences and in a great number of cases the evidence is found to be quite unreliable. Baron Gurney directed the jury on the law and contrasted the evidence of the girl Bolland and the witness Edwards, but his reference to the fact that Bolland might have been raped whilst she was insensible would seem to indicate that he disbelieved Edwards. The summing-up is so scanty, however, that it is quite impossible to make firm comments about it.

The whole case is full of doubtful points, and the doctrine of reasonable doubt might very well have applied. In a great murder trial R. v. Woolmington that went to the House of Lords on a point of public importance with the certificate of the Attorney-General, the doctrine of reasonable doubt was described by Lord Sankey, the Lord Chancellor, as 'the golden thread' that runs through the fabric of the criminal law in this country. The onus of proof is always on the Crown. It never shifts. Whether the defence brings evidence or not the Crown must still prove beyond all reasonable doubt that the accused person is guilty of the offence charged in the indictment, and if the jury is left with a reasonable doubt, the Crown fails and the accused person is discharged. In so grave a case as rape in the circumstances set out in the text it is fairly certain that a modern judge would have told the jury that 'they must be sure' before they convict, and whilst leaving the case to the decision of the jury, as he must, he would have indicated to them the view he was taking for their consideration and their guidance.

Robert Taylor, Convicted of Bigamy

On Monday, the 29th of June 1840, Robert Taylor, one of the most impudent impostors that we ever remember to have read of, was tried at the Durham Sessions for polygamy. The offender was a mere youth, between nineteen and twenty years of age, but his numerous matrimonial adventures and devices to obtain money, marked him as a person of singular cunning and dexterity. His plan seems to have been in all cases to practise first on the cupidity of his own sex, by holding out a pecuniary reward to any one who would procure him a suitable alliance, and then, by representing himself to be of aristocratic birth and heir to extensive possessions, to dazzle and win over the victim and her friends. To aid his views, he represented himself as a son of Lord Kenedy, of Ashby Hall, Leicestershire. He was furnished with numerous documents, framed to corroborate his misrepresentations. These, which he carried in a tin case, were found on his person when he was apprehended. Amongst them was a parchment, on which was written, in a fine clerkly hand, what purported to be 'The last will and testament of Lord Kenedy', &c. By this document Taylor appeared to be the heir to 1,015,000*l*, three per cent Consols, besides immense wealth in coal mines, salt factories, woollen factories, quarries, machinery, houses, plate, jewellery and even ships; and 'John Nicholson, Thomas Johnson and Mrs Robinson' appeared to have been constituted 'guardians of the said Robert Taylor'. The documents bore date 22nd of September 1829, and exhibited the signatures, first, of the supposed testator 'Kenedy', and then of the attesting witnesses, 'Samuel Robinson, clerk to James Lee, and John Turner' and 'William Cowley, barrister'. He had also an indenture certifying the correctness of the will, and describing his person by certain marks on his right arm, and elsewhere. He had sundry other papers ingeniously enough contrived for the purpose of aiding his deception, but, as he was a youth of coarse and vulgar manners, the success which attended his impostures can only be accounted for by the blind avarice of his dupes. At the time of his trial, six of his marriages, in several parts of the north of England, had come to the knowledge of the police, but there was good reason to suppose that there were many other instances in which he had successfully conducted his plans.

Like many who have pursued a career of base and unprincipled deception, this scoundrel affected great sanctity, and connected himself at different times with both the Wesleyan and Primitive Methodists. Indeed, one of his principal dupes was a Mr Fryer, a preacher in the last-named connexion, who, Taylor having promised a reward of 10*l* to any one who would procure him a young and religious wife, offered him the choice of his two sisters-in-law. Taylor chose the younger, a girl about eighteen years of age, and was married to her. This preacher not only failed to obtain the expected reward, but was swindled out of 12*l* which he lent to the roguish adventurer. This, however, proved the last of his exploits, for having made several fruitless attempts to run away from this wife, he was at length compelled to take her with him, and on his way through the county of Durham he was apprehended.

The budget of papers found in the prisoner's possession contained a multitude of curiosities besides those above alluded to, which our space will not allow us to particularize. It appeared from one of them, an indenture of apprenticeship, that at the agc of thirteen he had been apprenticed to a sweep and collier in Staffordshire till he should be twenty-one years old. The indenture described him as a poor child from Fatfield, in the county of Durham. There was several licences and documents relating to his marriages. One of these was a memorandum of an agreement between Robert Taylor and Mary Wilson, of Newcastle-on-Tyne, to marry in three months from October 16 1839, Taylor to forfeit 20,000*l* if he married any other woman and Mary Anne to forfeit one-third per annum of her yearly salary if she proved faithless. Annexed to this was a memorandum of a loan of 4*l* from Mary Anne's father, with an engagement, on the part of Taylor, to pay 1*l* per annum interest. Many of the papers related to the prisoner's connexion with the Wesleyan and Primitive Methodists, and with the Teetotallers, of which latter society he appears to have been a staunch adherent. The most curious paper was 'a memorandum of agreement made between Robert Taylor, Esq, son of the late Lord Kenedy, of Ashby

Hall, in the parish of Ashby de la-Zouch, and those he may engage as servants'. We regret that we cannot give this amusing document entire. It bears what purports to be the prisoner's signature, and from it he appears to have engaged an establishment of stewards, butlers, footmen, grooms, coachmen, gamekeepers, helpers, &c, sufficient for half a dozen princes at salaries of from 20*l* to 60*l* per annum. The stipulation of the engagement was, that the servants, butlers included, were to observe the teetotal pledge.

When the prisoner was placed at the bar to take his trial, the court was excessively crowded, and all eyes were fixed upon the young Lothario who had so readily succeeded in procuring half a dozen wives. Instead of a handsome, seductive gallant, there stood before the court a shabby-looking individual, with a face not merely ordinary but repulsive. He was evidently much amused at the sensation which his appearance produced, and joined in the smiles of the bystanders. He was perfectly unabashed and conducted himself throughout the trial with the utmost ease and unconcern.

The first case taken was that of the prisoner's intermarriage with Mary Ann Davidson, the sister-in-law of Mr Fryer, the Primitive Methodist preacher. John Wood, a wagoner of Birmingham, was called to prove the first marriage of which the authorities had any knowledge. It appeared, that this witness met the prisoner in Birmingham in 1838. The prisoner told Wood he was heir to 60,000*l* a year under the will of his father, Lord Kenedy. In proof of this assertion he produced papers. He said he had a great wish to be married to a respectable young lady, and if Wood could introduce him to such a one, he would make him a handsome present. Wood introduced him to Miss Sarah Ann Skidmore and to her father, who was a shopkeeper. The documents were shown to the young lady and her parents: the licence and the wedding-ring were procured that very day, and the couple were married the next morning. Shortly after, the prisoner went to London to settle his affairs. He subsequently returned and lived with his wife; but he had not been married more than six or seven weeks when he deserted her altogether.

As the prisoner was undefended, the court asked him if he had any questions to put to the witness.

Prisoner: 'I'll ax him one or two. I axed you if you knew a decent girl as wanted a husband and you said you did, you knew as how one Sarah Ann Skidmore wished to be married. And I told you I'd advertised and offered a reward of 10*l*. You took me to Benjamin Skidmore. Now, are you sure as how he saw the dockyments?'

Witness: 'Yes, quite sure: you showed him a document stating that you would have 60,000*l* a year when you came of age.'

Prisoner's mother (from the middle of the court): 'Robert, tell them thou's under age, and thy marriage can't stand good.'

The prisoner gave a lordly wave of the hand, accompanied by a significant gesture, intimating to his maternal parent to leave the management of the case to his superior skill. Then, turning to the witness, he said, 'Are you sure that you yourself saw the will?'

Witness: 'Yes.'

Prisoner: 'No, it was not the will: it was only the certicket of my guardians to show who I was and what property was coming to me.'

Here Mr Granger, the counsel for the prosecution, drew forth the tin case, which was a pitman's candle-box bearing the following inscription, 'Robert Taylor, otherwise Lord Kenedy'. From this case the learned counsel drew the 'dockyments'. The 'will' was rich alike in its bequests and its odours. It was a foul and filthy affair to look upon and to approach. Disregarding the usual long and dry prefaces in which lawyers are accustomed to indulge, it rushed at once into the marrow of the subject. Mr Granger tickled the ears of the court with a line or two. Thus: 'I give and bequeath to Robert Taylor, son of Elizabeth Taylor, single woman, 1,015,000*l* three per cent Consols and no more.' The will proceeded to bestow upon him four coal-pits, a woollen factory, two or three ships, and sundry other trifles, as before mentioned.

Mary Davidson, a neat, modest-looking girl, detailed the circumstances which led to her marriage with the prisoner. The latter, she said, was introduced to her at the house of her father, on the 4th of April, by Benjamin Fryer, her brother-in-law, who was a preacher among the Primitive Methodists. The latter said he had known the prisoner some time, and he recommended him as a pious young man whom he had brought to the house on purpose to marry her. The prisoner said he was the son of Lord Kenedy, and the moment he arrived in London with a wife he would have 700*l*, and 20*l* a year till he was of age, when he would have 60,000*l* per annum. He showed her several documents, one of which was a certificate that he was Lord Kenedy's son and would have 60,000*l* a year when he came of age. He had previously seen her unmarried sister, whom he rejected in favour of her. They were married by licence the very next morning. They lived together three weeks, during which time the prisoner had made several attempts to get away; and many times, in the night, he had endeavoured to slide the ring off her finger. While they were together, he lived upon the money which he borrowed from her brother-in-law, to whom he owed 22*l*.

The prisoner being again directed to ask the witness any questions he pleased said, placing his hands upon the bar and leaning forward in a counsellor-like attitude, 'Now, Mary, are you certain that I had 22*l* from your brother-in-law?' Witness: 'You had 12*l* in money and you were to pay him a reward of 10*l*.'

Prisoner: 'You say I had 12*l* in money, Mary. Now there was 10*s* to be paid for the ring, 5*s* for fees, 3*l* 10*s* for the licence, and 8*l* I had in money, which makes 12*l* 5*s*. So you see, Mary, you are wrong. You was also wrong when you said I told you I was to have 20*l* per annum per year.' Witness: 'You said 20*l*.'

Prisoner: 'No, Mary, I said 150*l* per year per annum. And I wish to ax you if I didn't say, "Will you have me, money or no money?"' Witness: 'No, you did not.'

Prisoner: 'Yes, Mary, I axed you, would you have me, money or no money, and you consented either way.'

The prisoner spoke at considerable length in his defence, giving a rambling account of his various migrations from the north to 'Brummagem', from 'Brummagem' to the north, &c, with some amusing particulars of his marriages and courtships, whereby he wished to make it appear that all the young ladies he came near wanted to have him, and that he had been in every instance inveigled into wedlock for the sake of his possessions. His main defence was that he was under age, and that all his marriages were illegal; and his conclusion seemed to be that having contracted one illegal marriage, he thought himself perfectly justified in contracting a hundred.

The prisoner's mother having expressed a wish to give evidence, and the prisoner having consented, she took her place in the witness-box, and deposed that she was now the wife of Michael Rickaby. The prisoner was not born in wedlock; she had him in a love affair. But she would not say who his father was. She had not come there for that. He was under age.

The jury found the prisoner 'Guilty'.

The prisoner was next indicted for having, in October 1839, married Mary Ann Wilson, daughter of George Wilson, a tobacconist of Newcastle. The marriage to Miss Skidmore was again proved by the certificate, which bore his lordship's mark. The prisoner, it appeared, had advertised for a wife in the Newcastle papers. In that town he appears to have attached himself to the Wesleyan Methodists. By his professions of religion and his teetotal pledges, he obtained a high character for morality and sanctity. Miss Wilson said she first saw the prisoner in October at a Methodist chapel in Newcastle. On the same day she met him at a class meeting. On the 16th of October she was introduced to him by a friend, when he promised to call upon her at three o'clock that afternoon. He did so, and as soon as he sat down, he pulled out a tin case which was marked 'Robert Taylor, otherwise Lord Kenedy'. He said he was entitled to 60,000*l* a year and other hereditaments. The following day he made her an offer of marriage and she accepted him. He said if he could get the loan of some money, they would be married the next morning. Her father lent him 4*l*, a licence was bought, and they were married the day but one after she had accepted him and three days after her introduction to him. Eighteen days after this he deserted her, and she heard no more of him till he was in custody.

The jury returned a verdict of 'Guilty'.

The court having spent some time in deliberation,

The chairman said: 'You have for some time been going about the country in a most unprincipled way, marrying weak and unsuspecting girls and bringing misery upon them and their friends. We have seriously considered whether it is not imperative upon us to visit you with the severest penalty that the law allows. We have determined, however, to stop short of this; but you must be punished with great severity for your wicked conduct. For the first offence of which you have been convicted, you are sentenced to be imprisoned one year to hard labour, and for the second, to be imprisoned eighteen months to hard labour, making altogether two years and a half.'

Prisoner: 'Gentlemen, when I come out again, will any of my wives have a claim upon me?'

The court declined to answer the question, and he then requested that his 'dockyments' might be restored to him.

The court thought it better to make no order: they might be placed in the hands of the governor of the jail.

The mother of the prisoner, on quitting the court, finding herself an object of some attraction, became somewhat communicative on her family history. Among other things, she stated that her son was one of General Evans's 'Legion', and that she had sent a letter into Spain, which had the effect of procuring his return to England. She had come from Workington, in Cumberland, a distance of one hundred and fifteen miles, to attend the trial, for 'her son was her son', and she could not rest without coming. One thing she would not allow curiosity to penetrate—and that was, the mystery which hung over the prisoner's birth. She had 'kept the secret' nineteen years and was not going to reveal it in the twentieth. All that she would say was, that 'she had him to a real gentleman'.

The Earl of Cardigan, Tried at the Bar of the House of Lords, for an Assault with intent to Murder

On Tuesday, February the 16th 1841, the Right Hon the Earl of Cardigan was tried by his peers at the bar of the House of Lords, for an assault with intent to murder, alleged to have been committed by him in fighting a duel with Mr Harvey Garnet Phipps Tuckett.

In introducing this case to our readers we do not deem it to be necessary to enter into any minute or extended discussion in reference to the circumstances which preceded this trial, but it will be sufficient to point out the general facts by which the duel which was the subject matter of the investigation was brought about.

In the year 1840, the Earl of Cardigan held the rank of Lieutenant-Colonel of the 11th Regiment of Hussars, of which His Royal Highness Prince Albert had recently received a commission as colonel. It appears to have been the object of the Earl of Cardigan to advance the discipline and general conduct of his regiment to such a state as to entitle it to be esteemed in the light in which it was held—that of a favourite regiment. The earl had been appointed to the regiment in the year 1838, while it was serving in India, but in the spring of the ensuing year, the usual period of service abroad having expired, the 11th Hussars were ordered home, and soon after received the title of 'Prince Albert's Own'. While stationed at Brighton, in the course of the year 1840, some differences arose between the noble earl and the officers under his command, which, whether justly or unjustly, procured for the former a considerable degree of notoriety and placed his character as the commander of a regiment in an unenviable position. Complaints to the War Office were the result of these misunderstandings, and the subject became matter of discussion in the various newspapers of the day. Amongst the journals which took a prominent part in these debates was the *Morning Chronicle*, and in the columns of that paper a series of letters appeared under the signature of 'An Old Soldier', which eventually proved to be the contributions of Mr Tuckett, formerly a captain under the command of the Earl of Cardigan. Many of these letters undoubtedly contained matter highly offensive personally to the Earl of Cardigan, and the noble earl having discovered their author, called upon him to afford that satisfaction usually deemed to be due from one gentleman to another under circumstances of insult or other provocation.

A meeting took place at Wimbledon Common, on the 12th of September 1840, the respective combatants being attended by seconds, the result of which was that, at the second shot, Captain Tuckett was wounded. The whole affair was witnessed by some persons resident in the neighbourhood, and the parties were all taken into custody, and eventually bound over to appear to answer any charge which might be preferred against them at the ensuing Sessions at the Central Criminal Court.

A police constable was directed to institute a prosecution, and bills of indictment were laid before the grand jury against Captain Tuckett, and Captain Wainwright, his second, and also against the Earl of Cardigan, and Captain Douglas, who had attended him in the capacity of his friend. In the cases of the two first-named individuals the bill was ignored, but a true bill was returned against the Earl of Cardigan and Captain Douglas.

The extent of jurisdiction of the judges at the Old Bailey prevented them from trying the Earl of Cardigan, whose alleged offence the noble earl was entitled to have inquired of by his peers, and the investigation of the case against the parties indicted was therefore postponed from session to session until the sitting of Parliament, the court declining to enter upon the case of Captain Douglas until that of the principal to the offence had first been disposed of. Parliament assembled on the 16th of January 1841, and then, so soon as the forms of the House of Lords would admit, the bill of indictment was removed by *certiorari*, in order to be disposed of by their lordships. The customary preliminary forms having been complied with, the trial took place on the day above named, namely, Tuesday, the 16th of February.

The public had been made acquainted with the fact that the trial would not take place in Westminster Hall, and that the Painted Chamber, in which the peers had met for parliamentary business since the destruction of the old House by fire, was under preparation for this solemn and imposing scene. The smallness of the apartment, and the general desire amongst the peeresses and the various members of the nobility and rank of the land to be present upon so important and interesting an occasion, rendered it necessary that very extensive alterations should be made to secure sufficient accommodation, and considerable ingenuity had been exercised in order to accomplish that object, every corner and nook from which a glimpse of the court could be snatched being provided with sittings. But the capacity of the building prevented the architect, with all his skill, from making the supply equal to the demand. The benches, galleries, and floor, were covered with crimson cloth, and the walls themselves with paper, in which that colour was predominant, and the effect was to make the gorgeous robes of the peers and the splendid dresses of the peeresses stand out in dazzling relief. When the court had opened and the chamber was filled, the *tout ensemble* was magnificent.

At a quarter before eleven o'clock, the Lords' Speaker (Lord Denman), having robed in his private room, entered the House. A procession was formed in the usual manner, his lordship being preceded by the purse-bearer with the purse, the sergeant with the mace, the Black Rod carrying the Lord High Steward's staff and Garter carrying his sceptre.

Garter and Black Rod having taken their places at the bar, the Lord Speaker proceeded to the Woolsack, where prayers were read by the Bishop of Lichfield.

The clerk assistant of Parliament then proceeded to call over the peers, beginning with the junior baron.

This necessary ceremony being completed, the clerks of the Crown in Chancery and in the Queen's Bench jointly made three reverences, and the clerk of the Crown in Chancery, on his knee, delivered the commission to the Lord Speaker, who gave it to the clerk of the Crown in the Queen's Bench to read. Both clerks then retired with like reverences to the table.

The sergeant-at-arms then made proclamation, and the Lord Speaker informed the peers that Her Majesty's commission was about to be read, and directed that all persons should rise and be uncovered while the commission was reading.

The commission appointing Lord Denman as Lord High Steward was then read, and Garter and Black Rod having made their reverences, proceeded to the Woolsack and took their places on the right of the Lord High Steward, and both holding the staff, presented it on their knees to His Grace.

His Grace rose, and having made reverence to the throne, took his seat in the chair of state provided for him on the uppermost step but one of the throne. Proclamation was then made for silence, when the queen's writ of *certiorari* to remove the indictment, with the return thereof, and the record of the indictment, were read by the clerk of the Crown in the Queen's Bench. The Lord High Steward then directed the sergeant-at-arms to make proclamation for the yeomen usher to bring the prisoner to the bar.

The Earl of Cardigan immediately entered the House, and advanced to the bar, accompanied by the yeoman usher. He made three reverences, one to His Grace the Lord High Steward, and one to the peers on either side, who returned the salute. The ceremony of kneeling was dispensed with. The noble earl, who was dressed in plain clothes, was then conducted within the bar, where he remained standing while the Lord High Steward acquainted him with the nature of the charge against him.

The prisoner was arraigned in the usual form, for firing at Harvey Garnet Phipps Tuckett, on the 12th of September, with intent to kill and murder him. The second count charged him with firing at the said Harvey Garnet Phipps Tuckett with intent to maim and disable him; and the third count varied the charge —with intent to do him some grievous bodily harm.

The clerk then asked, 'How say you, James Thomas Earl of Cardigan, are you guilty or not?'

The Earl of Cardigan, in a firm voice, replied, 'Not guilty, my lords.'

The clerk: 'How will you be tried, my lord?'

The Earl of Cardigan: 'By my peers.'

The noble prisoner then took his seat on a stool within the bar, and His Grace the Lord High Steward removed to the table, preceded by Garter, Black Rod and the purse-bearer, as before.

Mr Waddington opened the pleadings, stating the nature of

the offence as set out in the indictment, and added that the noble prisoner had, for his trial, put himself upon their lordships, his peers.

The Attorney-General addressed their lordships as follows: 'I have the honour to attend your lordships on this occasion as Attorney-General for Her Majesty, to lay before you the circumstances of the case upon which you will be called to pronounce judgement, without any object or wish on my part, except that I may humbly assist your lordships in coming to a right conclusion upon it, according to its merits.

'An indictment has been found against a peer of the realm by a grand jury of his country, charging him with a felony, the punishment of which is transportation or imprisonment. That indictment has been removed before your lordships at the request of the noble prisoner, and, I must say, most properly removed, for an inferior court had no jurisdiction to try him. The charge is, upon the face of it, of a most serious character, and it would not have been satisfactory if it had gone off without any inquiry. The policeman, however, who was bound over to prosecute, fulfilled his recognizances by appearing at the Central Criminal Court and preferring the indictment. It is possible that in the course of this trial, questions of great magnitude on the construction of Acts of Parliament or respecting the privileges of the peerage may arise, which it is of great importance to this House, to the Crown and to the community, should be deliberately discussed. According to all the precedents that can be found, whenever a peer has been tried in Parliament, the prosecution has been conducted by the law-officers of the Crown. Fortunately, we have no living memory on this subject. It is now sixty-four years since any proceeding of this sort has taken place, and I am rejoiced to think that on the present occasion the charge against the noble prisoner at the bar does not imply any degree of moral turpitude, and that, if he should be found guilty, his conviction will reflect no discredit on the illustrious order to which he belongs. At the same time, it clearly appears to me that the noble lord at the bar has been guilty of infringing the statute law of the realm, which this and all other courts of justice are bound to respect and enforce. Your lordships are not sitting as a court of honour, or as a branch of the legislature; your lordships are sitting here as a court bound by the rules of law, and under a sanction as sacred as that of an oath.

'The indictment against the Earl of Cardigan is framed upon an Act of Parliament which passed in the first year of the reign of her present Majesty. It charges the noble defendant with having shot at Captain Harvey Tuckett, with the several intents set forth in the indictment. I think I shall best discharge my duty to your lordships by presenting to you a brief history of the law on this subject.

'By the common law of England, personal violence, when death did not ensue from it, amounted to a mere misdemeanour, and if the wounded party did not die within a year and a day, no felony was committed. The first act which created a felony where death did not ensue was the 5th of Henry IV. By that act certain personal injuries, without death, were made felonies without benefit of clergy. Then came the Coventry Act, the 22nd and 23rd of Charles II, whereby any person lying in wait for and wounding another with intent to maim or disfigure, was guilty of felony without benefit of clergy. Under both these acts no offence was committed unless a wound was inflicted, and it was not until the 9th George I, commonly called the Black Act, that an attempt, where no wound was given, was made a felony. By that act it was enacted, that if any person should wilfully and maliciously shoot at any person in any dwelling-house or other place, he should be guilty of felony without benefit of clergy, although no wound were inflicted: but it was determined upon that statute—and in fairness to the noble prisoner it is my duty to remind your lordships of it—that unless the case was one in which, if death had ensued, it would have amounted to murder, no offence was committed under the statute.

'The law continued on this footing until an act was passed in the 43rd of George III, which is commonly called Lord Ellenborough's Act. This act did not repeal the Black Act, but greatly extended its operation, and, among other enactments, contains this: "That if any person or persons shall wilfully, maliciously and unlawfully shoot at any of His Majesty's subjects, or shall wilfully, maliciously and unlawfully present, point or level any kind of loaded fire-arms at any of His Majesty's subjects, and attempt, by drawing a trigger, or in any other manner, to discharge the same at or against his or their person or persons . . . with intent in so doing, or by means thereof, to murder, or rob, or to maim, disfigure, or disable such His Majesty's subject or subjects, or with intent to do some other grievous bodily harm to such His Majesty's subject or subjects, he shall be guilty of felony without benefit of clergy." This act, however, has the following express proviso: "Provided always, that in case it shall appear on the trial of any person or persons indicted for the wilfully, maliciously, and unlawfully shooting at any of His Majesty's subjects . . . with such intent as aforesaid, that such acts . . . were committed under such circumstances as that if death had ensued therefrom the same would not in law have amounted to the crime of murder; then and in every such case the person or persons so indicted shall be deemed and taken to be not guilty of the felonies whereof they shall be so indicted, but be thereof acquitted."

'Next came the statute of the 9th of George IV, cap. 31, which, I believe, is generally called Lord Lansdowne's Act, that noble lord having introduced it into Parliament when he was Secretary for the Home Department. This is an act for consolidating and amending the statutes relating to offences against the person. It repeals the Black Act and Lord Ellenborough's Act, but it contains provisions similar to those of the latter. Things remained on this footing till the act was passed on which the present indictment is framed. That act, which received the royal assent on the 17th of July 1837, is the 1st of Victoria, cap. 85, and is entitled "An Act to amend the laws relating to offences against the Person". By the second section it is enacted: "That whosoever shall . . . wound any person, or shall by any means whatsoever cause to any person any bodily injury dangerous to life, with intent . . . to commit murder, shall be guilty of felony, and being convicted thereof, shall suffer death." Therefore, to shoot at a person and inflict a wound dangerous to life, remains by this act a capital offence. The fourth section enacts: "That whosoever unlawfully and maliciously shall shoot at any person, or shall, by drawing a trigger or in any other manner, attempt to discharge any kind of loaded arms at any person . . . with intent . . . to maim, disfigure, or disable such person, or to do some other grievous bodily harm to such person . . . shall be guilty of felony, and being convicted thereof shall be liable, at the discretion of the court, to be transported beyond the seas for the term of his or her natural life, or for any term not less than fifteen years, or to be imprisoned for any term not exceeding three years." This act contains no such proviso as is found in Lord Ellenborough's Act, and that of the 9th of George IV, a circumstance which it is material your lordships should bear in mind when you come to deliberate on your judgement with respect to the second and third counts of the indictment.

'I am happy to say that the indictment contains no count on the capital charge. A wound was inflicted, but the prosecutor has very properly restricted the charge to firing at with intent, without alleging that any wound dangerous to life was inflicted. The first count charges, that the Earl of Cardigan shot at Captain Tuckett with intent, in the language of the law, to commit the crime of murder. The second count charges his lordship with the same act with intent to maim, disfigure, or disable Captain Tuckett, and the third count charges him with the same act with intent to do Captain Tuckett some grievous bodily harm. It will be for your lordships to say whether, upon the facts which I shall lay before you, and which I am instructed to say can be clearly made out in evidence, each and every one of the counts must not be considered as fully established.

'The substance of the evidence in this case is that, on the 12th of September last, the Earl of Cardigan fought a duel with pistols on Wimbledon Common with Captain Tuckett and wounded him at the second exchange of shots. It will appear that about five o'clock on the afternoon of that day, two carriages, coming in opposite directions, were seen to arrive on Wimbledon Common, and a party of gentlemen alighted from each. It was evident to those who observed what was going on, that a duel was in contemplation. The parties went to a part of Wimbledon Common between the road that leads to Lord Spencer's park and a windmill. The seconds made the usual preparations: the principals, the Earl of Cardigan and Captain Tuckett, were placed at a distance of about twelve yards: they exchanged shots without effect: they received from their seconds each another pistol: they again fired, and Captain Tuckett was wounded by the Earl of Cardigan. Mr Dann, who occupied the mill, and his son, and Sir

James Anderson, a surgeon who was standing close by, went up immediately. The wound was examined: it bled freely but most fortunately—and I am sure that no one rejoices at the circumstance more than the noble prisoner at the bar—it proved to be not of a dangerous nature. Mr Dann, the miller, who was a constable, took the whole party into custody. The wound was again formally examined, and Sir J. Anderson pressed that he might be set at liberty and allowed to take Captain Tuckett to his house in London, which was immediately acceded to upon Captain Tuckett promising to appear before the magistrates when he recovered. The miller retained the Earl of Cardigan and his second, Captain Douglas, as well as Captain Wainwright, the second of Captain Tuckett. The Earl of Cardigan had still a pistol in his hand when the miller approached him, and two cases of pistols were still on the ground, one of which bore the crest of the noble earl and was claimed by him as his property. The parties in custody were conducted before the magistrates at Wandsworth, when the Earl of Cardigan made use of these words: "I have fought a duel: I have hit my man I believe, but not seriously." Then pointing to Captain Douglas, he said, "This gentleman is also a prisoner and my second." He was asked whether the person he had hit was Captain Reynolds, upon which he replied, "Do you think I would condescend to fight with one of my own officers?" His lordship was compelled by the magistrates to enter into recognizances to appear when called upon, which he did from time to time, till at last the matter was carried to the Central Criminal Court.

'The witnesses I shall call before your lordships are the miller, his wife and son, and the policeman named Busaine, who was at the station-house and will speak to the declarations made by the Earl of Cardigan. I can offer no evidence respecting the origin of the quarrel. Captain Douglas is to take his trial for his share in the transaction. He, as your lordships will observe, is jointly indicted with the Earl of Cardigan. A bill was also preferred against Captains Tuckett and Wainwright, but the grand jury have thrown it out. Those gentlemen, however, are still liable to be tried, and it would not be decorous to summon them before your lordships to give evidence which might afterwards be turned against themselves, probably, when they would be on trial for their lives. I shall call Sir J. Anderson, who has hitherto spoken fairly on the subject and, I suppose, will now make no objection to state all that fell within his observation. Upon these facts it will be for your lordships to say whether all the counts of the indictment are not fully proved and supported.

'With respect to the first count, it is painful to use the language which it necessarily recites, but it will be for your lordships to say whether, in point of law, the noble prisoner at the bar did not shoot at Captain Tuckett with intent to commit the crime therein mentioned. I at once acquit the Earl of Cardigan of anything unfair in the conduct of this duel. Something has been said respecting the noble earl's pistols having rifle barrels, whilst those of Captain Tuckett had not such barrels. However that may have been, I have the most perfect conviction that nothing but what was fair and honourable was intended, and that the Earl of Cardigan most probably imagined, when he carried his pistols to the field with him, that one of them would be directed against his own person. Nor do I suppose that there was any grudge—any personal animosity—any rancour or malignity on the part of the noble earl towards his antagonist. Whether the noble earl gave or received the invitation to go out, I believe his only object was to preserve his reputation, and maintain his station in society as an officer and a gentleman. His lordship is in the Army—he is Lieutenant-Colonel of the 11th Hussars—and no doubt he on this occasion only complied with what he considered to be necessary to be done according to the usages of society. But if death had ensued under these circumstances it would have been a great calamity; and although moralists of high name have excused and even defended the practice of duelling, your lordships must consider what, in this respect, is the law of England.

'There can be no doubt that by the law of England parties who go out deliberately to fight a duel, if death ensues, are guilty of murder. It will be my duty to state to your lordships a few of the leading authorities on this point. I will mention the highest authorities known to the law of England—Hale, Hawkins, Foster and Blackstone.

'Hale, in his *Pleas of the Crown*, says, "If A and B suddenly fall out, and they presently agree to fight in a field, and run and fetch their weapons and go to the field and fight, and A kills B, this is not murder, but homicide, for it is but a continuance of the sudden falling out, and the blood was never cooled; but if there were deliberation, as that they went on the next day—nay, though it was the same day, if there was such a competent distance of time that in common presumption they had time of deliberation—then it is murder." In the 1st vol. of *Hawkins' Pleas of the Crown*, cap. 13, sec. 21, p. 96, the law on this subject is thus laid down: "It seems agreed, that whenever two persons in cold blood meet and fight on a precedent quarrel, and one of them is killed, the other is guilty of murder, and cannot help himself by alleging that he was struck first by the deceased, or that he had often declined to meet him, and was prevailed upon to do it by his importunity, or that it was his intent only to vindicate his reputation—or that he meant not to kill, but to disarm his adversary—for since he deliberately engaged in an act highly unlawful, in defiance of the laws, he must at his peril abide the consequence thereof."

'Sir M. Foster, in his discourse on homicide, says: "Upon this principle deliberate duelling, if death ensues, is, in the eye of the law, murder, because it is generally founded on a feeling of revenge. And if a person be drawn into a duel, not from motives so criminal, but merely for the protection of what he calls his honour, that is no excuse for those who, in seeking to destroy another, act in defiance of all laws human and divine."

'Blackstone, in his fourth volume, p. 199, thus writes, when describing and defining the crime of murder: "This takes in the case of deliberate duelling, where both parties meet avowedly with an intent to murder: thinking it their duty, as gentlemen, and claiming it as their right, to wanton with their own lives and those of their fellow-creatures; without any warrant or authority from any power, either divine or human, but in direct contradiction to the laws both of God and man; and, therefore, the law has justly fixed the crime and punishment of murder on them, and on their seconds also."

'Those are the highest authorities known to the law of England, and they are uniformly followed by the English judges.

'Such being the definition of murder constantly given from the bench on trials for life and death, ought not your lordships to suppose that the legislature has made use of the word "murder" in the same sense, and that when we find the expression "with intent to commit murder", it means with intent to do that which, if accomplished, would amount in law to the crime of murder. The legislature, and your lordships as part of it, must be taken to have well known what was the legal definition of murder, and to have used the expression, in a judicial act, in its legal sense. However painful the consideration may be, does it not necessarily follow that the first count of the indictment is completely proved? The circumstances clearly show that the Earl of Cardigan and Captain Tuckett met by appointment. The arrangements being completed, they fired twice: the Earl of Cardigan took deliberate aim, fired, and wounded his antagonist. He must be supposed to have intended that which he did. If, unfortunately, death had ensued, would not this have been a case of murder? The only supposition by which the case could be reduced to one of manslaughter would be that the Earl of Cardigan and Captain Tuckett met casually on Wimbledon Common—that they suddenly quarrelled, and, whilst their blood was hot, fought. But your lordships will hardly strain the facts so far as to say this was a casual meeting, when you see that each party was accompanied by a second and supplied with a brace of pistols, and that the whole affair was conducted according to the forms and solemnities observed when a deliberate duel is fought.

'With respect to the second count I know not what defence can possibly be suggested, because even if it had been a casual meeting, and if death had ensued under circumstances which would have amounted only to manslaughter, that would be no defence to the second and third counts. I presume to assert that, on the authority of a case which came before the fifteen judges of England, and which was decided, two most learned judges doubting on the occasion but not dissenting from the decision. The two judges who doubted were His Grace the High Steward, who presides over your lordships' proceedings on this occasion, and Mr Justice Littledale. It would not become me to say anything of the learning and ability of the noble High Steward in his presence, but with respect to Mr Justice Littledale, I will say that there never was a more learned or acute judge than he was, whose retirement from the bench the bar have lately witnessed with reluctance and regret. I therefore attach the greatest weight even to doubts proceeding from such a quarter. But the thirteen other judges entertained no doubt upon that occasion, and came to the conclusion that, upon the 4th section of the act upon which the present indictment was framed, it is not necessary for a conviction that if death ensued the offence should amount to murder.

'I apprehend that the judges probably reasoned in this manner —the intention of Parliament being to make offences, before capital, punishable only by transportation, the quality of the offence is not precisely the same as before, so that if a person maims another, or disables him, or does him some grievous bodily harm, even though it were an unpremeditated act arising out of a sudden scuffle, it should nevertheless be an offence under this act, which gives a discretionary power to the court either to transport for fifteen years, or to imprison for a single hour. The judges, doubtless, considering this discretionary power, and the omission of the proviso which was in the preceding acts—seeing that the capital punishment was abolished, came to the conclusion that the offence was committed, even though if death had ensued, it would not, under the circumstances, have amounted to the crime of murder. Looking at the authority of this case, I know not what defence can possibly be urged with respect to the second and third counts.

'I rejoice, my lords, to think that the noble prisoner will have an advantage upon this occasion which has never before been enjoyed by any peer who has been tried at your lordships' bar—an advantage which neither Lord Lovat, Lord Ferrers, nor the Duchess of Kingston, could claim. He will have the advantage of the assistance of my most able, ingenious, zealous and learned friend, Sir William Follett, who will address your lordships in his behalf on the facts and merits of the case. This privilege is secured to the noble prisoner under the admirable law your lordships passed a few years ago, by which, in all cases, the party has the advantage of addressing, through his counsel, the tribunal which is to determine on his guilt or innocence. Notwithstanding, however, all the learning, ability and zeal of my honourable and learned friend, I know not how he will be able to persuade your lordships to acquit his noble client on any one count of this indictment. My learned friend will not ask your lordships—and if he did, it would be in vain—to forget the law by which you are bound. Captain Douglas stands on his trial before another tribunal, and his trial has been postponed by the judges on the express ground that the same case is first to be tried by the highest criminal court known in the empire. Your lordships are to lay down the law by which all inferior courts are to be bound.

'I beg leave, on this subject, to read the words made use of at this bar by one of my most distinguished predecessors, who afterwards for many years presided with great dignity on the Woolsack—I mean Lord Thurlow. When Lord Thurlow was Attorney-General, in addressing this house in the case of the Duchess of Kingston, he made use of this language: "I do desire to press this upon your lordships as an universal maxim: no more dangerous idea can creep into the mind of a judge than the imagination that he is wiser than the law. I confine this to no judge, whatever may be his denomination, but extend it to all. And speaking at the bar of an English court of justice, I make sure of your lordships' approbation when I comprise even your lordships sitting in Westminster Hall. It is a grievous example to other judges. If your lordships assume this, sitting in judgement, why not the King's Bench? Why not commissioners of oyer and terminer? If they do so, why not the Quarter Sessions? Ingenious men may strain the law very far, but to pervert it was to new-model it—the genius of our constitution says judges have no such authority, nor shall presume to exercise it."

'I conclude, my lords, with the respectful expression of my conviction, that your lordships' judgement in this case, whatever it may be, will be according to truth and the justice of the case, and that you will preserve the high reputation in the exercise of judicial functions which has so long been enjoyed by your lordships and your ancestors.'

The evidence of the various persons who had witnessed the transaction of the duel, and which supported the statement made by the learned Attorney-General, was then produced, but, at the close of the case, it was objected by Sir William Follett, on behalf of the Earl of Cardigan, that there was no evidence to show that the person against whom the shot was discharged was Mr

Harvey Garnet Phipps Tuckett. The card of 'Mr Harvey Tuckett' had been put in, but this might be quite another person from the individual pointed to by the indictment.

The Attorney-General was heard on the other side, but, after a short deliberation, the Lord High Steward announced that the evidence which fixed the identity of the individual was insufficient, and the peers thereupon declared the noble defendant 'Not Guilty'.

At the Central Criminal Court, on Wednesday, the 3rd of March, Captain Douglas was put upon his trial, before Mr Justice Williams, upon the indictment which had been found against him; but the jury, in the absence of positive evidence to identify Mr Tuckett, came to the same conclusion as that which had been arrived at by the House of Peers, and a verdict of acquittal was returned.

The proceedings in this case are made almost unintelligible by the verbiage of the Attorney-General, who seems to have been overcome by the solemnity of the occasion and opened at quite inordinate length.

If Cardigan had been charged at common law with the misdemeanour of issuing a challenge to a duel he could have been tried at the Old Bailey, but because the indictment was in this form he had perforce to be tried in the House of Lords. It is to be observed that before the Indictments Act of 1915 the form of the indictment was all important, for after all the fuss and bother of transferring this case of Cardigan from the Old Bailey to the House of Lords, it was finally decided on what most people would now regard as the silliest point imaginable, but which was regarded at that time as of first importance.

The indictment was for shooting at Harvey Garnet Phipps Tuckett with intent to murder. Now at that time the name of the person who was shot at was a material averment, as it was called, and therefore the averment must be strictly proved as laid. The criminal procedure of that day provided that if there was any variance between the statements in the indictment, and the evidence given in support, the accused person could not lawfully be convicted, and some very remarkable illustrations are recorded in the books. There was a later case in 1855 where a man was indicted for having by night, in pursuit of game, entered the lands of George William Frederick Charles Duke of Cambridge. A witness proved that two of the names, George William, belonged to the Duke, and it was proved that there were others but no proof was given what the others were. The court having refused to amend the indictment by striking out the words 'Frederick Charles' the conviction was subsequently quashed on appeal. In Cardigan's case there was evidence that the man shot at was Harvey Tuckett but no evidence was given that he bore the full names set out in the indictment. It was unanimously held by the House of Lords that the variance was fatal and Cardigan was acquitted.

The Attorney-General in the case was Sir John Campbell, afterwards Lord Campbell, Lord Chancellor and Lord Chief Justice. We are fortunate in having many of the letters and diaries of Lord Campbell, and in a note to the speech which he made for the Crown he appended this interesting account:

> *The facts were proved substantially as above stated; but an acquittal took place on the ground that there was not sufficient proof of the Christian name of Captain Tuckett. The counsel for the Crown at the consultations before the trial had distinctly pointed out the necessity for evidence to prove that Captain Tuckett's name was the same as stated in the indictment . . . and in the Briefs delivered to counsel before the trial there was abundant evidence of the full name. The deficiency arose from the witnesses . . . not giving the evidence expected of them. Blame was very lavishly cast upon me for the result—some not scrupling to say that there had been a premeditated scheme to secure an acquittal. This absurd charge did not give me one moment's uneasiness—but I was, I confess, much hurt by an accusation from very respectable quarters that my address contained a defence of duelling and had a tendency to encourage that practice . . . I consider that to fight a duel must always be a great calamity, but it is not always necessarily a great crime.*

So far as the character of Cardigan was concerned there is a speech made in the House of Commons by Macaulay, then Secretary-at-War, in a debate in 1841 when he said:

> *Could Lord Cardigan go to a theatre that he was not insulted? Could he take his place in a railway-train without having a hiss raised against him? Was there ever a case in which a man was*

more violently assailed? Without wishing to assert that Lord Cardigan is faultless (on that point I do not give an opinion), if he had been Hare the accomplice of Burke, or any other person impugned on the most criminal charge, instead of being charged with faults of temper or manner, could stronger or more violent or more intemperate means be taken to mark the public aversion?

It should also be mentioned that had Lord Cardigan been convicted it was expected that he would claim benefit of clergy and peerage (as the Duchess of Kingston did after her conviction for bigamy). There was a doubtful point in law whether a certain provision under the statute of Edward VI had been repealed by a statute of George IV, and immediately after the trial a short Act was passed expressly repealing the statute of Edward and providing that 'peers against whom any indictment may be found, shall plead to such indictment, and shall, upon conviction, be liable to the same punishment as any other of Her Majesty's subjects'.

A very full report of the case is contained in Vol. 4 (New Series) of the State Trials *including the letters written by Captain Tuckett of which Lord Cardigan complained.*